COLLISION COURSE

Inside the Battle for General Motors

Micheline Maynard

A Birch Lane Press Book

Published by Carol Publishing Group

A Birch Lane Press Book
Published by Carol Publishing Group
Birch Lane Press is a registered trademark of Carol Communications, Inc.
Editorial Offices: 600 Madison Avenue, New York, N.Y. 10022
Sales and Distribution Offices: 120 Enterprise Avenue, Secaucus, N.J. 07094
In Canada: Canadian Manda Group, One Atlantic Avenue, Suite 105, Toronto, Ontario M6K 3E7
Queries regarding rights and permissions should be addressed to Carol Publishing Group, 600 Madison Avenue, New York, N.Y. 10022

Carol Publishing Group books are available at special discounts for bulk purchases, sales promotion, fund-raising, or educational purposes. Special editions can be created to specifications. For details, contact: Special Sales Department, Carol Publishing Group, 120 Enterprise Avenue, Secaucus, N.J. 07094

Designed by Ardashes Hamparian

Manufactured in the United States of America

10 9 8 7 6 5 4 3 2 1

Library of Congress Cataloging-in-Publication Data

Maynard, Micheline.
    Collision course : inside the battle for General Motors / Micheline Maynard.
        p.   cm.
    "A Birch Lane Press book."
    Includes index.
    ISBN 1-55972-313-0 (hardcover)
        1. General Motors Corporation.   2. Automobile industry and trade—United States.   I. Title.
HD9710.U54G47464   1995
338.7'6292'0973—dc20   95-4694
                                                                          CIP

To my mother, Bernice Maynard,
and to the memory of my father, Frank H. Maynard

What Is Leadership?

"The first responsibility of a leader is to define reality. The last is to say, 'thank you.' In between the two, the leader must become a servant and a debtor. That sums up the progress of an artful leader."

Leadership Is an Art, by Max DePree

CONTENTS

ACKNOWLEDGMENTS

I have been fascinated with turnaround attempts since 1989, when, as a Knight-Bagehot Fellow for Business and Economics Journalism at Columbia University, I took a very difficult management course in the Graduate School of Business called Turnarounds. The professor was a demanding, insightful, and kind management expert named John Whitney. The lessons I learned in that course echoed during the two and a half years I have spent on this project. Certainly, the General Motors story can't be told in a single volume. Someone—perhaps even myself—should follow the changes that Jack Smith has tried to make in his three years as GM's chief executive officer to see if they come to fruition. GM's success or failure cannot be judged completely for another five years. At the very least, this book is a guide to show the crisis GM faced and the solutions Smith and his team selected in the wake of financial chaos.

In writing this book, I have been very fortunate to have had the cooperation, however wary, of many of the people who played a role at GM over the past five years. Because of the sensitivity of the issues involved, several requested that I not identify them by name. But the vast majority of people whom I interviewed were willing to discuss GM on the record. First of all, I would like to thank Jack Smith for his help, and his wife Lydia for her assistance, support, and photographs. Smith's sisters Sally Mahoney and Mary Carroll Smith assisted me in writing about his family background. Jack's many friends in Worcester were more than generous with their time. I particularly want to thank Joseph Lane, alumni director at St. John's Academy, in Shrewsbury, Massachusetts.

At GM, I am particularly grateful to Mark Hogan, president of GM's Brazilian operations, and Robert Purcell, executive director of GM's Electric Vehicle Program, for helping me understand the philosophy behind Fundamental Change and

ix

the elements that comprised the plan. In GM's corporate and North American operations, I would like to thank all those whom I interviewed, including G. Richard Wagoner, Harry Pearce, J. Michael Losh, J. T. Battenberg, Robert Hendry, Michael Grimaldi, Wayne Cherry, Vince Barabba, Jay Wetzel, Richard LeFauve, Roy Roberts, Jim Perkins, John Rock, Kenneth Baker, Heidi Kunz, Maureen Kempston Darkes, David Viano, Ron Haas, Gary Cowger, Thomas Gottschalk, George Peapples, Jim Taylor, Gerald Collins, Harold Kutner, Elizabeth Vanzura, Gerald Knechtel, Arvin Mueller, Joe Spielman, and John Rines for their time and assistance. In GM's public relations department, I would particularly like to thank Jack Harned for his work shepherding this project. Thanks also go to Bill O'Neill for his early support and suggestions, Ed Lechzin, Toni Simonetti, Stewart Low, Linda Cook, and Bruce MacDonald.

In GM's international operations, I must first thank Louis Hughes for allowing me to visit nearly every corner of GM's European operations and witness firsthand the success GM has enjoyed in Europe. Special thanks to Kenneth Levy, director of GM Europe public relations, for backing this project at a crucial point in its infancy, and to his assistant. Thanks also to Peter Hanenberger, David Herman, Charles Golden, Jurgen Stockmar, Richard Ruzzin, Richard Donnelly, Richard Nerod, and Eric Stevens.

I wish I had gotten the chance to interview GM chairman John Smale, who declined my requests to talk with him. Among people not associated with GM, grateful credit must first go to David Cole, director of the University of Michigan's Office for the Study of Automotive Transportation. He ran interference for me on at least three occasions when GM's cooperation was in doubt. Moreover, Dave was an instrumental link with a number of people who helped me gain a better understanding of where GM had been and what it was trying to do. Next, I must thank Robert Stempel for his generous time, as well as his assistant Sylvia. I'd like to thank a number of others, including Roger Smith, Bill Hoglund, Robert T. O'Connell, Donald Ephlin, Stephen Yokich, Joseph Phillippi, Steve Girsky, Ted Shasta, Christopher Cedergren, Ron Pinelli,

Nicholas Colas, John Whitney, George Borst, Nancy Garvey, Lawrence Bossidy, Jack Welch, J. Davis Illingworth, Mike DaPrile, Russell Scafede, Alexander Trotman, Dennis Pawley, Kenneth Whipple, and Bill and Judy Stevens, at whose cottage on Cape Cod this book came to life. Special thanks to Walter Hayes, whose support and guidance have been invaluable in my career. And I would especially like to thank two others who have requested to remain anonymous. They know this is their book as much as mine.

I must thank John Hillkirk, managing editor of the Money section at *USA Today*, , for his years of encouragement and his firm belief in the philosophy of empowerment. Thanks also go to his predecessor, Hal Ritter, to deputy managing editor Rodney Brooks, to automotive editor Paul Wiseman, and my auto team colleagues Jim Healey, Mike Clements, and Earle Eldridge for their brainstorming support. Also, thanks to my newsroom buddies Alma Mister, Ellen Neuborne, and Patricia Edmonds for their frequent help and pep talks. Warm thanks to MaryFran Tyler, whose extensive contacts in Worcester, Massachusetts, were invaluable in telling the story of Jack Smith's early years. A big thank you to the *USA Today* library staff.

I would like to thank my editor at Birch Lane Press, Jim Ellison, and my agent, Russell Galen. Thanks also to my great friend Kevin Lahart for introducing me to Russ. For their constant reassurances that I would finish this book, I must thank Judith Burns, Kathleen Kerwin, Keith Naughton, and John Guiniven.

Finally, I would like to thank my family, beginning with my wise and understanding mother, Bernice Maynard, my brother Frank, his wife Lisa, their son Benjamin, their baby Parker, and my godmother, Maxine Clapper. In closing, I want to salute the memory of my uncle, John Mordas, who died the summer before I began this book. His legacy enhanced this project (although he probably would have preferred that I invest in something with a guaranteed return). As a lifelong Cadillac owner, I am sure he would have been deeply interested in reading about the company that built his cars, and he might have had just as many questions for GM as I had.

FOREWORD

The American automobile industry is undergoing a transition of immense proportions. This process of change has not been easy, has not been pretty, and is certainly not over. Indeed, one of the most remarkable sagas in the restructuring of this industry is the story of General Motors, the world's largest industrial organization. For those of us who were brought up in Detroit, in the heart of the industry, the events of the past few years have been truly remarkable. It is difficult to find any part of General Motors that has not undergone fundamental change, and the change is continuing.

Few organizations in American industry have had the long-term success that General Motors enjoyed. During the 1950s, 60s, and much of the 70s, GM was the industry's low-cost producer because of its powerful economies of scale. With nearly 60 percent of the car market, its most challenging problems seemed to revolve around concerns that the Justice Department would try to break up GM because of its dominant market share. But in the 1970s, two energy crises, important new government regulations, and significant sales gains by the Japanese were followed by real and far more substantive challenges in the 1980s. The size, strength, and tradition of General Motors became its curse.

During the 1980s, GM tried to capitalize on the weakness of its U.S. competitors, Ford and Chrysler, with unprecedented investments in new products, facilities, and advanced technology. However, the path that was charted for GM almost brought the corporation to its knees in the early 1990s. The prevailing view inside of GM was that money and power could solve problems. This was a sharp contrast to the Toyota philosophy, which focuses on solving problems with technology that's cheaply and easily available before spending money on new high-tech equipment.

But perhaps the greatest problem within GM was its lack of a sense of urgency, due largely to managers perceiving the organization as infallible. This wasn't always the view of

xiii

senior management: often, they understood too well what needed to be done. But those beneath them just didn't believe change was required. After all, GM was GM. I remember numerous discussions with executives who, I believe, really saw the need for dramatic change but were almost powerless to galvanize the company.

In the 1990s, true disaster hit General Motors. When Roger Smith retired, a new management team was installed, but the die was cast. Serious cash flow problems arose and threatened to bring the giant corporation to its knees. The GM board, which had become more assertive in the late 1980s, took charge and forced the early retirement of CEO Robert Stempel and president Lloyd Reuss. The now more active board placed Jack Smith in charge with the simple assignment of stopping the cash hemmorhage and turning the battleship around— quickly. Now, under Smith, the battleship is turning, but it is still not a speedboat.

Detroit and General Motors have always been a somewhat closed community. It is not easy to become assimiliated into this industry from outside, just as it has not been easy for this industry to see the world around it. Even journalists covering the industry struggle to see inside it, but few really gain access to the minds of the leaders of this industry.

Maynard succeeds in lifting the cast iron and steel curtain of General Motors. She was given unprecedented access to many of the key leaders engaged in a transformation that is absolutely massive and is continuing. No longer is it possible to use a simple snapshot to describe unfolding events, when a video is required. I believe this book is, indeed, a dynamic written video of GM. Her insight is particularly revealing and should be of interest to all who are concerned with the auto industry, the long-term competitiveness of our country, and an increasingly challenging world environment.

The combination of saga and soap opera at General Motors will continue for some time to come. Is the corporation on the right course? Only time will tell, but my guess is the future of General Motors is bright, indeed. And Micheline Maynard has painted a most revealing picture of important elements of this transformation.

David Cole, director, Office for the Study of
Automotive Transportation, University of Michigan

Collision Course

CHAPTER • 1

The Invisible CEO

Monday, October 26, 1992, began for Jack Smith as it often did, with a 7:15 A.M. breakfast meeting at the General Motors building just north of downtown Detroit. At that hour, it took the GM president only about thirty minutes to ride in from his modern home in Bloomfield Hills, the upper-class suburb where scores of U.S. auto industry executives live. GM's top executives rarely ate breakfast at home, since most mornings began with a meeting in one of the wood-paneled dining rooms on the fourteenth floor of "the building," as it's called by those who work there. Smith's meeting was actually starting later than some at the company.

In GM's vast empire of car and truck and auto parts factories, the workday started at 6 A.M. when blue-collar workers showed up for the first shift. Smith had gotten used to leaving his house before dawn and getting home close to midnight. The morning and evening drives to and from work were his only moments of solitude. Waiting on the backseat when his driver arrived were copies of the *Wall Street Journal*, the *New York Times*, and Detroit's morning newspaper, the *Free Press*. Sometimes he'd make a few telephone calls on his cellular phone, but normally he'd use the time to glance at the newspapers, then give a final review to material for the meetings he was set to attend that day.

First on Smith's calendar that Monday was a meeting with a group of GM strategic planners who had been responsible for the program that Smith prayed would stop GM's financial hemorrhaging in North America and head the giant car company back to profitability. Just ten days earlier, Smith had chaired a meeting of GM's top 100 executives at the GM Technical Center, in Warren, Michigan. Speaking in the broad tones of his mid-Massachusetts birthplace, he'd quietly outlined the series of painful steps GM had to take to assure Wall Street, its shareholders, and, most important, its revolution-seeking board of directors, that the company could be put back on the track to success.

The plan, dubbed Fundamental Change, culminated six months of work by his driven young crisis team, mostly white male middle managers in their twenties, thirties, and early forties. Smith cherished these "Young Turks,"[1] whose dedication to fixing GM was matched only by his own. The plan's roots were in a proposal first drafted in secret more than a year before. The outline was prepared months before militant Wall Street ratings agencies and frustrated GM board members forced GM's embattled CEO Robert Stempel to announce a shattering plant-closing and job-cuts plan to take effect in December 1992. The young managers' turnaround plan would ultimately serve as the blueprint over the next few years for GM's often difficult and dispiriting efforts to streamline its bloated operations and shake up its internally competitive corporate culture.

The October 16 session had been a difficult day for Smith, who'd joined the company thirty years earlier at a GM assembly plant in Framingham, Massachusetts, just a short drive from his hometown of Worcester. Though Smith had never been comfortable giving presentations or speaking to big groups, it fell to him to remind his management colleagues that GM faced a dire fate—perhaps even financial ruin—if steps weren't taken to stop the severe bleeding that had drained $12 billion in cash (or $1 billion a month, as much as it cost in the 1980s to develop a new car or truck) from its North American operations over the past year. A top-secret report from GM's financial staff, circulated only to upper-level finance executives and members of the GM board, warned that GM was in danger of going bankrupt.

Outlining the turnaround proposal, Smith told the group,

"This is probably the toughest speech I've ever made in my career." But Smith had assured the exhausted and shell-shocked executives that the plan would work. As the living symbol of the GM directors' displeasure with Stempel's original management team, Smith knew the plan had to be successful or his own job as GM president was in doubt. He asked his fellow executives to keep the turnaround plan a secret from even their closest colleagues, because GM was going to announce it after the board of directors held its next meeting in New York on November 2.

Before then, however, Smith needed to make sure the GM planners had put enough detail in the program so he could assure the board that it would not be ignored by the thousands of middle managers who still weren't convinced of the depths of GM's problems. That was the reason he had called the early-morning meeting in Dining Room No. 3. The small conference room, site of many emergency brainstorming sessions that year, shared a connecting door that led to the offices of GM's president and chief executive. Among those waiting for Smith when he got to work were strategic planners Mark Hogan and Bob Purcell, and Smith's administrative assistant Mark Schmitz. They'd come to the meeting directly from their cars, parked in the garage in the basement of the GM building. Still wearing their suit coats, as was customary in the tradition-laden dining room, the men were poured coffee in white china cups by waiters who would then bring them their heart's desire for breakfast. (A request for fruit in the dead of winter would bring forth silver bowls of strawberries, blueberries, and raspberries; the choices of dry cereal rivaled a Kroger supermarket.)

In between sips of coffee and bites of toast, the group was deep into discussion when Stempel appeared in the doorway at around 8 A.M. looking "white and jowly," as one of the people in the room recalls. Just a few weeks before, the GM chairman had been hospitalized briefly in Washington after a fainting spell at a meeting of the conference board, a high-level cluster of the top CEOs in the U.S. who met regularly to mull big business's positions on public policy questions. He'd been rushed to George Washington University Hospital, the same place where Ronald Reagan was taken after he was shot by John Hinckley Jr. outside the Washington Hilton in 1981.

The doctors who'd attended Stempel wanted him to remain several days so they could run a complete battery of cardiac tests. They feared he might need surgery. Stempel refused. Against the doctors' advice, he was transported on a stretcher to a waiting GM jet at the private aviation terminal at National Airport, amid the tightest protection that the airport's security chief can ever recall, including that for visiting heads of state. Stempel's attack came the same day the *Washington Post* reported that members of GM's board of directors, who'd dumped Stempel's managers and installed Smith six months before, now wanted him to get tough with the United Auto Workers or face losing his job, too. The report set off a firestorm of speculation about Stempel's future. He'd tried to ride it out. But the board moved brutally and quickly to undercut Stempel's position.

The previous Thursday, Stempel showed up for a long-scheduled speech at a hotel in Dearborn, Michigan. His appearance was mobbed by members of Detroit's feisty and aggressive automotive media. GM's public relations officials, perplexed by their inability to find out what was going on in the company's upper ranks, made arrangements for Stempel to escape through the kitchen after the speech. But the reporters followed in heated pursuit, slipping and sliding on the wet and greasy floor. One of them nearly knocked himself out when he stumbled almost on Stempel's heels. Before striding out the door and ducking into a waiting GM car, the tall CEO, known for his courtesy, paused and quietly admonished the reporter to be more careful.

He might outrun the press, but Stempel could no longer escape the displeasure of outside members of the GM board. John Smale, retired CEO of Procter & Gamble, cut the legs out from Stempel late that afternoon. Smale had been named chairman of the board's executive committee six months earlier, the first time that position had not been held by GM's sitting CEO. Advised by New York attorney Ira Millstein, Smale and non-company board members began playing a role unprecedented in American corporate governance—and one that would be copied by boards at IBM, Kmart, Sears, and Morrison Knudson in the years to come.

Smale had been all but invisible that tumultuous year. Now, he came forward to bring the crisis at GM to a head. On Thursday afternoon Stempel had asked GM's corporate spokesman, Jim Crellin, to put a statement together that emphasized GM was on track with its turnaround plan. Before the statement could be written, Smale had released his own. The words were tantamount to a vote of no confidence in Stempel's two-year-old administration.* During the weekend that followed Smale's terse proclamation, Stempel's plight was picked apart by radio talk show hosts, newspaper columnists, and television commentators. The courtly man who'd guarded his public image with such care was the number one subject of debate in shopping malls, restaurants, and at tailgate parties at the University of Michigan football game. Most of the comments weren't kind.

As Detroit was buzzing about him, Stempel decided to find out where he stood. Saturday and Sunday, he called board members to see whether he had any support left for remaining as CEO.[2] None of them specifically asked him to resign, but their collective unhappiness became clearer with every phone call. Stempel spoke with many of GM's senior managers, and had two conversations with Smith. Stempel did not tell anyone of his plans, yet his closest colleagues knew the calls were a way of warning them he was about to act. Despite her deep concern for her husband's welfare, Stempel's stylish wife, Pat, didn't try to sway her husband but left him alone to mull his options. With all the criticism ringing in his ears, lacking the faith of the board, worried about the paralysis that was gripping the company, and with his own deteriorating health to consider, Stempel threw in the towel. He finally made up his

---

*John Smale's statement was this: "The General Motors board of directors has taken no action regarding any management changes at GM. However, the question of executive leadership is a primary concern to the board of directors of any company and GM is no exception. The GM board of directors continues to carefully reflect upon the wisest course for assuring the most effective leadership for the corporation."

mind on Sunday night, October 25, that he would quit the next morning. And he wanted to tell Smith the news in person.

"Jack, can I see you a minute?" Stempel, standing in the door of the breakfast meeting, asked GM's president. Smith, without glancing at the others in the room, left and walked away with Stempel. About ten minutes later, he returned, his forehead drawn in thought beneath the pointed widow's peak in his dark hair. "We have to keep the meeting short because Bob has just resigned, and we need to work through that," Smith quietly told the young men.

Nobody in the room spoke for a moment. But all were thinking the same thought: Jack Smith is now in charge of General Motors.

In reality, Stempel's resignation on October 26 was simply the other shoe dropping in a management shakeup that had been thrust upon the company the previous April 6, Jack Smith's birthday. That Monday, as GM's board met in Dallas, home of the company's ED electronics subsidiary, Smith, who had been GM's vice chairman in charge of international operations, was named GM's president and its CEO in all but title. The day is not one Smith likes to discuss, even years later. Asked if it was true he'd told friends it was the worst day of his life, Smith replied, "I wouldn't want to have another one like it."[3]

The reason for the board's action was simple and bleak: GM was teetering close to financial ruin. It was a fate few inside the company wanted to believe, none more so than Stempel, the "car guy" who was supposed to put the company back on the track with standout cars and trucks. GM had been the symbol of American industrial might for more than eighty years, since its founding in 1908 by William Crapo Durant. Its sweeping organization touched almost every corner of the USA—and many nations across the globe. By the 1990s, GM had 750,000 employees around the world, two thirds of them in the United States. It had three times more employees in the U.S. than its closest rival, Ford. GM employed one of every five factory workers in the country. More than 2.1 million people fell under its generous health care plan, including active workers, retirees, and members of their families. Every GM job, the Commerce Department calculated, had a direct impact on five more jobs—suppliers who provided parts for GM cars, bankers who made car loans to GM customers, waitresses in coffee shops across the street from GM plants and offices. GM's sales approached a staggering $150 billion—nearly 50 percent more than Ford, and almost triple the sales of number-three Chrysler. GM had more than 300 factories, offices, and parts-supply operations spread across the world. Its single-spaced list of subsidiaries filled four pages in its annual 10-K financial report to the government. Its place at the top of the *Fortune* 500 list was unchallenged.

It had taken thirty years for GM's problems to come to a boiling point. In the 1960s, GM had held nearly 60 percent of the car market. The Justice Department regularly threatened to dismantle GM's operations, but the company wasn't really afraid of the government. With six car and truck divisions— Chevrolet, Pontiac, Oldsmobile, Buick, Cadillac, and GMC— more than ten thousand car dealers, and an advertising budget close to $1 billion a year, GM dominated the industry in a way that awed its competitors. Henry Ford II, who took control of his family's auto company after World War II and ran it until 1980, was fascinated by GM. He pinned GM's sprawling organization chart to his wall and would use it to intimidate employees who were afraid to thrust Ford into new lines of business.[4] Try as Ford might, with cars like Mustang and the Lincoln Continental, its 20 percent of the car market was no challenger for GM's empire. "GM was not just the market leader. It was hugely the market leader," says Walter Hayes, retired chairman of Aston Martin who served as vice chairman of Ford of Europe. "GM became an institution and not a company. It is difficult for anyone to cope with that burden."

Like other institutions of the time—the Pentagon, AT&T, IBM—GM was thick with bureaucracy and plagued by tunnel vision. The simplest decisions took inordinate amounts of time to push through to the top, where decision-making power was centered. To get a slight change in a headlight approved took fifteen meetings before the matter went to GM's president. If Chevrolet wanted to offer special financing deals to graduating college seniors, GM's management committee, headed by the chairman, had to approve the marketing plans. Divisions brutally competed against each other for customers, ignoring the rest of the industry in their quest to be GM's top-seller. "If you were at Oldsmobile, you didn't talk to the guys at Chevrolet," Stempel recalls. "[That attitude] was [encouraged] because that's where the competition was. If Buick and Olds could go head to head, that was for the good of the corporation. It went on a lot longer than it should have."[5] Meanwhile, as the executives focused on one-upmanship, the automotive world was rapidly changing. In response to the oil shocks of the 1970s, Japanese carmakers and Germany's Volkswagen introduced small, fuel-efficient cars that appealed to young buyers. GM, often likened to the *Queen Mary*, could not possibly turn itself around in such a narrow river of time. When the 1970s began, more than 90 percent of its cars were mid-sized and large models that averaged fourteen miles per gallon. GM tried to downsize its fleet, but its smaller cars couldn't compare with Japanese autos in quality or price.

Moreover, GM executives weren't convinced that the problems were real. Long into the 1980s, the prevailing mind-set within GM was that the young buyers might try imports while they were single, but when they began raising families, they would want the big cars GM sold. GM didn't need to change much because buyers would come to it. Meanwhile, GM thought it could rely on its huge stable of customers to come back for new GM cars and sustain the automaker's market share. But even the most loyal GM buyers had run out of patience. They began to desert the company in droves midway through the decade, buying aerodynamic Ford Tauruses, reliable Honda Accords, and appealing Toyota Camrys. Though GM's market share was clearly shrinking, the loss of customers did not spark a crisis within the huge company.

There's an easy explanation. GM is not like the rest of America. It thinks it is. But GM's America, like the one that Ronald Reagan thought he remembered and Newt Gingrich wants to restore, is still largely the America of the 1950s. GM may be the last place where white males can comfortably plan a career without fear that they might not receive a promotion because a minority or a woman was qualified and in the running. Women have almost no say in the GM world, minorities even less. There are four women and two blacks among GM's forty-seven vice presidents; all fifteen executives above them are white males. In the five steps of the management pyramid (the CEO forming the tip), the few GM women and minorities with authority are clustered at the base. Behind the scenes, however, GM could not survive without its extremely capable secretaries, who are instrumental in keeping their bosses' hectic schedules. Around GM, it's a common sight to see executives whip out three-by-five cards that fit into a suit pocket to check where they are supposed to be next. The administrative assistant juggles the twenty to twenty-five messages that flood in during the morning and organizes them by importance on her boss's desk so he can flip through them when he gets back from lunch. She knows where her boss is, day or night, and, since executives share their office suites, where other bosses are supposed to be as well. Few reporters get through this phalanx unless a boss has left instructions that it's okay to take a message. (And no GM car–owner with a problem stands a chance; they'd instantly be referred to a customer-assistance center whose young telephone operators are trained in anger diffusion.) Though GM has a state-of-the-art telephone mailbox system with many options—"Press one for urgent delivery, press two for normal delivery"—almost everyone prefers the ease of having an assistant take his messages.

GM can seem an unconnected and sterile place, the modern equivalent of those quaint 1950s ads in *Life* magazine where teenagers sit docilely on plaid stadium blankets sipping Pepsi-Cola and munching on potato chips. It's the world of television sitcoms—at least, the ones before *Roseanne*. It's a world based on values like conformity and relentless upward mobility. It's the world of the suburbs, preferably the new ones where seedlings are still struggling to get over ten feet tall. It's a world that still exists in only a few instances in the rest of America. For the most part, it's largely been obliterated by the women's movement, crime, poverty, AIDS, corporate downsizing, high technology, CNN, the Japanese auto industry, and the breakup of the nuclear family.

The culture of GM is a living, breathing thing that perplexes anyone who tries to change it. Over the past few years, GM has shifted much of its focus from the GM building to its sprawling Technical Center campus in suburban Warren, Michigan. The move has been touted as GM's way of getting closer to its customers. But in reality, GM merely traded an office building isolated in the city to a complex isolated in the suburbs. The chain-link fences around the Tech Center might as well be the limestone walls of the GM building for all that they keep out the world.

GM's culture, no matter where the office is located, is still extremely competitive. Before the mid-1980s, GM was a continent of fiefdoms. Each business unit and car division had its own identity and distrusted other parts of GM that might compete with it for resources. Each division had its priority: Chevrolet's was to build cars as cheaply as possible; Oldsmobile's was to pump a little luxury into those cars; Cadillac's was to grab every safety and gee-whiz innovation first to dazzle its well-heeled buyers. Says Stempel, "You knew at Chevrolet that you would kill your mother for a tenth of a cent."[6] All that was supposed to change when Roger Smith reorganized GM, and when Stempel, in one of his last actions as CEO, created GM's North American Operations, tying all its car development pieces together. But despite the best efforts by many to change internal competition to an atmosphere of consensus, it still exists. And, argues one company manager, the culture of looking inward is the biggest impediment to GM's progress.

Like the British royal family, it seems at times that an executive had to be born into GM to really be comfortable and accepted there. At the minimum, anyone who tries to rise must be willing to work long hours—probably ten hours a day, and even longer on the New York financial staff. The goal of every young staffer is to join the ranks of the "unclassified"—the GM equivalent of winning tenure at a university. Unclassified status makes a staffer eligible for an annual bonus, stock options, and other goodies that send annual pay into the six-figure range. Savvy staffers who've managed to gain notice from their superiors quickly learn to demand unclassified status when they are offered transfers and promotions. But the designation can also be a curse. It means giving up a life outside the office for years, at least during the week. If you're based in Detroit, there's no time for socializing unless it's a business dinner or a professional meeting, like the Society of Automotive Engineers or the Harvard Club. That's true for all the auto companies, not just GM. Though Detroit is home to one of the finest symphonies in the world, whose broadcasts on classical music stations are sponsored by GM, it's rare to find more than a couple of people who admit to attending the DSO's concerts on a regular basis.

Many people who follow the industry are information junkies, devouring newspapers and magazines, cruising television news programs and radio stations, searching for the latest auto industry tidbits. That's not the case at GM, where more briefcases carry copies of the *Detroit Free Press* than of the *Financial Times*. The *Free Press* is the first newspaper forty-year-old NAO president G. Richard Wagoner, who oversees a staff of 300,000 employees, picks up each morning. He also glances at *USA Today* and the *Wall Street Journal*, but that's the end of his daily information flow unless he's traveling and has time on his hands. Wagoner says he doesn't listen to radio on the way to work, so he misses Detroit's talk radio shows and the in-depth reporting of National Public Radio. He gets home too late for local television news, and if he watches anything, it's a basketball game.[7]

That kind of a world no longer sounds very appealing to the millions of people who've turned their backs on corporate America to start new careers from home offices, where they control their own destiny. But, for decades, a job at GM was the biggest brass ring a young, ambitious business school student could grab. Once he got to GM, he found that instead of worrying about beating outside competition, many executives spent more time figuring out how they'd climb GM's corporate ladder. Getting to the top required a combination of tenacity, ingenuity, patience, and networking. GM executives devoted their lives to plotting their careers, finding the right mentors, taking the right transfers, putting themselves in line for the crucial promotions, and making sure they got the right amount of visibility, but not too much, so they could keep advancing. They coveted offices on the fourteenth floor of the GM building, in the executive wing. And the ultimate goal was the CEO's office in the southeast corner of the GM building, facing downtown Detroit and Canada beyond. Everybody gossiped about who was in, who was out, who was rising, who'd been frozen out of competition. Detroit's newspapers and the auto industry trade publication, *Automotive News*, at times resembled the *Daily Racing Form*, because they'd handicap the odds of senior executives who were vying for the chairman's job.

Jack Smith may have been the first GM chief executive who never entered the race. Indeed, with GM close to running out of cash in the fall of 1992, it was hard to understand why anybody would have wanted the job. Says UAW president Stephen Yokich, "He inherited the worst-case scenario of a company in this country." Until Stempel took control in 1990, GM's CEO had been a dictator, so authoritative that his statements could move stock markets on Wall Street, in London, and in Tokyo. Running GM was as difficult as running the Kremlin, and its leader had to deal with as many blocs as any Russian leader ever faced. No CEO could ever count on full support from both of GM's factions—the finance men, derisively called "bean counters," and the operations men, or "car guys." Until Stempel, an engineer, became CEO, the top GM job had always gone to a finance man. The number-two job belonged to a car guy, who in theory should have had tremendous influence on company direction. But the final decisions were up to the chief executive, whose operations experience was usually pretty limited.

Choosing Stempel was supposed to be a sign GM would put a renewed focus on developing leading-edge cars and trucks that would stop its market share plunge. He knew firsthand what it was like to sit at a drawing board. When he was still a high school student, his first job had been as a mechanic in New Jersey, and, until the complex power plants with their computer controls became the norm in the 1990s, he could tear down an engine as well as any of its creators. Stempel, who'd attended Worcester Polytechnic Institute in Smith's hometown, joined GM as an engineer at Oldsmobile in 1958. On his first day he was asked to design a wheel for a rear-wheel-drive Oldsmobile then under development. "Here I was, a graduate engineer, and I'm reinventing the wheel," he recalls.[8] Stempel made a sketch and handed it to his boss, who asked him what he'd learned. Stempel replied, "Nothing. This is pretty dumb." And his boss replied, "You should learn something from everything." Stempel literally went back to his drawing board (in the days before computer-aided design took over many of the tasks engineers used to perform by hand) and researched everything he could learn about wheels. "By the time I finished that project, I knew an awful lot about wheels," he says. He went on to work on the first Oldsmobile Toronado, head Oldsmobile engineering, and move up the GM ladder. GM chief executive Roger Smith named him GM president in 1987, and in 1990 he followed Smith to the top job.

By the time Stempel took over, GM's market share had fallen to little over half what the company held when he first went to work there. The descent had accelerated through the 1980s. In 1987, when Stempel became president, GM began the year with 42 percent of the car market. It lost five percentage points of market share that year, the equivalent of 500,000 sales, even though automakers were near the peak of their mid-1980s boom cycle. And the losses continued. By the time financial crisis loomed in 1992, GM held barely 34 percent of the car market, a loss of eight points in five years. Yet GM's factories in theory were able to build enough cars and trucks to fill a 66 percent market share. Stempel knew from the day he became president that GM had to close plants. In the late 1980s, the company had shut five assembly plants, including the one in Framingham where Jack Smith began his GM career.

Late in 1991, Stempel tried to mollify GM's board by announcing a gut-wrenching plan to slash 75,000 jobs and close twenty-three assembly and parts plants. But the directors, particularly those who didn't work for GM, did not think he was moving fast enough. They decided the company had to have a leader with broad management experience who could take hold of the problems and turn GM in the right direction. That winter, board member Smale interviewed several levels of GM executives, trying to figure out who had a handle on the crisis facing the giant auto company. He was looking for an insider who was also an outsider. He wanted someone who understood GM both from a finance and an operations stand-point. He was seeking someone who had a following within the company, but somebody who had an outside view as well. He wanted somebody with discipline and a strong disdain for the creative bookkeeping that had become the norm at GM.

Jack Smith fit the bill almost perfectly. Born in 1938, he'd spent his lifetime at the world's biggest carmaker, rising from a job as a payroll clerk in the Framingham factory to GM's savvy New York treasurer's office, a training ground for the com-pany's top financial minds. Roger Smith, GM's treasurer in the 1970s, likes to take credit for discovering Jack Smith and placing him in key jobs. Had he merely progressed in his financial path, Jack Smith's rise to the top might have included a stint as GM's chief financial officer, possibly on the way to becoming CEO sometime when he was close to sixty. But instead Jack Smith's career path turned overseas. He negoti-ated the company's ground-breaking joint venture with Toyota to build small cars in California. He went up to Canada to run GM's auto plants and marketing operations, gaining valuable knowledge about manufacturing and marketing. He turned GM Europe from a mediocre money-loser into a market leader. Summoned back to Detroit in 1988 by then-CEO Roger Smith, Jack Smith took charge of GM's international operations and made it a solid performer. When Roger Smith retired in 1990, it was rumored Jack Smith had a shot at the president's job. But he lost out to Lloyd Reuss, one of Stempel's closest GM colleagues and an inveterate believer in GM's market dominance.

With GM's car and truck operations in the United States stalled out and losing billions, Jack Smith's success overseas made him the perfect candidate in Smale's eyes to take charge of the company. Inside GM Jack Smith already had amassed a solid crew of young managers and seasoned executives who fought for the chance to work for him in New York in the 1960s and 1970s, and who later followed him into key jobs as he quietly climbed the GM ladder. Smith dislikes the insinuation that he has a clique—"I don't only [promote] the guys I grew up with," he says[9]—but many of the people in GM's top two dozen jobs worked for him at some point years ago in a finance job or in Europe.

Just as his global background set him apart from his predecessor, Smith's style, too, has been a complete change for GM. As a boss, he does more listening than talking, never ruling out an idea if it is worthy of investigation. In the 1970s at GM, complained former executive John De Lorean, top managers were deluged with paper, often taking home 600 to 800 pages a night to read before dawn. But Smith doesn't want lengthy reports, only a one-page summary of a proposal. If he likes an idea, he'll often scribble, "Go ahead, JFS" on it and shoot it back through inter-office mail. He returns phone calls within minutes if the matter is urgent. He prefers that managers make decisions affecting their particular parts of GM on their own. But when a major decision faces the company, he wants the issue to be discussed by everyone involved.

"He absolutely had the kind of style of leadership that we needed," says planner Purcell, one of the young men who met with Smith on the day Stempel resigned. "He's a plainspoken kind of nuts-and-bolts manager. He's not flamboyant or showy, no. He's ultimately believable."

"His leadership style is something else," says NAO president Wagoner, whose own open manner has been compared to that of Smith. "If you work for him, you feel one hundred percent empowered to do the right stuff. Ninety percent of the time, he's very predictable. There's no mystery here. You don't lay out sixty-six options and go into his office and wonder how it's all going to come out."

"Jack has taught me to be a leader by his example," says Hughes, president of GM's International Operations, who first worked with Smith in the treasurer's office in the 1970s. "In his quiet, unassuming way, he inspires people to want to do their best for him."

"Jack is just Jack," says David Cole, director of the University of Michigan's Office for the Study of Automotive Transportation, whose father, Edward Cole, was GM's president in the turbulent 1970s.

One of Smith's most famous sayings among the people who know him is, "Deeds, not words." He is a firm believer in the idea that GM's accomplishments during his tenure should speak for themselves, that hype is not the way to make them happen. It is a crucial philosophy, for GM has always been a company of big dreams and poor execution. Every time it trumpets a goal, it trips over itself trying to achieve it. Smith has deliberately tried to break that pattern. Of medium height, with dark hair and usually merry but sometimes haunted-looking blue eyes, Smith may easily be the most reflective of GM's chief executives.

Early in his tenure as CEO Smith gave a commencement address at Quinsigamond Community College in his hometown that he wrote by himself, with help from his sisters, Sally and Mary Carroll, both teachers and scholars. Smith told the graduates that to prosper, they had to keep their health, and they needed the support of their families. "You also need to have a *purpose* in your life. And that purpose has to be something beyond yourself—a greater good. Try to find a greater good for yourself." In words that were obviously close to his heart, Smith said the graduates would need to be competent. They would have to work very hard. "I think you also have to be humble. Believe me, if you're not humble now, life has ways of making you humble," he said. He told the graduates they would see highs and lows. They'd be disappointed, defeated. "You will be, but fight back! Keep your feet on the earth." A sense of humor was important. And he said the graduates should not be afraid to take chances, and to show leadership. "When you can bring out the best in people, you can be a leader," Smith said.

In the 1980s, Roger Smith preached teamwork while practicing tyranny. Stempel tried to stress the importance of his management team, only to see his group disbanded when GM went to hell. Jack Smith, on the other hand, embodies the concept of consensus that is a frequent topic of lectures by quality gurus. Rarely now is an important call made at the company without discussion by the board of managers who are involved in carrying it out—the North American Strategy Board, the European Strategy Board, or the International Strategy Board, for issues involving GM's global operations. Such sharing of authority is clearly Smith's attempt to break the destructive patterns of self-preservation that made GM's top management worried more about competing with each other than with the outside world.

Yet as the years of his leadership go by, Smith is little more known and understood than he was the day he took the job. Smith clearly is no Lee Iacocca, basking in the spotlight, or Jack Welch, happy to have another opportunity to spread his gospel of efficiency. Although he has a constituency of 750,000 employees and triple that number of retirees and family members, he simply has not seemed convinced that public displays are that important. It could be a reaction to the blaze of publicity that followed his selection as president and subsequently CEO. Or it may be that his concept of leadership is different from that of the typical CEO. On a stone in his office are the words of Chinese philosopher Lao-tzu.

> A leader is best
> When people barely know he exists.
> Not so good when people obey him and acclaim him.
> Worse when they despise him.
> But of a good leader
> Who talks little, when his work is done
> And his aim fulfilled,
> They will say,
> "We did it ourselves."

Clearly, he doesn't want the focus on himself. Embarrassed by a flattering 1993 *Business Week* cover story, he left the magazine on the kitchen counter at home for two weeks before picking it up. Any other company would have ordered 50,000 reprints of *Fortune* magazine's 1994 saga, "GM's $11 Billion Turnaround," and shared them with opinion leaders. Not Smith's GM. It was probably just as well that GM's public relations department didn't trumpet the comeback story, because soon after the magazine hit the newsstands, GM's third-quarter earnings headed south, along with its stock. In the days that followed, people began to wonder whether the overhaul that Smith had directed since 1992 had been completely successful.

It is not an unreasonable question. Thus far the Smith years at GM have been a time of raised hopes, probing examinations, and continued uncertainty. Under Smith, GM's team of financial experts attacked the company's bleeding balance sheet and brought torrential losses under control. In 1994, GM earned record corporate profits that likely will continue for the next few years if the economy cooperates. Yet within GM's vital North American Operations, which constitutes 65 percent of its revenue, Smith's team has had trouble with the company's most basic mission: getting new cars and trucks off the ground cleanly, efficiently, and on time. There are many questions about the direction the world's most complex auto company will take in the years to come. And even Smith, the man thrust in charge of a company he never schemed to lead, may not begin to know all the answers.

CHAPTER · 2

A Car for Every Purse and Purpose

The 1936 movie *Dodsworth* opens to the strains of "Auld Lang Syne" and the sight of a solitary figure of a man, standing at the window of his office, gazing at an auto factory. The company's name, Dodsworth, is stretched across the side of the screen in tall, silver art deco letters. The man, who we realize is the factory's owner, seems to imperceptibly tremble. The camera pans to his desk, where we see a newspaper, the *Zenith Times-Advocate*, whose headline proclaims, "Dodsworth Motors Sold to U.M." A kind voice breaks the reverie. "Mr. Dodsworth, the men are ready," the secretary tells the executive. The scene then shifts to a courtyard of the great auto factory, where a giant winged emblem boasting "Dodsworth 6" is emblazoned on a wall. Men in coveralls and working clothes respectfully shake their boss's hand and wish him good luck. "Hate to see you go, Sam," and "Good luck, Sam," they tell him. Finally, Dodsworth is shown in his limousine, headed to his mansion, the newspaper on the seat next to him. Through the back of the car, we see the towers of the plant billowing steam into the air. Dodsworth takes a final look, sighs, and picks up the newspaper, undoubtedly to read the story of his sellout.

It may have been the movies, but it was a scene repeated dozens of times in the early 1900s as General Motors built its empire. Unlike Ford, whose founder Henry Ford was a widely recognized mogul by 1910, or Chrysler, whose Walter P. Chrysler was nearly as renowned, General Motors never had a figurehead. It was begun as a collection of companies designed to combine the strengths of each in a powerful force that could dominate the industry. William Crapo Durant often is called the founder of GM, but he acted in consort with New York bankers and financiers whose blood coursed not black with motor oil but steely cold with silver and gold. GM's roots were not in carriage-making as Durant's own had been. It was not the culmination of a dream, like the automakers founded by Olds or Nash. It was merely a good business deal.

Durant founded GM on October 1, 1908. He'd wanted to call it United Motors but changed his mind at the last minute. (GM would find a use for the name seventy-five years later, when it formed a joint car venture with Toyota.) GM was a holding company. Buick and Oldsmobile were acquired the first year; Oakland, later known as Pontiac, and Cadillac followed in 1909. Durant had big plans for the combined operation, but in 1910 he ran into a financial crisis and had to give controlling interest to a group of East Coast bankers. But Durant wasn't through yet. He joined up with Louis Chevrolet to form a car company whose vehicles were intended to appeal to people on limited budgets. Sales were good, and soon the bankers wanted shares in their company. Durant traded stock, little by little, for shares in GM and within four years he had enough to launch a proxy fight.

Yet he ran into some formidable forces. Delaware's DuPont family, always looking to build on its chemical fortune, was intrigued by the idea of investing in the growing motor industry. The bankers appealed to family scion Pierre DuPont to represent their interests. They made him chairman of the company, and the DuPonts began snapping up shares. Eventually, they held 30 percent of GM and remained the car-maker's biggest shareholder until the 1950s, when the Justice Department forced the DuPonts to divest. With DuPont at the helm, GM kept growing through World War I, adding Fisher Body, forming a subsidiary in Canada, and creating General Motors Acceptance Corp., which would become a financial powerhouse at its own.

Durant was the catalyst for the founding of GM, but it took until the 1920s for the company to have a leader that set it on the course it would follow for decades to come. Alfred P. Sloan, often called one of America's greatest business minds, took control in 1920 after a boardroom coup not much different from the one that would occur in 1992. He was charged with sorting out GM's array of acquisitions. Like Jack Smith seventy years later, Sloan saw that GM was staggering under its own weight. It had bought everything in sight, only to be stuck with clumps of car and auto parts companies that had little in common and whose duplication was mindboggling. Its 1921 product lineup, for example, showed ten cars from Chevrolet, Oakland, Oldsmobile, Scripps-Booth, Sheridan, Buick, and Cadillac. Prices of many models were similar and so were the cars' features; the divisions even copied one another's magazine ads.

Sloan put an end to the floundering and established two guiding principles. Sloan wanted GM to be a car company that could offer a full range of carefully designed vehicles, from small and cheap to large and luxury, making money on nearly all the cars it sold. To do that, the automaker had to have strict financial planning and controls.

Sloan decreed the company should never lose a customer. When the buyer outgrew a car on one level, he could move up a notch. The ultimate goal, naturally, would be to climb to the top of the ladder. Sloan called it "a car for every purse and purpose." In his 1964 book, *My Years at General Motors*, which is still taught in countless business-school classes, Sloan laid out a hypothetical lineup of cars in price ranges of $400 to $600, $600 to $900, $900 to $1,200, $1,200 to $1,700, $1,700 to $2,500, and $2,500 to $3,500. (Just multiply these figures by twelve and you'll get a similar lineup for the 1990s.)

The point of setting up price categories, Sloan said, was to keep limits on the number of vehicles a company offered. But he didn't want big gaps in price between the categories. His thought was that GM should lure buyers into spending just a little more money than they'd originally planned. They could look at the lineup and see the cars that beckoned from atop the product pile. By just spending a little more per month, the buyers could have more features, comfort, and status. (That was the flawed idea behind LaSalle, which was designed to be a "poor man's Cadillac" between Buick and Cadillac. It turned out that even poor people knew the difference—they'd rather have a Cadillac.) Sloan, however, didn't want GM to focus all its efforts on selling the more expensive models and its luxury cars because he knew the company couldn't sell enough to stay in business. He thought GM should put its greatest emphasis on the middle of the market. If GM had listened to Sloan, people who worked for Smith said decades later, the 1990s overhaul might never have been necessary.

All this was a moot point when Sloan came up with his theory, because GM was getting killed in the marketplace by Ford. In 1920, for example, Ford had 60 percent of the market for mid-level cars and trucks; Chevrolet, later to become Ford's chief competitor, had just 4 percent of the car market. Sloan knew that GM had to put its focus on the vehicles it would build in the mid-1920s and beyond. GM borrowed $83 million—a staggering amount for the 1920s—to pay for the development of these key models. But Sloan didn't want designers and engineers guessing at what the market wanted, and he didn't want GM introducing vehicles just to compete with what Ford brought out. He set up strict criteria for new car projects:

- Is it logical and necessary to the lineup?
- Has it been properly developed technically?
- Will it benefit the corporation—not just its division?
- How much money will it make, compared with other cars in the works?

To keep control over the outlay, Sloan set up a practice that would be etched in the stone of the GM Building almost as deeply as the "D" that is all that remains of Durant's dream. Sloan decided that the executive and finance committees of the board of directors would have control over car projects. Managers of the programs could spend small amounts of money without having to ask for permission, but anything major had to be approved by the board. He felt he had good reason to do this: Sloan discovered that GM's cash management was dismal.

Each division controlled its own finances, banking all its income and paying its own bills. Since only the divisions sold vehicles, money never got to the corporation. Sloan changed it so that all the money flowed through one central accounting office. Soon, under Sloan, it was clear that the finance operation was GM's real nerve center. His intent was to free the divisions and car-program managers from having to be concerned with cars' finances. He wanted the stylists, like Harley Earl, who joined GM in the 1920s, to have complete freedom—within the identity of each division.

It did not take long for Sloan's new organization to pay off. By 1927, GM had earned the biggest corporate profit to date: $235 million. Just before the stock market crashed, GM had grabbed the market back from Ford. In 1928, one of every three cars sold was a GM product. Every car sold generated a profit of $150—something that GM couldn't manage to do sixty years later. By the New York Auto Show of 1929, GM's lineup included a six-cylinder Chevrolet, two truck lines at Chevrolet and GMC, an all-new Buick, and new transmissions for its top-of-the-line Cadillac and LaSalle luxury cars. But when financial disaster occurred, GM was not immune. In late 1929 it lost its leadership to Ford and tried to stimulate the market with deep price cuts. Nothing worked. GM's stock, which stood at $73 a share in early September, fell to $8 within three years.

Yet GM's size worked to its advantage during the Depression. While other companies were suffering, its market share climbed above 40 percent, although of a market half the size of the pre-crash one. By the middle of the decade, thanks to New Deal programs and the National Recovery Act, people were beginning to buy cars again, and GM could offer the most choices.

But just as the market got better, GM faced the first of what would be many labor crises with the fledgling United Auto Workers union. The UAW, which would face a tough organizing fight at Ford along with its battle at GM, began a drive for reforms in GM plants that continues to this day. Its original demands included weekly payment to workers, a limit to speedups on the assembly line, and guarantees of job security. GM saw no need to give in, and the union decided to close the company down. Using a tactic it still draws upon with success in the 1990s, the union looked for factories that built parts used in many GM cars. Shutting down a parts plant would have a broader effect than just closing one assembly plant, since many factories needed the parts built there. The UAW chose GM's Fisher Body Plant No. 1 in Flint, Michigan, which built body stampings for Buick, Oldsmobile, Pontiac, and LaSalle cars. The UAW planned to add other parts plants to the strike if the shutdown lasted.

Early in January 1937, workers at Fisher Body No. 1 sat down at their jobs and refused to do more work. A mile away, workers at Fisher Body No. 2 joined the shutdown. Other plants stopped work as GM shut factories that could not operate without the key parts. Within a few days, more than 105,000 workers were on strike. All seemed peaceful until January 10, when a fight broke out between plant guards and strikers. Door hinges, bolts, and car parts flew through the air. Police turned a high-pressure hose on the strikers, and then several officers opened fire. One worker was seriously hurt and thirteen more suffered flesh wounds. The next day, Michigan governor Frank Murphy arrived in Flint with 1,200 National Guard troops. Murphy offered to arbitrate and convinced the workers to leave the plants in order to hold formal talks. But the plan fell through because of rumors that GM was going to fire anybody involved in the strike. President Franklin Roosevelt and Labor Secretary Frances Perkins tried to talk Sloan into participating in negotiations with the workers. But Sloan got mad when word of the meeting became public. He issued an ultimatum to the workers: leave the plants or no negotiations.

The workers refused and unexpectedly grabbed control of GM's Cleveland Plant No. 4, which built Chevrolet engines. That shut down all of Chevrolet, GM's biggest division. Threats and court injunctions flew between the sides. Some at GM favored sending in the National Guard, but cooler heads managed to prevail. Finally, the workers' representatives and company officials agreed to let the union sign up as many members as it wanted; the company would discuss the union's demands and GM retained the right to deal with other unions. That first walkout, one of many to come at GM, cost the company $175 million in revenue from 280,000 cars it couldn't build. More than 150,000 GM employees had been laid off because of the walkouts. And a tense labor-management relationship, which never much improved, got off to a rocky start.

By the end of the 1930s, Chevrolet had built its twenty-five millionth car; LaSalle was close to extinction, and Harley Earl emerged as one of the industry's most talented designers. Millions of people flocked to the 1939 World's Fair in New York to visit GM's beautifully designed exhibit, with its cars of the future and their streamlined look. But threats of war were wafting toward the United States from Europe. In early 1940, Chevrolet got its first order for war materials, and GM president William Knudson resigned to head the Defense Department's Office of Production Management. GM's plants were told to aggressively bid for any government contracts for war materials. By February 1942, when Roosevelt ordered a halt to all automobile production, the auto industry's new role was clear. Detroit became the arsenal of democracy. GM plants quickly converted to building jeeps, troop carriers, and armaments: tanks, ships, fighter planes, guns, and cannons. GM built nearly two thirds of the trucks used by U.S. troops. Its overseas operations, like Vauxhall in England, built tanks and munitions for use by American and British troops in Europe. The Cleveland plant that the UAW had shut down built diesel engines for destroyers and their warships. As male auto workers signed up for duties overseas, women took their places, some the first ever hired at their plants. GM factories were churning out war materials so rapidly that when the war ended it took nine thousand rail cars to haul away every bit of war work that was in progress on the assembly lines.

With the war over, 1946 should have been a year of celebration and regrouping at GM. Instead, the union and the company were battling yet again. With plants cranking up to meet the postwar demand for cars, UAW president Walter Reuther thought his workers deserved a bigger raise than GM was offering. GM president Charlie Wilson was willing to talk but found the union's demands unreasonable. The pair, who'd had a warm relationship throughout the day-and-night production of the war, sat down to resolve their differences. They came to within one cent an hour, and Reuther figured GM would cave in to the demand rather than risk a walkout with so many buyers in line for new cars. He was wrong. Wilson refused to pay the extra penny, and the UAW struck GM for 101 days. Ultimately, GM did give in and Wilson learned a valuable lesson about dealing with Reuther. Just two years later, the two agreed to a milestone in union-company relations. In 1948 GM agreed to pay cost-of-living allowances as well as raises, giving workers more money as inflation grew. The three-year contract cost GM a bundle but the company had bought labor stability. "General Motors may have paid a billion for peace, but it got a bargain," *Fortune* magazine said.

Now GM could get on with its postwar business, and the company boomed. "If ever there was a symbol of America's industrial might in those years, it was General Motors, so powerful that to call it merely a corporation seemed woefully inadequate," wrote David Halberstam in *The Fifties*. It was a time of fins and chrome, of new highways, of subdivisions popping up from farmland as though Paul Bunyon had walked along the fields, sprinkling seeds that grew into tract houses. Everybody wanted two cars to fit in their new garages. GM, which dominated the market like it never had before the war, was dictating everything, from styling to prices to which of its dealers should get its hottest cars. GM's arrogance was so widely known that Wilson, who'd left to become President Dwight D. Eisenhower's secretary of defense early in the decade, was reported to have said, "What's good for General Motors is good for the country." It may have been what he and his colleagues at GM believed, Halberstam wrote, but Wilson wouldn't say that out loud. What he did say was, "We at General Motors have always felt that what was good for the country was good for General Motors as well." Nonetheless, perception became reality in Wilson's case. And GM's legend was fueled once more.

Still, the stylists, engineers, marketers, and manufacturers had much to be proud of. All across its model lineup, GM was creating classics. Buick had its top-of-the-line Roadmaster, equipped with portholes and the super-smooth Dynaflow transmission. Oldsmobile aimed for power with its Rocket V-8 engine and the Holiday hardtop sedan. Pontiac had its own transmission, the Hydramatic, and it launched its first Wide Track suspension, which added five inches to the car's wheelbase width. Chevrolet had its hot rod Bel Air, and Cadillac its fin-adorned luxoboats. Every year, GM put on a party, called "Motorama," to celebrate its latest stars. The touring gala was a chance for GM to flaunt the designs its stylists were drafting in their spacious new quarters at the GM Technical Center in Warren, Michigan. The complex was the postwar work of architect Eero Saarinen, who had been in residence at nearby Cranbrook Academy of Art and Design in Bloomfield Hills. (The GM design building, which faced a block-long reflecting pool, boasted a teakwood-paneled office for the design director that looks modern to this day. Touch a button and the lights dim; touch another and the curtains draw closed; touch a third and what looks to be a coffee table rises to dining-room-table height.) The first Motorama of the year always was held in a ballroom at the Waldorf-Astoria in New York, and the exhibits were then packed up to visit other cities. GM hired orchestras and chorus lines, invited celebrities, and beamed searchlights at the Manhattan skies. In 1953, the Motorama star was a little two-seater sports car called the Corvette. It was simply a styling exercise to see if GM could come up with something that could battle with Britain's Triumph and MG sports cars. The little auto had a white body, round headlights, and a red-leather interior. Reaction to the convertible was instantaneous, and GM was flooded with requests for Corvettes. Among the people who gazed at the Corvette on its turntable at the Waldorf was a young Ford product planner who'd been trying to convince his bosses to go ahead with a two-seater on its drawingboards. When Donald Petersen got back to Dearborn, he argued that the reaction to the Corvette meant there would be plenty of buyers interested in his car. Petersen got the go-ahead. Two years later, Ford's Thunderbird made its debut. And thirty years later, Petersen became Ford's CEO.

In the 1950s the 'Vette was the exception to the rule at GM, which was cranking out big, heavy four-doors, coupes, and convertibles loaded with chrome and decorated in spirited colors like turquoise, pink, and malachite. Nearly 98 percent of the cars it sold were full-sized cars that averaged less than ten miles per gallon (hardly anything to worry about in an era of fifteen-cents-per-gallon gasoline.) Whitewall tires were the rule. And buyers could pretty much get anything they wanted in the way of looks and engines; in 1957, GM offered seventy-five different cars that could be packaged with 450 different options. GM's market share was climbing, even as the Justice Department warned regularly that the company was getting too big. By the end of the 1950s, Chevrolet alone controlled 25 percent of the car market—as much as Ford does in the 1990s. GM owned 52 percent of the market and was headed for 60 percent. GM was a money machine: Its sales topped $1 billion as the decade began, and the cash kept rolling in. GM earned a 25 percent return on every vehicle it sold. That gave it a comfortable cushion with which to launch price wars with Ford when it suspected the number-two car company was getting too close to Chevrolet.

As the decade came to a close, no car seemed to typify what GM had become more than the 1959 Cadillac. It was daunting, the steamship liner of the road, bulky, powerful, a sign of the decade's conspicuous consumption. Its front grille was impressive, but its distinctive feature was its fins—long, pointed, topped with red taillights that gleamed in the dark, a beacon of success glowing across American highways. That rear end could seem threatening, even deadly, and sometimes the fins could maim or even kill in particularly bad collisions. GM didn't pay any attention, since its executives simply believed buyers weren't all that concerned about safety. It didn't matter that Ford and Chrysler had added seat belts as an option in 1955, or that Alabama congressman Kenneth Roberts tried to make seat belts standard equipment on autos in the late 1950s. Certainly some of its engineers were calling for changes in some of the cars that GM was preparing for the 1960s. And if the men at the top had listened, GM's fall from dominance might never have begun.

In 1961, Edward Cole, who'd led Chevrolet during its 1950s sales boom, was set for a promotion. One of the last cars on which he'd worked while at Chevrolet was a little rear-engine bug aimed at hanging on to some of the young buyers who were beginning to wander over to the Volkswagen Beetle. The car had what some people called a soapbox shape. Its six-cylinder "pancake" engine was air-cooled, like the Beetle's, and Chevrolet had high hopes for turning the little car into a convertible, a station wagon, and even a small van. Cole was glad to be able to fill a market niche. But Cole's replacement at Chevy, Semon "Bunkie" Knudson, wasn't happy with the way the Corvair had turned out. Most of its 2,400 pounds were concentrated on its rear end, where the engine sat. The suspension on the car was simply too light to balance the heavy rear end with the nearly empty front end. As a result, tests showed the Corvairs tended to swerve and even to flip over. Knudson demanded some changes, but the quickest GM could get them on the cars was 1965. There was nothing much that could be done to stabilize the 1964 model.

GM's decision to launch the 1964 Corvair cost people lives, irreparably damaged GM's image, and almost singlehandedly created the auto safety movement. This time, it wasn't poor faceless buyers who were suffering. GM executives found out the cost of the Corvair firsthand. Knudson's niece was critically hurt in a Corvair; executive vice president Cy Osborne's son suffered brain damage in an accident involving a Corvair, and Cadillac general manager Cal Werner's son was killed riding in one. Ralph Nader, a young attorney from Connecticut, was stunned by the number of accidents involving the Corvair and the terrible injuries that were resulting. He made the Corvair the centerpiece of his book, *Unsafe at Any Speed*, an indictment of the auto industry's lack of interest in safety matters. Nader charged that GM knew of the problems with the Corvair's light suspension, yet deliberately introduced the car. He found a receptive audience, in part because GM and other automakers were under fire in Congress. Senators Abraham Ribicoff and Robert Kennedy had convened the first real hearings on auto safety to question top companies on their commitment to the issue. One after another, GM executives appeared before the committee to insist the company put safety first in developing its cars. But the committee's staff had done its homework. It discovered that the doors on GM cars tore off 6,300 percent more often in accidents than doors on Chrysler cars and 8,500 percent more often than Ford's car doors. GM pointed out it spent $1.25 million a year on safety studies—an uncertain claim, since nobody really knew how much the company put into safety research. But the senators fired back that GM had earned $1.7 billion in 1964. If GM's case was torn then, it was shredded by Nader's appearance. He had offered to share his research on Corvair with other people who were suing GM over the car. More than 100 people came forward.

GM, panicking, made a tactical error. It hired a private investigator to tail Nader, not an unusual practice. But the PI went overboard, tapping Nader's phone and trying to trap him in compromising situations. Nader found out about the investigator, told the committee, and all hell broke loose. GM president James Roche was forced to publicly apologize to Nader, and Ribicoff was able to line up the support he'd lacked in the past for the first National Traffic and Motor Vehicle Safety Act. It created a new government safety bureau that could set standards for automotive safety—and order companies to recall cars that didn't meet those standards. In just the first year, carmakers had to recall 4.7 million vehicles, and by the late 1960s nearly one third of all cars sold each year were recalled to fix safety defects. The car that sparked the uproar—the Corvair—faded from view. GM, which had sold 1.5 million before the Congressional hearings, sold just 125,000 afterward.

The Corvair was the beginning of the end of GM's unquestioned dominance of the car market. It had some styling successes, like the mid-1960s versions of the Corvette, and its muscle cars like the Pontiac GTO and Firebird brought baby-boom buyers into showrooms. But in the decades to come GM would be remembered more for its product mistakes than its product successes. And competition—from Ford and Chrysler and from Japan and Europe—would deal the company's lineup a blow from which it has yet to recover. By the early 1970s it was clear that the world was changing, and not to GM's liking. Volkswagen, which GM had ignored during the 1960s, was selling half a million cars a year. In 1970 Toyota's sales passed the 100,000 mark for the first time. Ford Mustang had grown in size and power but was still selling more than 300,000 a year.

GM was still a company where large cars were the center of attention and there was a prescribed way of life for the executives who made it to the top. Unless they were division general managers, whose job it was to keep dealers happy and keep pushing products, they stayed out of the limelight. "The GM chairman is actually one of the least recognized businessmen in America," said John De Lorean, who ran Pontiac and Chevrolet before leaving GM in the early 1970s to embark on an ill-fated automotive venture of his own.[1] During the 1970s, two Ford executives—chairman Henry Ford II and president Lee Iacocca—were the best-known automotive leaders. GM's chairman, Thomas Murphy, and its president, Elliott "Pete" Estes, were all but invisible to the public. This did not mean that they were shadowy figures to people inside GM. On the contrary, executives were GM's royalty. No one visited a city without being greeted by an entourage of zone managers, district managers, and public relations representatives. The bigger the boss, the bigger the welcoming committee. De Lorean made the mistake of neglecting to pick up Estes at the San Francisco airport the morning he flew in for a meeting with Pontiac engineers. He was taking an early morning shower when his bathroom door suddenly flew open, almost tearing off the hinges. Shocked, De Lorean threw back the curtain[2] to find Estes fuming. "Why the hell wasn't somebody out to meet me at the airport this morning? You knew I was coming, but nobody was there. God damn it, I served my time picking up my bosses at the airport. Now, you guys are going to do this for me," Estes raged.

Fawning over the boss—called "loyalty" in GM terms—was crucial to survival in GM because bosses had all the power and the CEO had more power than anyone. If a CEO or president lost interest in a new car or truck program, its development could halt in its tracks. If a top executive got behind a program, it would speed through the tangled GM development system and reach the market ahead of vehicles that rightly preceded it in market importance. Up until the early 1990s, this was the way GM did business. A strong program manager who had the backing of key executives could expect his car to move forward; a program manager who tangled with his superiors over a car's features or the buyers at whom it was targeted could see his budget cut and his funding delayed. Nine times out of ten, the cars that caught top executives' fancy were sports cars or luxury models with high profit margins. Even in the 1970s, with America reeling from two energy crises, GM executives kept their focus on big cars to the detriment of the small cars that consumers badly needed. Why? Because big cars made money and small cars didn't. It took just as much time and money to develop a small car as a big one, and GM's manufacturing costs were basically the same no matter the size of the car. There was so much competition in the small car market from Ford and the imports that GM could not sell the car for enough to cover its costs and make a profit. Every time it tried to do so, it met with defeat.

Like the Corvair before it, the Vega was a prime example. In 1968, GM president James Roche promised that within two years GM would introduce a small car that would be lighter than the VW Beetle, cost the same, and leap ahead of it technologically. The announcement shocked Ford, which was working on the Pinto but wasn't close to being ready to introduce it. Roche's announcement was meant to show that GM, which had fumbled with the Corvair, wasn't going to be surpassed by foreign competition. But engineering work on the Vega hadn't reached a point where Roche should have made such promises. Among the ideas for the car was an aluminum engine, revolutionary for a mass-produced car of the era. Even in the 1990s automakers are still refining ways that the lighter metal can be used in place of cast-iron engine parts. Aluminum's biggest advantage is its weight, which is one-third that of iron. That is crucial in a small car, which must be kept light in order to maximize its fuel economy. Its disadvantage is that it does not wear as well as iron and can be distorted in the heat generated by an internal combustion engine.

Technology was nowhere advanced enough to allow GM to introduce an all-aluminum engine, so developers settled for a hybrid that combined aluminum and iron, looked bulky, and during tests did not seem to wear as well as a conventional engine. And it was expensive: $400 a car more than if GM had used a cast-iron engine. That meant GM couldn't introduce Vega at anywhere near the $1,800 price of a Beetle, or $1,919, the amount Ford's Pinto was expected to cost. The Vega was priced at $2,091, which sounds cheap now but wasn't in 1971, when the average large car cost $5,000. De Lorean, who had to defend the expensive, overweight car at a press conference, was cringing as he touted its price as "in the ballpark" of what GM had promised. Reporter Dan Fisher of the *Los Angeles Times* raised his hand. "Would your boss accept a ballpark estimate of your anticipated expense budget at Chevrolet for the next year that was a plus or minus twenty-five percent?" he asked.[3]

It was a stunningly accurate point, and one that typified the atmosphere at GM. As was the company's nature, GM had promised big things with the Vega and failed to deliver.

Soon after the Vega hit the market and flopped, De Lorean simply gave up. Many people at GM were glad to see him go. From dirt-poor beginnings in a bad Detroit neighborhood he'd zoomed through the ranks by bucking tradition, embarrassing the conservative executives and their wives by his flamboyant lifestyle. Keeping more in tune with Hollywood than with Detroit, he'd dyed his hair jet-black, wore silky patterned shirts opened to the navel and gold jewelry, hung out with celebrities like O. J. Simpson, and even posed for a magazine portrait barechested. He'd married, and quickly divorced, twenty-year-old Kelly Harmon and begun another relationship with model Christina Ferrare, who would become his third wife and subsequently his third ex-wife. De Lorean had broken the code by becoming more visible than the executives to whom he reported.

Yet he had an almost clairvoyant sense of the problems

that GM would face twenty years in the future. Before he left GM in 1972, he wrote a long memo to then-chairman Richard Gerstenberg. The fourteen-page single-spaced report detailed what De Lorean saw as GM's major problems, both culturally and in its operations. GM, De Lorean wrote, was racked by poor morale. "We no longer have a highly motivated team or the team spirit that built GM." Executives rose to the fourteenh floor not because of their talent, but because they had learned how to play the system. Except at Chevrolet, he wrote, "We have virtually no marketing expertise. Contrary to Mr. Sloan's teachings, we do not use the best information available to make decisions. None of the modern marketing tools are used regularly or extensively. When they are, the results are generally discarded. We seem to forget that a cloistered executive whose only social contacts are with other executives who make $500,000 a year, and who has really not bought a car in years, has no basis to judge public taste."

De Lorean thought the problems lay in three areas: incompetent management, a lack of planning, and the absence of good management development. GM moved its executives along far too fast for them to get a good grip on the car business. And it promoted executives who could not run a car factory or design an automobile themselves. "We are an automobile company, but we have not developed executives capable of insuring the future success of GM's automotive business. There is a genuine concern for General Motors' future. GM has an unbelievably great potential—but it is not being realized."

De Lorean did not just lecture and analyze. He came up with a seven-step plan he thought could save GM $1.35 billion and improve its profits by $3 billion over three years. Among his ideas:

1. Better management, management motivation, and morale. Savings: $200 million.
2. On-time tooling and better planning. Savings: $250 million.
3. Least-cost standardized parts. Savings: $300 million.
4. Smooth model startups. Savings: $200 million.

5. Low-cost manufacturing techniques. Savings: $100 million.
6. Coordination of suppliers and divisions. Savings: $200 million.
7. Cut order response time by fourteen days. Savings: $100 million.

De Lorean never got an answer to his memo. It would not have made any difference. "The company I so revered was no longer the company I was working for. And so I left." Not every young executive felt so displaced, however. At the time that De Lorean was attracting attention, and beginning to put his foot out the door, a young manager in GM's New York finance operations was building his own career. In two decades' time he would use ideas very much like De Lorean had suggested in his own attempt to reshape the company. First, however, GM had to endure one of the most tumultuous eras in its history: the chairmanship of Roger Smith.

These days, Roger Smith's image is that of a despot who terrorized his employees and nearly ruined the giant automaker just to make the balance sheet look good and fatten his bonus and pension income. His foes universally describe him as the worst CEO to ever lead the company, both in terms of strategy and the devastation he wreaked on GM's relationship with its union. He was a perfect target for filmmaker Michael Moore, whose search for Smith was the subject of his stinging satire, *Roger & Me*. Says Ralph Nader: "Roger Smith's tenure was one of the darkest in General Motors' history, for customers, workers, and for residents of GM's factory towns."

Yet to completely condemn Roger Smith's decade is short-sighted and simply wrong. Roger Smith had vision. He saw trends coming before others in the industry could spot them, and he tried to take steps to meet them. From technology to organization to diversification, Roger Smith saw the seeds of the future and tried to plant them at GM. His biggest mistake may have been believing that he was the only man smart enough to run the company, say some who worked with him.

"Roger had two problems," says a retired GM executive. "He didn't trust people and he didn't understand the car business."

People who met Roger Smith for the first time were always amazed that he was the most powerful business leader in the country. Of medium height, fond of brown or plaid suits, Roger Smith had a pink, blotchy face, scraggly reddish hair, and a high-pitched, squeaky voice. He looked more like a car dealership's sales manager than a chief executive, and was fond of language last heard in Andy Hardy movies of the 1940s. His vocabulary was peppered with expressions like "Jeepers!" and "How about that?" and "Humdinger." He'd drive his public relations staff crazy, bounding over before the weekly meetings of the Economic Club of Detroit to expound to reporters about the most sensitive issues. Anything Roger Smith said was a story, and he was famous for shoot-from-the-hip quotes that frustrated GM lawyers and labor relations officials. At a crucial point during 1982 concessions talks with the UAW, Roger Smith vowed to reporters that he'd "close a lot of plants" if the union didn't give in. He infuriated Ford's then-CEO, Phillip Caldwell, by neglecting to inform Caldwell in a pre–union-negotiations strategy session that GM planned to offer to pass any concessions it got from the union through to car buyers as rebates. Caldwell refused to match the rebate offer and ultimately got his revenge when talks broke down at GM, prompting the union to forge a deal with Ford. The contract gave the union a greater say in company affairs than Smith would have ever granted, and GM was forced to accept the same contract. But on the very afternoon GM and the union signed the deal, which froze workers' wages for two years, GM's proxy statement to shareholders disclosed a proposal to make it easier for executives to earn bigger bonuses. Former UAW President Douglas Fraser, who retired in 1983, got so frustrated he vowed to find "a zipper for Roger Smith's lips."

Smith didn't seem to care. GM was his and he'd run it the way he saw fit. Other CEOs had been just as tough, only not as public. Smith's climb to the top took thirty-two years, from the day he joined GM in 1949 as a general accounting clerk in the Detroit central office. Like Jack Smith, his path to the corner office was through the finance staff. He spent almost no consequential time in an operations job in GM's automotive business. He served seven years in New York and became the treasurer in 1970. In the decade before he became CEO, Smith was in charge of the finance staff, public relations, GM's non-automotive business, and other staff functions. He joined the GM board in 1974, and by the time CEO Thomas Murphy was ready to retire in 1981, it was clear that Smith was the right finance guy to replace him.

When he got to the top in 1981, Smith talked teamwork and even brought famed quality expert W. Edwards Deming to GM for his empowerment-focused seminars. But Smith ruled GM with an iron hand encased in a steel glove. To solidify his control of the company, Smith eventually put five GM executives on the GM board. (One of the first moves GM's outside directors made when they kicked out the early-1990s management team was to slash the number of insiders from five to two. And after William Hoglund retired in 1994, only one, Jack Smith, remained.) A wrong word from a staffer in Roger Smith's presence could end a career, even if the comment was true. Veteran GM executive William Hoglund can pinpoint almost to the minute the day Roger Smith turned against him. In 1988, Hoglund attended a meeting with other GM executives to try to figure out why the Chevrolet-Pontiac-Canada group, created in a massive 1984 reorganization of the company, was losing $3 billion a year. None of the executives wanted to answer Smith's probing questions. Finally, Hoglund spoke up. The big problem was because GM had replaced the low-cost Chevrolet Celebrity, a no-frills early-1980s alternative to GM's gas-guzzlers, with the Lumina, which cost far more to build. Now, said Hoglund, GM was losing close to $2,000 per car. Lumina was also one of the cars in the GM-10 program that Smith had pushed for in order to battle Japanese automakers. Hoglund had dared to trash one of the chairman's favorite projects. Other executives turned on him, too, for breaking with the "good news only" code that top management lived by. From then on it was as if Hoglund were in Siberia, an untouchable. Only when Jack Smith became CEO was Hoglund's blunt-spoken place in the GM hierarchy restored.

Others also learned it was unwise to question the red-haired CEO's judgment. Convinced that sport utility sales were going to explode in the early 1990s, a trio of young product planners put together a presentation for Smith in 1989 on the need for a four-door version of the Chevrolet Blazer. They knew that their colleagues had tried twice before to convince the chairman to approve the project, but they figured their market data and profit projections made a strong enough case that Smith couldn't say no. If he approved the idea, Chevrolet could probably put the vehicle on the market in 1991, about the time that Ford planned to bring out a consumer-friendly sport utility called Explorer. As they changed their transparencies in a darkened fourteenth-floor conference room, the staffers watched Smith for a reaction. There was none. Finally, when the lights came up, Smith's hand slammed down on the desk. "I do not want to see a presentation on this vehicle ever again!" he declared. The three planners quickly left. None of them lost their jobs, but they learned a painful lesson: don't challenge the boss. "That was a career-limiting presentation," recalls one of the group. Eventually, Chevy got its four-door, but it hit the market two years after the Explorer, which had become the best-selling people hauler in the United States.

Smith, with almost no instinct for the car market, was just as capable of ordering his staffers to build something they didn't think would sell. In the mid-1980s GM was preparing the new series of mid-sized cars internally dubbed the GM-10s. They were supposed to be GM's best bet to fight the sales inroads being made by Ford Taurus, Honda Accord, and Toyota Camry, but the program had been delayed by a cash crunch, and GM couldn't afford to produce both the two-door and four-door versions at the same time. It could introduce one version, then follow it later with the other. It would be more expensive to do the four-doors first, but marketing experts argued GM needed them more because baby boomers were beginning to have children and didn't want coupes. Sales of four-door Accords demonstrated that that was what they wanted. Smith looked the cars over and decreed that GM would introduce the two-door versions first. They were cheaper. And besides, in the 1950s and 1960s, when the Smiths were raising their children, nobody under forty wanted to drive a four-door car; coupes were all the rage for the younger buyers that GM wanted to attract. If they wanted more room, GM dealers could simply show them bigger cars. The GM-10s, led by the Chevrolet Lumina, were doomed the day they hit the market. Buyers didn't want the two-doors and by the time the four-doors hit the market, there were few customers. GM had to unload many of the poor-quality cars on rental-car companies at a loss. Later, Smith contended that market research data showed buyers wanted two-door cars, and that was why GM built them first. People inside GM knew better.

He might not have viewed the automotive market in a way that the product planners would have liked, but Smith had his own brand of business strategy. "You've got to put Roger Smith into perspective," says Bob Purcell, a student of GM history and one of the planners who helped write Jack Smith's NAO turnaround program. "He put some thought into intellectual leadership. If he had been successful, he would have transformed the industry."[4]

Smith was dazzled by technology, especially the kind that was coming out of Japan. He wondered at Sony's ability to introduce the Walkman personal stereo, the Watchman personal TV, and the compact disc players that were fast replacing phonographs. Smith marveled at robots' ability to take over tasks that auto workers long abhorred, like spot welding and windshield placement. Smith put GM on a technology drive, spending $9 billion during the 1980s to overhaul GM plants and build new ones. He bought up dozens of small high tech companies, and launched a robotics joint venture with Japan's Fanuc robot company that was called GM Fanuc. He sent Jack Smith off to forge a deal with Toyota, thinking he'd pick up more manufacturing technology that way.

Smith's zest for high tech was a reason he pushed ahead with reorganizing GM. He called it "reindustrializing GM." The 1984 reorganization was one of Smith's better ideas that, like so many others, was badly implemented. When he took charge of GM in 1981, the company was a series of fiefdoms.

One of the most elite was Fisher Body, the car-engineering division that also built car bodies at its plants. These were then shipped to assembly plants, where undercarriages were added and engines, transmissions, and interior features were installed. The Fisher Body people, corporate descendants of the Fisher Brothers who were auto industry pioneers, were proud of their work and disdainful of what happened once car bodies left their factories and engineering specifications left their offices. Much of their ire was targeted at the General Motors Assembly Division. The quality of the vehicles assembled in GMAD plants was notoriously bad. Until the 1970s, car divisions had supervised some of the factories, called "home plants." Usually, cars at the upper end of the price scale were built in home plants while GMAD factories churned out cheaper models in bulk. When he ran Chevrolet, John De Lorean discovered GM's parts plants knew they could not send defective parts to home plants.[5] Instead, they got rid of them in GMAD factories. Meanwhile, GMAD partisans, fuming at years of abuse, maintained the end results would have been better if Fisher Body's engineers had been more precise in creating car bodies and vehicles. Nobody ever sat down to thrash out the issue. "That was what was killing us—[the lack of coordination between] Fisher and GMAD and the car divisions," said Smith. "A guy at GMAD said to me, 'Fisher throws it over the wall to us and says to hell with it.'"

Despite their differences, Fisher Body and GMAD had one destructive thing in common: If managers did not like an idea that engineers had come up with for producing a car, they could refuse to pass the design along until a new system was put in place. This meant having to order new parts for the cars far too late in the product-development cycle; it meant delays in introducing new vehicles and it meant higher costs. And by the time a vehicle had reached Fisher Body or GMAD, it had already spent five years on the drawing boards and computer screens that were just appearing in GM's design studios. The rivalries weren't just between Fisher Body and GMAD; divisions fought each other for cars and trucks they claimed their dealers needed to be competitive. They'd hold price wars with each other, undercutting parts of the same company. And nobody, if you asked them, said they worked for GM. Engineers worked for Fisher Body, manufacturing experts worked for GMAD, and the divisions each had a cherished identity of their own.

Smith wanted to put an end to the in-fighting and focus GM on the kind of profits he knew a more streamlined organization could yield. "Change, change, change. That was what we needed," he said. He had a vision of a car industry in the future that virtually ran itself, able to adjust to competition from places like Japan, and factories that would be able to operate without the reams of paperwork that clogged filing cabinets and ended up in huge canvas carts to be toted away. Smith and his president, F. James McDonald, tried to find a way to fix the company on their own, using Opel's operations in Germany as a model. But in the end they called in consultants McKinsey and Company for suggestions.

The result seemed to make sense on paper. GM was grouping its car divisions by size: Chevrolet-Pontiac-Canada and Buick-Oldsmobile-Cadillac. In an instant, GMAD and Fisher Body were no more, their operations split between the two car groups. CPC and BOC each would have their own layer of management on top of the bureaucracy already in place. But what Smith miscalculated was just how deep-seated the loyalties were to the divisions that had now disappeared. "People were calling me at home, crying on the phone. They'd say, 'I used to work for Fisher Body and now it's gone. What am I supposed to do?'" Smith recalled. "One thing we didn't understand was how firm and set people were in their ways." It took more than a year just to sort out the job titles—a precious year that was lost getting cars and trucks out of the design studios and development labs and onto dealers' lots. Meanwhile, GM earned more than $4 billion in 1984, executives and managers took home millions of dollars in bonuses, and the momentum just wasn't there to drive the reorganization. Sighs Smith: "Wouldn't it have been wonderful if we could have flipped a switch and it would have been done?"

At the same time, Smith was taking even bigger steps outside the auto industry with two massive acquisitions. In

1984, GM bought Electronic Data Systems, the data processing company founded by H. Ross Perot, for $2.5 billion. And a year later, it paid $5 billion for Hughes Aircraft, the telecommunications and defense contractor put on the block by the Howard Hughes Medical Institute. In each case, GM created a new class of stock that would trade according to the fortunes of the two new subsidiaries—Class E for EDS, Class H for Hughes.

Smith was fascinated by what Perot had been able to accomplish with his straight-shooting, conservative group of computer whizzes. He was enthralled by the tale of the trip by Perot's private army to Iran to save EDS employees. He thought Perot, whose Texas twang was almost a southern copy of Smith's own nasal tones, was a genius. GM had a pressing need to do something about its data processing operations. With the computer age breathing down the company's neck, parts of GM simply couldn't communicate because they did not share the same technology. Smith's first thought was to set up his own data processing center. "Our plan was to buy a defunct college in Iowa and train [employees] there," Smith said. "Then we started looking at all the computer companies. We couldn't buy IBM, obviously. But then we heard we could buy EDS. Everybody said you've got to watch it, they were wild people down there. We said we need somebody who was wild."[6]

When he bought EDS, he put Perot on the GM board. And that was where the trouble started. Smith seemingly had none of his predecessors' problems with outsiders. He thought GM could benefit every so often from fresh blood and fresh views. That was why he brought Chicago attorney Elmer Johnson into the corporation from Kirkland & Ellis, GM's law firm. And Smith thought Perot's business acumen could help GM. Perot thought so, too, but not in a way that Smith found palatable. He opposed GM's 1985 purchase of Hughes Aircraft because he couldn't see any way spending the $5 billion would benefit GM. His digging found that two thirds of Hughes' annual net income came from 1 percent of its defense contracts. Perot did not think this was a business GM should be delving into. His was the lone vote on the GM board opposing Hughes, which

Smith maintains was a brilliant buy. "Hughes is going to pay off down the road. It's a long, long term thing. In the year 2000 the country will be short of engineers, but GM won't be. There is some great talent at Hughes."

In 1986, Perot got far more vocal. He did not like the intrusion of GM's finance staff into EDS's affairs. It seemed incredulous that Perot would sell his company to GM, then not let its bookkeepers in the door. But Perot viewed the deal as a business combination, not a GM takeover. He wanted to keep his company's culture and operations intact. He'd had a close look at the inner workings of GM and he didn't like what he saw. Within months, Smith and Perot seemed at war and it was not just over EDS. Perot began to publicly criticize GM. "It takes five years to develop a car in this company. Heck, we won World War Two in four years," he jibed. To *Business Week,* Perot jabbed at GM's corporate culture. "The first [EDS employee] to see a snake kills it. At GM, the first thing you do is organize a committee on snakes. Then you bring in a consultant who knows a lot about snakes. Third thing you do is talk about it for a year." Perot insisted that his attacks were meant to wake up GM and set it on a path to improvement. Smith was puzzled because he says Perot did not voice many of his complaints to him. "A lot of things printed between Ross and me were pure baloney," Smith said. "He never said much at a board meeting. We'd go around at every meeting and ask them if they had any questions. He never had any." But Smith said the breakup was inevitable because of the "uncomplimentary" things Perot said about GM. He chalked the complaints up to Perot's lack of knowledge about how GM operated. "He'd say, 'Hey, I've got a new design for a brake, let's put it on tomorrow.' I'd say, 'Hey, Ross, we've got to test that a million miles.' He'd say, 'Hey, you guys are too slow.' There were things he didn't understand about the auto business," Smith said.

Behind the scenes, Perot was negotiating to get out of GM. He listed his grievances in a letter to Smith in May, and then proposed some solutions. One was for GM to sell EDS, either back to EDS shareholders or to somebody else. Another was for GM to buy his EDS stock.[7] The pair battled for months, until finally, in December, they agreed to a stunning breakup. GM would pay Perot $700 million—about the cost of restyling a small car—for his stock. He was to leave the GM board. And he could not criticize GM management or he'd risk losing up to $7.5 million. (One couldn't help but picture Perot throwing $100 bills into a big bucket every time he opened his mouth to knock GM.) For five years, Perot was banned from buying GM stock or trying to influence company management. There were actually fears among some people at GM that he would try to take over the company. Perot never did so, but he fired one last shot at GM. He actually berated GM's board for approving the payoff, saying he'd been given the equivalent of enough cash for "a spanking new car plant and the jobs that go with it." The battle shredded GM's reputation at a time when the company already was having enough trouble selling its cars and trucks. In summer 1995, GM moved to spin off EDS as a separate entity. Nonetheless, Smith says he isn't sorry GM bought the company, which is now worth seven times what GM paid for it.

By 1987, the year after the Perot blowup, GM was in a swift and steady decline. Even though U.S. car and truck sales reached a record 16.4 million in 1986, GM's share was falling. When Smith became CEO, GM held 46 percent of the car market. When 1987 began, GM had 42 percent. In 1987, a year before the GM-10 cars were to be introduced, GM's market share fell five full percentage points to 37 percent. It was a sales disaster; never in the history of the modern auto industry had one of the major companies lost so much market share. It meant half a million fewer people bought GM cars in 1987 than in the year before. Smith thought critics were making too much of the market share decline, since GM was posting record profits. "I'd rather be remembered as the guy who lost market share and increased profits than the guy who increased market share and lost profits," Smith said. The reasons for the slide were obvious. GM cars' quality was wretched. The company was being strangled by a lineup of "lookalike" cars that resembled one another externally yet had no interior similarities. From Cadillac to Chevrolet, every division was saddled with cars that were indistinguishable except for cushier options. And every one was assembled using different parts that could not be used interchangeably. It was just the opposite of what Smith should have done: built cars whose sheet metal was different, but whose components were common.

Buyers fled in horror. Ford, relishing the confusion at a time when it had just brought out its distinctive "jellybean" Taurus and Sable sedans, tweaked GM in a classic advertisement of the late 1980s. In it, a well-heeled man approaches a valet to ask for his Buick Century. Another comes up looking for his Oldsmobile Cutlass Ciera. A third asks for his Chevrolet Celebrity. The three cars drive up and none of the men can tell which is his. A fourth patron, asking for his Lincoln, slides behind the wheel and quickly drives away as the trio are arguing over whose car is whose. GM was furious at the ad and Ford eventually pulled it from the airwaves, but the delicious point had been made.

Strangely, none of the chaos showed up at the bottom line. While GM's market share was sliding and its operations were in turmoil, the net income numbers simply got bigger. In 1980 GM had lost $785 million. But in the years that followed, GM earned billion-dollar profits, climbing to $4.5 billion in 1988 and $4.2 billion in 1989. It was hard to tell if all those profits were pure; almost every year during the mid to late 1980s, GM took special charges, made accounting changes, and booked gains that made year-over-year comparisons nearly impossible. If there were optimistic assumptions to be made, GM would err on the rosy side. Smith defends every adjustment as standard and acceptable accounting procedure. "The wrong ones were after I left." In all, GM earned nearly $25 billion during the Roger Smith years, $55 billion if the values of EDS and Hughes were factored in. (The number, at least $10 billion higher than Wall Street analysts will acknowledge, came from a study by University of Southern California business school students.) Those numbers were ammunition enough for Smith to battle his critics. Pressed to defend his record in a 1990 interview with the author, Smith yanked open his desk drawer, whipped out a copy of the annual report, and showed her a bar chart illustrating GM's earnings over the past decade. "I look at some of these things, and I don't think they're too bad," he declared. "Sure, some of the long-term things will take a while. But I think there's plenty of evidence" of GM's success.

Every time he was challenged, Smith would demand the questioner to wait five years before writing the ultimate summation of the Smith years. "I don't expect them to build a big stone monument to me. That's not my goal in life," Smith said. "I'd like to think that if I did anything extraordinary, it was the work that we did in getting the corporation ready for the twenty-first century." That's certainly what Smith had in mind, says GM manager Purcell, looking back on what Smith saw in his flawed crystal ball. "He was trying to go beyond production. He wanted to go to a highly automated environment. I don't think he had enough operating experience to understand how to do it," Purcell says. Today, Smith points to the $55 billion figure as his legacy. "They want to blame me for the financial problems at NAO? When I left there in the first half of 1990, they were still in the black. So, don't look at me. And where would they be without that $55 billion?"

Despite all the things that Smith did wrong, he did at least two things right. One of them was the Saturn Corporation, which did more to create goodwill for GM in the early 1990s than anything else. It created a new sense of teamwork among dealers tired of treating customers like dirt. It showed that GM and the UAW could get along—even if this meant ripping up the old GM contract and trying a new way to cooperate. It became a training ground for a whole generation of GM managers. Smith stuck by the division when even members of the GM board, like Elmer Johnson, wanted to kill it. For that, says former UAW vice president Donald Ephlin, "Roger Smith is my hero."[8] Though the execution of Saturn would later prove to be flawed, and subsequent leaders at GM would question its mission and focus, Smith's belief that U.S. automakers could try anew may be his saving legacy.

Saturn was dreamed up in July 1982, in the midst of one of the worst slumps in industry memory. Battered by recession and high gas prices, sales of GM's full-sized cars had plummeted. Yet lines formed outside Japanese car dealers and Volkswagen dealers who had stocks of fuel-sipping small cars, the kind that Detroit had long laughed at. Magazines like *Consumer Reports* were laving praise on these small Toyota Corollas, Honda Accords, and Nissan Sentras, while scoffing at Motor City iron. What's more, buyers under forty, just starting to hit their peak earning power, were snapping up these cars. In California, Japanese cars climbed to 50 percent of the market. GM and its American rivals had small cars—Ford Escort, Chevrolet Chevette, Dodge Omni—but they couldn't compete in quality and reliability. The Big Three were losing money on each small car they sold—while Japanese and VW dealers were charging sticker price and more.

GM already was investigating a joint car-building deal with Toyota. Its bargainers, headed by Jack Smith, were holding talks in Nagoya, Japan, on a production venture. But Roger Smith wanted GM to be able to build a profitable small car on its own in the United States. In June 1982 Smith told staffers on GM's Advanced Product and Design Team to prepare a report on a future small car. It was finished around Thanksgiving. Just before Christmas, Smith directed GM executive vice president Alex Cunningham to proceed with "Project Saturn." He plucked staffers from various GM divisions—Jay Wetzel and John Middlebrook from Pontiac, Guy Briggs from Oldsmobile, Tom Manoff from GM's Delco electronics division, Joseph Sanchez from Oldsmobile, and Reed Rundell from Holden Motors, GM's Australian subsidiary. Sanchez was placed in charge.

They hadn't all met each other when the project began, but they had one thing in common: During Christmas vacation each learned that he was now attached to Saturn. In letters formalizing their new assignments, Cunningham explained that the project's name came from the Saturn rocket that helped propel men to the moon in the 1960s. Cunningham said their project would be similar because Saturn would take U.S.-built cars to new heights of excellence.

From the beginning, Saturn was supposed to be different. It was to be a paperless company, where staffers would communicate by computer. There would be no red tape—disputes would be settled quickly, in person, without committee meetings. Memos, debates, and politics were banned. Saturn would have no bureaucracy—there would be just a handful of steps between factory worker and top management. The creators overlooked just one thing: there was no way to pay the bills. So the six founders each were handed American Express cards. Every month, the Saturn officials tallied up what they'd spent on parts, consulting fees, office equipment, and telephones. They turned the charges in on the same expense reports they used for gasoline and lunch tabs. Sometimes the bills would be $20,000 or $30,000 a month. "My wife Marty said to me once, Is this any way to start a car company?" laughed Wetzel, who later would become GM's North American chief engineer.

The Saturn team had to scramble to find a home because nobody at GM had set aside a floor for the new project. At first they lined up desks side-by-side in a garage at the GM Tech Center. Six months in, they found some space in a GM office building. "Our [first] real office was a conference room," Wetzel recalled. The group worked twelve-hour days for six months, crafting the outline of the new company. Their first task was to write a mission statement that defined Saturn's goals. Today every company, large and small, has a mission statement. In some companies, it's posted inside the front door and in every office. In others, it's quickly forgotten. But when the Saturn founders were starting, mission statements were a new concept, designed to make sure everybody on a team understood the company's goals. Eventually Saturn's mission statement would be printed on credit card–sized white and red laminated cards, which Saturn officials whipped out at every opportunity. Writing on a yellow legal pad, with a blue felt-tipped pen, the Saturn founders set down their goals:

> We, the Saturn team, in concert with the UAW
> and GM, believe that meeting the needs of Saturn
> customers, members, suppliers, dealers and
> neighbors is fundamental to fulfilling our mission.
>   To meet our customers' needs, our products and
> services must be world leaders in value and
> satisfaction.
>   To meet our members' needs, we will create a

sense of belonging in an environment of mutual trust, respect and dignity. We believe that all people want to be involved in decisions that affect them. We will develop the tools, training and education each member needs. Creative, motivated, responsible team members who understand that change is crucial to success are Saturn's most important asset.

To meet our suppliers' and dealers' needs, we will create real partnerships. We will strive for fairness, trust and respect with them, and we will work with them to help them feel ownership of Saturn's mission and philosophy.

To meet our community neighbors' needs, we will be a good citizen, and protect the environment, and we will seek to cooperate with the government at all levels.

By continuously operating according to this philosophy, we will fulfill our mission.

The team grew rapidly; within a month after the first six founders were picked, Saturn had fifteen people; within three months, 150. By the end of the first year, there were 800 GM staffers working on Saturn. (Though it's the size of some computer software companies, and roughly as big as Ben & Jerry's Famous Ice Cream, that was a typical size for a group in GM working on a project that would eventually lead to a car.) Each week, when newcomers arrived, there would be a staff meeting and mini pep rally during which each Saturn staffer would stand up, introduce himself, and explain what he did. Officials say there was more interest outside GM in Saturn than inside the carmaker; the core group was made up of believers in the Saturn concept, but hot-shot designers and ambitious engineers with short-range brains wanted to stick with car and truck projects already approved and slated for GM's lineup. Smith coined the phrase "no-year car," meaning GM wasn't under any pressure to get it on the road. To some, "no-year" was a codeword for "never happen," which was why many saw the project as yet another hare-brained scheme by their CEO. Eventually, the Saturn team got big enough so that GM relocated the project in leased offices in a new building near Oakland Mall in Troy, Michigan.

The Saturn founders had made a point to include the UAW in the mission statement, although it seemed too much to hope that the union would give Saturn much of a boost. Relations between the UAW and GM were at their nadir. GM had been forced to accept the contract the union reached at Ford after talks broke off at GM, where some executives scoffed at the cooperation-building sections of the pact. But in a stroke of luck for the Saturn founders, Donald Ephlin, who'd helped negotiate the Ford contract, was named to run the UAW's GM operations.

White-haired Ephlin, fond of Bailey's Irish Cream (he'd later quit drinking and switch to non-alcohol beer), had faith in the project from the start. Ephlin wielded considerable influence in the union. He'd been a favorite of about-to-retire UAW president Doug Fraser. He'd gotten his start at the same Framingham, Massachusetts, plant where Jack Smith had his first job, although the pair never met. Ephlin was well liked by the press for his sly wit, friendly grin, and quotability. After he lost to Owen Bieber for the top union job, UAW insiders would say Ephlin's cosiness with a small group of auto-industry reporters was to blame for his downfall. Ephlin, in fact, had conducted his UAW presidency quest through the media while Bieber had done it the old-fashioned way—visiting union halls and regional offices, slogging through miles of campaigning with nary a notice from reporters. When it came time to count the votes among members of the UAW Executive Committee, Ephlin got one vote: his own. Nonetheless, Ephlin had vision. He knew Saturn was a chance the union had long dreamed of—to have a say in the way cars were built and the company was run. "It's the greatest visual demonstration that the American auto industry is alive and well and can be competitive," he says. Ephlin and GM vice president Alfred Warren, head of GM's labor relations department, began to line up UAW officials and GM labor relations staffers to work on Saturn. There were ninety-nine people—so they adopted the name "Group of 99." Among Saturn loyalists, membership in the Group of 99 became a badge of honor—much as attending St. John's was a unifying force among the men of Jack Smith's Worcester boyhood.

Before benchmarking—measuring yourself against the performance of your competitors—became part of business lexicon, the Group of 99 did it. In two months the group traveled two million miles and spent 50,000 hours in meetings, conversations, and seminars, trying to figure out the secrets to the best companies' success. They went to Disney World and Ritz-Carlton hotels, Nordstrom department stores, and Motorola factories. What they found was that the best companies shared the same philosophy:

- Quality was the key to keeping customers happy, and customer satisfaction was everybody's responsibility.
- Total trust between workers and management was a must.
- Workers didn't need to ask bosses for permission every time they wanted to try something new.
- Employees were treated like company assets, not liabilities.

The key role of employees and factory workers at the companies they visited made the Group of 99 realize that the standard UAW-GM contract was too restrictive. It was a small paperback book, with pages of clauses, limitations, job restrictions, and side letters dictating the kind of duties each factory worker would have. Saturn would need something else. So, in 1985, negotiators hammered out a unique labor agreement.

Saturn workers wouldn't be paid by the hour, but receive salaries. They'd get only 90 percent of wages paid to other GM workers, but they could get bonuses based on the Saturn cars sold and could earn a share of Saturn's profits. (In hindsight, it would have been better for Saturn workers to take hourly pay. Saturn finally earned money in 1993 and remains profitable, but has hardly hit the levels that its founders hoped for.) Saturn would have just a few job titles, compared with dozens at a typical GM plant. The multiple job titles had been a tactic by the union in years past to build employment levels. Workers weren't allowed to do more than one task in a traditional plant because the UAW's goal was to have as many people around as possible. That meant a GM worker could spend months, even years doing the same job. But at Saturn, assignments could change daily. Workers would need to know how to do a number of different things—and the people they worked with would know exactly who was trained to do what. That made the work more interesting, and Saturn would have more leeway in making job assignments.

Before workers were even hired, however, candidates would go through hours of employment interviews and seminars to make sure they understood the company's "team approach." They were interviewed by other Saturn workers as well as managers. Saturn vowed that all the decisions on the plant floor would be made in consensus between UAW members and GM managers. A GM executive would run the factory, but the president of Saturn's UAW local, Mike Bennett, would have nearly equal say. Saturn pledged, further, that no layoffs would take place under "unseen or catastrophic events or severe economic conditions." If jobs had to be cut—no one expected that to happen in the first decade—GM managers would suffer, too. If Saturn was shut temporarily by slow sales, Saturn workers would attend training classes, sweep floors, fix machines, and perform other duties.The workers were taking the biggest gamble of all. By joining Saturn, they were giving up their recall rights to other GM factories. That meant that if Saturn was a bust, their ties with GM would be cut forever. Moreover, they couldn't simply transfer from Saturn back to their home plant. This winnowed down the candidates to a crop of workers who really wanted to work at the Saturn plant.

The UAW's executive board grudgingly approved the contract at a special meeting called in Chicago in the spring of 1985. As they were meeting, the first word of the location of the Saturn factory began to float around: a little town in Tennessee called Spring Hill, not too far from Nashville. It was almost an anticlimax to the site-choosing circus in which Roger Smith reveled. Throughout 1984, Smith's office on the fourteenth floor of the GM building might as well have had a revolving door. Mayors, governors, senators, state senators, planning commissioners—more than 1,100 people in all—tried to win the factory for their states and towns. Billboards from different states went up on I-94, I-96, and I-75, the highways GM executives took on their way to work. Every day, an official would call a press conference, pitching his municipality to yawning reporters. None of this was really necessary. From the start Saturn had a specific list of what it wanted: about 10,000 empty acres, with no development, what the industry calls a "green field site." Saturn needed to be near major highways so components could be easily delivered. Some people argued it should be built in California, because that was where Saturn's potential customers were most plentiful. Others said GM owed the factory to Detroit, or Flint, because hundreds of thousands of jobs had been lost. But the Saturn founders wanted the factory to be away from heavily union towns where people would have preconceived notions. And they favored a place in the middle of the country—if not the Midwest, then the Mid-South, where Honda, Nissan, and Toyota were to build plants.

Not too many people had heard of Spring Hill, Tennessee, except maybe for Civil War buffs. Horses galloped and cows grazed on the site where the factory would rise. Tourists occasionally wandered into quaint little Franklin just a few miles away to see the town square, visit the cemetery, or shop for antiques. More important to GM officials, Nissan had built the biggest car plant in the country on the other side of Nashville. The small cars and pickups that the plant churned out were equal in quality to Nissans built in Japan. The work ethic among the Tennesseans seemed strong. And the hills and greenery of Nashville seemed welcoming to the Detroiters, used to a city built on concrete. With universities like Vanderbilt, the country music industry, and the beautiful mansions nestled nearby, the Nashville area seemed ideal.

Once the contract was signed and the site was selected, Smith went into public relations overdrive. He hyped Saturn—still five years away from the market—as the car to end all cars. He rolled out what was supposed to be a Saturn prototype for President Reagan to drive during a visit to the GM Tech Center early in his second administration. There was no Saturn prototype because the car was still being sketched.

The red car was simply a Chevy with a few styling changes, but Reagan gave it a thumbs up. Saturn officials were embarrassed—and frustrated because the project was getting so much attention so far ahead of schedule. "How do you think it felt to be a chief engineer at a car project when there wasn't even any car?" says Wetzel. Morale at Saturn was deeply shaken in 1985 by Sanchez's death. The first Saturn president and one of the six founders, he died at his Lansing, Michigan, home of a heart attack. His replacement was GM executive Hoglund, general manager at Pontiac, who years later would become number two to Jack Smith. But Hoglund held the job only for a few months. Stability came in the form of Richard S. "Skip" LeFauve (pronounced le FOE), who'd been running GM's AC/Rochester electronics subsidiary. Though a GM lifer, LeFauve had signed on to the team concept of running things at Rochester, where relations with the UAW were far friendlier than in other parts of GM. A lookalike of sportscaster Curt Gowdy, with a sharp eaglelike gaze but easygoing manner, LeFauve said he had no idea how big the task would be. "It's one thing to say you're going to do this, another to do it," said LeFauve. "We had to develop the trust over time. We had to learn to trust each other."[9]

Finally, with LeFauve at the helm, attention began to turn to the car itself. Though Smith had repeatedly said Saturn would be a "no-year" car, it was slated to be introduced in 1989 or 1990, the year Smith would retire. There was intense pressure for Saturn to be a styling sensation, a head-turner, something radical. Ford was just about to introduce the Taurus, with sleek, aerodynamic lines that would become an industry sensation. (Later, people would criticize Taurus for launching a series of lookalike "jelly beans," but that was far in the future.) Meanwhile, GM's styling reputation was suffering because of its lookalike cars, all with sloping noses and boxy rear ends, similar on the outside, but different inside, where GM could have saved money. They were disasters in terms of both looks and quality. In a single year, 1987, GM's market share slumped five points. The lookalikes increased the pressure on Saturn to look different. Some people even suggested it be an electric car or a gas turbine car.

But the Saturn team argued that futuristic looks and flashy features would defeat their purpose. For months, they'd ridden around in 110 Honda Civics, Toyota Corollas, and Mazda 323s. They made notes on how the cars handled, how the engine sounded, where the radio and climate control buttons were placed, and even tape-recorded the sound of the doors closing. One of Wetzel's neighbors, watching him pull into his driveway each night in a Honda, strolled across the street one evening to talk to him. "Did you leave? Are you with Honda now?" the neighbor wondered. Wetzel grinned and assured him he was still at GM, just conducting some "competitive analysis," as Big Three executives call it when they take home other companies' cars. The Saturn officials didn't borrow the cars, as was standard industry practice, but bought them at dealerships. They found that the Japanese cars' showrooms were nothing like most GM dealerships, where lots were flooded with inventory and salesmen pressured buyers to make a deal that night. Sometimes there weren't many cars in stock, and buyers had to come back. The Japanese didn't fool around naming colors things like "Moonbeam" and "Stardust"—they used words like "navy" and "teal." Nor were there dozens of interior features like tinted sunroofs and power memory seats. Japanese cars usually came in just two or three versions—DX, LX or EX. Most were already loaded with options.

Saturn decided to do the same. Saturns were introduced in just three styles—a no-frills sedan, slightly upscale four-door, and a coupe. Later on, the line added a station wagon. Colors stayed basic: red was red, unless it had a metallic coating. Then, it was metallic red. "Less is best," says Donald Hudler, Saturn vice president of sales and marketing. "We were aiming for harmony and simplicity."[10] The resulting car was bland-looking, a little bit like a Pontiac, not sexy and nothing that was a head-turner. Saturn officials, who loudly defended their choice of a non-threatening car, were nervous. "Frankly, we were sweating bullets," said Hudler. But he had fought against giving Saturn an aerodynamic look. He calls such models "marshmallows"—"They look like you put them in a microwave on high for twenty seconds."

Roger Smith supported the Saturn team every step of the way, to the consternation of many executives inside GM who saw the funds they needed for their programs diverted to Saturn. The small car eventually would cost GM $5 billion by the time the Spring Hill factory opened in 1990—at least double what GM would publicly admit to spending on other ground-up car projects. Even while he spent billions of dollars on acquisitions, including $5 billion for Hughes Aircraft and $2.5 billion for EDS, Smith would emphasize that Saturn was in no danger. "It will be finished on time and underbudget," he repeated, parrotlike. But persistently, the rumors circulated that Saturn was going to be scrapped. GM's market share was plunging, the company's cash was being depleted by Smith's buying spree, and GM was laying out hundreds of millions of dollars in rebates and other incentives, trying to keep its car sales afloat. LeFauve recalls his mother once called him to ask if Saturn was okay. "Are you sure you have a job?" she asked.

If it had been up to Elmer Johnson, LeFauve might have been working elsewhere. Johnson, brought in by Smith to run GM's legal operations, was Saturn's biggest opponent on the GM board. The Chicago lawyer, tall and courtly yet with an independent streak, thought Saturn was a waste of GM's time and resources. In the fall of 1987, Johnson decided to launch a last-chance challenge to Saturn, hoping to keep the company from spending billions on its development that it needed to fund what he thought were far more important projects. On October 19, the stock market crashed 500 points and Johnson saw an opportunity to use the crash as cover for canceling Saturn. He tried to convince GM president Bob Stempel and executive vice president F. Alan Smith to join him in confronting Roger Smith. But everybody in GM knew that Smith would never abandon the project. In fact, he saw support for Saturn as a test of loyalty among the candidates who might hope to replace him.[11] During a meeting of the board's finance committee on December 7, 1987, Johnson gave a stinging denunciation of Saturn. GM was "lying wounded on the battlefield" and should refocus its efforts on projects in the works, not those it had barely even begun. But Smith disagreed. Sure, GM could cancel the project, but then who would prove that an American company could compete in the marketplace against the Japanese? Joining him was John Smale, Procter & Gamble's CEO. "If GM doesn't take this bold step, nobody else will," Smale said. Funding for Saturn was approved, although as a compromise GM officials decided to cut the plant's capacity back from the 500,000 cars a year that Smith wanted to build to a more conventional size of 240,000 cars, which could rise to 300,000-plus if a third shift of workers was hired. Johnson, who had once been in the pool of possible candidates to replace Smith, knew that his opposition to Saturn meant his GM career was over. Only six months later, he quit GM to return to his Chicago law firm, Kirkland & Ellis.

With the money approved, Saturn's development team went to work on the small car, designing an all-new engine as well. The process began in 1987 and was completed by 1990—as fast as any Japanese company could then get a car to market, and twice as fast as any GM vehicle generally made it onto the street. Meanwhile, the Spring Hill site was prepared and the skeleton for the sprawling factory began to rise in the foothills of the Smoky Mountains. Despite the fears of some locals, the factory didn't spoil the landscape. Tennessee built a parkway to connect the Saturn complex to the main highway. Tall grass and tree- and shrub-covered berms hid the plant from view. One day in 1989, Saturn executives stood on top of one of the hills to look at the huge concrete floor of the plant spread out at their feet. Holding the layout for the plant in their hands, they could tell where the paint shop would be, where the engine casting would take place, and even where the cars would roll off the end of the assembly line. It was like a scene from a Hollywood movie, Wetzel recalled. "That's when it really hit me," he said.

With the project heading forward, it was time to pick the dealers who would sell Saturn cars. Saturn sent market researchers out to benchmark customer service standards. It wasn't enough just to study Chevrolet dealers or Cadillac showrooms. Saturn was after people who owned Honda Civics and Toyota Corollas, men and women in their mid-thirties, college-educated, with an income of $40,000 and up. These were members of the "lost generation" who'd never bought a

Detroit carmaker's product. Saturn officials knew it would be a tough fight to convince Japanese-car owners whose autos were proven to be reliable to try an all-new car built by a company owned by GM. At the minimum, Saturn would have to offer consistent, high-quality customer service just to get people to visit showrooms. Even the Japanese-car dealers weren't yet offering this kind of service; Toyota's Lexus and Nissan's Infiniti hadn't yet been introduced, while Honda's Acura hadn't been around long enough to make its mark. Saturn assembled small groups of consumers and asked them dozens of questions about what they liked and hated about buying a car. Overwhelmingly, people told them they hated not knowing if they'd gotten a good deal. They were never sure whether they'd paid too much for the car that took them three weeks of comparison shopping to select. And women were vocal in their loathing of the whole car-buying process. Dealers would ignore them, condescend to them, or routinely ask them to come back with their husbands. Both sexes were angry at dealers' frequent practice of "qualifying" or looking them over when they walked into a showroom. If they looked prosperous, they'd get waited on. If they were dressed in sweatpants or jeans, they were often left to wait, fuming, for a salesperson.

From the focus groups, Saturn came up with its own customer-service philosophy:

- It banished the practice of asking shoppers whether they wanted to buy a car "that day." Every customer that walked into a showroom was to be greeted cordially and handed over to a salesperson, whether or not they came to look or to buy.
- Before going on a test drive and long before prices were discussed, Saturn salespeople were to give talks on Saturn's history. Often, they'd invite customers to watch a video about the founding of Saturn. Salespeople went into as much detail as a customer could bear. If they left a name and address, they'd get a thank-you letter and a phone call from their salesperson a few days later.
- Saturn decided to give customers 30 days to return their

car, no questions asked, and get a replacement. Each buyer is deluged with questionnaires asking how they like their car. They're sent postcards reminding them it's time for routine maintenance and each gets an annual pamphlet talking about Saturn's progress.

In 1987, Haywood "Huddy" Hyman Jr. was sitting in his Richmond, Virginia, Buick dealership, reading *Automotive News*, when he spotted an article on how to apply for a Saturn franchise. Hyman was a second-generation Richmond dealer— his father was a pillar of the Richmond community. And he'd done well, too; his Buick dealership was one of the biggest in Richmond, and he'd bought a Porsche-Audi showroom just as sales of the sports cars to Richmond's yuppies were skyrocketing. Hyman, then in his late thirties, fit the profile of the kind of dealer Saturn wanted. He has the relaxed, friendly air of a fraternity boy who's popular with his pals and a gentlemanly teaser with his female friends. Drawings by his children are tacked on the walls of his office. He's the kind of person who, hearing a visitor is interested in Confederate history, sends along brochures on Civil War Richmond. Intrigued, Hyman wrote to Saturn headquarters in Troy, Michigan, for a Saturn information package. Back came a brochure with a black cover and a letter signed by Skip LeFauve: "We are seeking people who believe that although there is often good in the old way, there's no room for the excuse, 'but we've always done it that way.'"

Flipping through the brochure, Hyman found a quiz. It asked, "Do you have a proven record of high customer satisfaction and strong sales? Are you willing to take on new challenges, learn and grow, and actively seek change? If your answers are yes, we would like to hear from you." That packet started Hyman on a two-year journey that culminated in his being selected one of the first fifty Saturn dealers to open for business on October 25, 1990. Saturn was extraordinarily choosy in selecting the dealers. First, their finances had to be in order because each franchise was going to cost an average of $1 million—and those in California closer to $4 million because of then-expensive real estate costs. Saturn wanted its dealers to be willing to build brand-new showrooms based on an architectural model it hoped would set the pattern for the typical Saturn dealership. In fact, many dealers found they couldn't afford new showrooms and initially launched their Saturn business from empty showrooms they'd simply leased or bought from other dealers who went out of business.

Hyman was impressed when Saturn officials took a good, hard look at his business history. They calculated his debt-to-equity ratios to be sure he was't burdened with loans on his other dealerships. Then Saturn sent interviewers to speak with his managers, his salespeople, and his customers, asking them to rate Hyman's dedication to quality and customer service on a scale of one (worst) to five (best). All of his scores averaged four or better, they told him. Hyman went to Spring Hill and to Troy, talking to LeFauve, Hudler, and the other executives, keeping his fingers crossed. And two years from the day he read the article in *Automotive News*, Hyman got a letter via Federal Express telling him he'd been selected for a Saturn dealership. In training classes over the next year, Hyman and the other forty-nine Saturn dealers were given details on how Saturn planned to operate.

First, dealers would be assigned a single market area. Saturn deliberately limited the number of showrooms, to keep administrative costs low and dealer profits high. Like church parishes, dealers are assigned to serve all potential customers in a specific region. People can buy cars wherever they wish, but dealers usually suggest they shop in their neighborhood and take their cars there for service. "The first time I sent a customer to [another dealership], I said to myself, 'I can't believe I'm doing this!'" said John Covell, general manager of Saturn of Seekonk, Massachusetts.

Saturn wanted two-way communication with its dealers. Like other GM divisions, Saturn has a dealer advisory board, called the Franchise Operations Team, that has a say in decisions about the cars. Saturn founders decided they couldn't give the UAW a role in running Saturn without including the people who sell the cars. Customers might not think this matters, but the FOT is one way their complaints get to the top.

Through the FOT and in all its bulletins to dealers Saturn

stresses its no-hassle selling philosophy. Saturn guarantees dealers profits of 12 to 15 percent on each small sedan or coupe. In return, dealers are to sell the cars at the moderate list price—originally $7,995 for the no-frills car, a figure that climbed to about $11,000 by 1995. Every customer is given the car at the same price, and shown a list of options and their prices. The only haggle at most showrooms is over the value of the trade-in. And those showrooms are designed to be wide open. Salespeople don't go into back rooms to cut deals. The sales manager sits on the showroom floor, in a cubicle in plain view of the customers.

Saturn took as much care in choosing its first group of workers as it did in selecting its initial crop of dealers. Early recruits began to arrive in Spring Hill in 1989. Some of them had been indefinitely laid off from their GM factories, with no hope of a job anytime soon. Some came from factories that GM had closed. Others watched as GM shut down plants, wondering if their line would be next. One of the people who took a chance was Catherine Willingham, a black single mother from Chicago. She came fresh with memories of the day GM eliminated half the jobs in her factory. "It hurt a lot— but it didn't hurt me half as much as it hurt them," she said. The job cuts prompted her to look into a Saturn job; soon she was loading up her car for the daylong drive. It was a tough adjustment for Willingham, her daughter, and her grandchild. She settled in a quiet suburb nothing like the busy Chicago neighborhood where she could find something to do day or night. In Nashville, she laughed, it was hard to find an all-night grocery store. But the move turned out to be a smart one: GM closed the Chicago factory two years after she got to Saturn. Coworker Carl Eppler, who went to Tennessee when GM closed his Flint, Michigan, plant in 1990, says it took a while to get used to the idea of workers having an equal say in decisionmaking. "People used to say, 'No way I want you working here. I'll kick your butt out the front door.' But here, it's different," he says. One thing Eppler liked was Saturn's focus on its Japanese competitors. When he worked at Flint, the joke was that the initials BOC—Buick, Oldsmobile, Cadillac—actually stood for "big old cars" that nobody wanted to buy. "The market isn't just hemmed in by the Atlantic and the Pacific. It's a world market," says Eppler.

All the hopes and dreams of Saturn executives, employees, auto workers, and dealers had built came to a head on July 30, 1990, the day before Smith was set to retire. In his last public move as GM CEO, Smith went to Spring Hill to see the first Saturn roll off the asssembly line. Hoping to keep the car shrouded in secrecy, Saturn let only the nose be seen by photographers. It wasn't quite time for Saturn to be introduced, but it was time for Smith to go. The management team that would replace him had been chosen. And it was up to them to make sure Saturn—and GM—were ready for the challenges of the 1990s.

Among the executives about to take charge at GM was a man whose career Roger Smith had helped develop over the past twenty-five years. Although others helped him, too, Roger Smith took credit for discovering him—his second great accomplishment. Had he not mentored Jack Smith, there is no way to know to whom GM would have turned for help when it needed it most.

CHAPTER · 3

From Worcester to Zurich

Worcester, Massachusetts, where Jack Smith was born in 1938, was and is the second-largest city in Massachusetts. Home to Holy Cross, Clark University, and the Worcester Polytechnic Institute, its downtown streets are quiet and a little tattered now. But the buildings are imposing—like the massive municipal auditorium, the courthouse, and the art museum, one of the best in New England. Worcester (locally it sounds like "wuss-tah") has always had a mix of people: descendants of French immigrants who'd come before and after the Revolutionary War, Irish who came to America before and after the Potato Famine of 1840, and Italian and Portuguese workers who came in the late 1890s and early 1900s for factory and construction jobs. Worcester had mills and munitions factories. The giant Herrington and Richardson plant hummed full-time during World War II, turning out armaments for the war effort. It lacked the patrician airs of Boston, but Worcester had an energy and prosperity of its own.

Both sets of Smith's great-grandparents had come from Ireland in the mid-1800s, settling on lush green dairy farms in western Massachusetts. So prevalent were the farms—and so successful—that motorists driving on old U.S. 20 or some of the backroads got used to stopping to let the contented dairy cows meander across the road. Smith's father, Francis, known as Frank, was one of eight children. Born in 1910, he grew up on a farm outside Worcester, even though his father owned a bicycle shop in town on Green Street. The shop did a booming business in bike rentals. Customers would throw their jackets on the floor of the shop for collateral, take the cycles for a spin in Elm Park, and return late in the day to collect their wearable deposits.[1] Business was so good that Frank Smith even worked on the day his sister got married.

Frank Smith was a quiet man, a little shorter than average, who talked his whole life of becoming a country doctor. But he ended up studying public health at the University of Massachusetts, then joining his brothers in another family venture. The Smiths had a small chain of ice cream stores, known as Smithfield's Famous Ice Cream. In a state where fights can take place over whose ice cream is tops, Smithfield had a reputation as a tasty, premium product, the Ben & Jerry's of its time. "Take home a half gallon, today!" read the signs on the big white trucks—"Phone Pl4-4309 for home delivery."

Worcester folks from the era can recite, at an instant's notice, who married whom, dated whom, moved away, moved back, made it big, went broke, and how they died. Well, as everybody who knew them will tell you, Frank Smith married a Sullivan. His wife Eleanor came from a family whose male members were policemen and politicians—some of them prominent. Her brother, Charles F. "Jeff" Smith, was the mayor of Worcester and later lieutenant governor of Massachusetts. When Jack Smith was a boy, he'd travel with his uncle, go to political rallies, watch his uncle shaking hands, ask him questions in the big sedan as it bowled its way across Massachusetts, soak up the way his uncle had time for anybody, whether elite Bostonian or western Massachusetts farmer.

Eleanor Sullivan met her future husband when she went to work in a Smithfield Ice Cream store. She scooped ice cream, and one day stopped to admire Frank Smith's work decorating ice cream cakes. Conversation led to dates and soon they became a steady couple. Two years after he graduated from UMass, the pair were married in 1934. Their first child was a daughter, Mary Carroll, born in 1935; Jack came next in 1938, followed by Michael in 1943, and the baby, Sally, in 1945. The Smiths lived on Chandler Street in a "three-decker." That house is gone, but dozens of them remain in Worcester: towering three- and four-story frame houses with front porches often shadowed by big oak and maple trees.

Far from the dim tenements of New York, the creaky flats of Detroit, or the monotonous row houses of Baltimore, these multifamily dwellings were roomy, comfortable, and well-built. Each floor had a single apartment, sometimes with three or four bedrooms. Doctors, lawyers, insurance men, and shopowners like Frank Smith brought up their families in three-deckers. It was an event to move to a house shared by just two families, and unlike the Sullivans, hardly anybody in the neighborhood lived in a house by themselves. Like the brownstones of Brooklyn, three-deckers made for little privacy—but then, with big families of six or eight kids fairly common in the pre–Vatican II era, it would be hard to expect any.

In the afternoons, when they weren't at church guild meetings, moms and grandmothers sat on their front porches, keeping an eye on neighborhood kids, wearing checkered aprons, knitting and chatting, occasionally yelling out to their children. At night, when dads came home in these days before television, they'd sit out front reading the Worcester paper or the *Boston Globe*, smoking a cigarette. Everybody seemed to smoke—there's a saying among New Englanders, "It's just a cigarette away," meaning that the trip only takes as long as it takes to smoke a cigarette. (The Smiths' house was about half a cigarette away from their closest ice cream store.) As the children played, sounds of Boston Red Sox broadcasts or the news on WBZ or Jack Benny's Sunday-night show would waft out front windows from big console radios with glowing golden dials.

Smith's childhood was filled with basketball games and trips to Elm Park or sprawling Chandler Hill Park for skating and snowball fights in winter, baseball in spring and summer, touch football and leaf fights in the fall. His friends would stand on the sidewalk and yell for "Smitty" to come down for a game of hoops. His mother, who kept house, would call from the front railing, "Jack will be right down," says boyhood friend Donald Moran. Smith especially loved basketball. "He was a nifty little point guard," says Moran. He had a lasting passion for the Boston Celtics, renowned in the late 1940s and early 1950s for players like Bob Couzy. That passion still burns. Decades later, Smith bought stock in the Celtics' limited partnership, and you can always start a conversation with him by asking about the Celts' season.

The boys played parish-league basketball on one of the best courts in the neighborhood, at May School, which still stands. It boasts one of the first poured concrete floors in Worcester, and the gym—big by elementary school standards—echoes with shouts of youngsters past and present. The solid brick building, where children make big maple leaves out of colored construction paper and tack them to windows in the fall, has another claim to fame: student radical Abbie Hoffman was educated there. Hoffman, a few years younger than Smith, grew up just a couple of streets away and attended the neighborhood synagogue. (He was still a fugitive from justice when his father died, and FBI agents were spied sitting in cars outside the synagogue, expecting Hoffman to show up. If he did, they didn't see him.)

Smith and his siblings went to grade school at Blessed Sacrament, where the nuns were strict. The children were expected to show up on time, have clean faces and hands, and keep quiet in class. They stood up when a priest came in the room, answered, "Yes, Father," or "Yes, Sister," and many children blessed themselves when they walked by the front of a church. Sally and her brother attended school together for only one year—Jack in the eighth grade, Sally in the first. But she still laughs, remembering the day she misbehaved and was sent to stand in the hallway at the end of the day, her face to the lockers. She heard the sound of footsteps and realized it was her brother, joining other school crossing guards heading out to their posts. Down the hall, her brother's voice rang out, "Boy, you're going to get it when you get home!"

When the Smith children got older, they were expected to help out at home and in the eight ice cream stores, including the main one on Chandler near their house, the others on Lincoln and Mulberry and Hamilton and in the outlying towns. The workload was heavy because for years Frank Smith also ran the Worcestor department of health. Jack Smith tried a turn at the front counter, where Smithfield sold a generous scoop of premium ice cream for ten cents—Popsicles were a nickel. But he didn't much like dealing with customers. He preferred working in the back of the shop, mixing ice cream and lugging the big tubs to the front when his sisters needed more. "He did all the grunt work," says Sally.

Holidays were hectic: On Christmas Eve the family didn't go to Midnight Mass with everybody else, but would stay up until 1 A.M. making up ice cream orders, filling half-gallon boxes with their pink-and-black printing, carving the vanilla slices to be served with pumpkin pie and Indian pudding after Christmas dinner, and churning festive flavors like Peppermint Stick. The next morning the deliveries started at 8 A.M. The Smiths often had to hustle to catch the final Christmas mass of the morning before they'd trudge home to open their presents.

Frank Smith liked family vacations, when the whole crew would take off for weekends and holidays to Hampton Beach, to the Poconos, and once to New York City. The family spent several days there, climbing the Statue of Liberty, visiting Central Park, walking down Fifth Avenue. On these trips, Eleanor Smith got time to read. She loved mysteries with a passion—"She always had a book going," says Sally—and she'd read aloud to the children or take them down to the library to bring home a load of books.

Everybody in the family was bright, but Mary Carroll, the oldest, was particularly smart. She had a thoughtful manner, excelled at writing, and diaplayed a deep intellect, even in grade school. Her parents hoped she would become a doctor. Unlike some parents of the day, who thought girls should be sent to community colleges, if they went at all, Frank Smith was willing to pay for eight years of schooling. But Mary decided in high school that she was going to become a nun. She begged to go to the convent after graduation. In some Irish families her decision might have been honored, and there might have been pressure on one of the Smith boys to become a priest. But Frank Smith refused her request to join a convent after high school and sent her to school at Trinity College in

Washington, D.C. Mary took her vows anyway soon after graduation.

As an adult she became a feminist author, earned a doctorate in Sanskrit and Indian languages, and wrote several books, ultimately leaving the sisterhood to teach at Vassar and the University of North Carolina and to live on Cape Cod. Years later, Jack Smith got stuck next to a bore on an airplane who boasted continuously about his accomplishments. Smith cut him off with, "My sister is an author"—not mentioning he himself was a fast-rising GM executive.

Once Mary was off to college, Smith came into the family spotlight. He wanted a business career, maybe working for Hood Milk and Ice Cream, the big regional dairy. He decided as soon as he got to high school that he'd go to Cornell to get his business degree. The idea didn't thrill his mother, who still bore memories of business failures during the Depression. She thought becoming a teacher was a more stable and high-status career. Eventually Sally would do so, as did her sister Mary Carroll; brother Michael went to work for GM and ended up vice chairman of Hughes Aircraft, which GM bought in 1985.

Smith spent his high school years at St. John's Academy, then as now an all-boys school. Today it sits upon a hill in Shrewsbury, the upper-crust town one over from Worcester. But the St. John's that Jack Smith attended was downtown in Worcester, not too far from one of the munitions plants. It was run by the Xaverian Brothers, whose church was built by the famed architect Charles Bullfinch, the designer of Boston's State House. While it was private, St. John's wasn't anywhere the equal of the elite boys' schools that dotted New England. "This wasn't like going to Exeter or Phillips Andover, where the Kennedys went," says classmate George Sullivan. "Our dads were judges and liquor store owners and tavern owners and dentists and doctors."

Smith went to the second of three St. John's buildings— the original one, built before the turn of the century, was used as a grade school. The school Jack attended was the big, three-story redbrick St. John's that was built in 1928—called the "new building" to differentiate it from the original school. Built by Portuguese bricklayers just before the Depression began, the building didn't withstand wear and tear very well. The week before he started high school, in 1953, Smith drove down with some of his pals to look around. As the car pulled up to the big red, weary-looking building, there was a silence in the car until Smith piped up, "They've got a lot of nerve calling this place the 'new' building!"[2]

At St. John's, Smith made friends for life. The men who knew him then, now all in their mid-fifties, tell Jack Smith stories as if they'd graduated last week, and if you get one of the group started, the others chime in with even taller tales. "The ties are hard to break," says Sullivan, who now runs one of the most successful insurance agencies in New England. Because Smith worked after school, it was hard to get him to go out during the school year. He didn't make it to many of his high school football games because he was helping out at Smithfield's. "We'd say, why not go to a record hop? Or a show? You couldn't move him," says Richard Quinlivan. And as for politics, like running for class president, forget about it, says his friend Moran. "I could see him working as a man behind the scenes, but I could never, never see Jack Smith asking for votes," he says. Adds Quinlivan, "That's exactly the opposite of his personality." The poise, grace, and ease with strangers that Smith would acquire later in life wasn't there in high school.

At St, John's, the boys sat in alphabetical order at wooden desks that they were warned not to carve their initials upon— "If you carved it, you bought it," recalls classmate Joseph Lane, now alumni director for the school. There were green chalkboards, the mahogany trim around the doors was thick, and a statue of St. Francis Xavier sat in a corner, watching over the class. The brothers wore brown monks' habits, complete with hoods and sandals in warmer months (in the winter they wore heavy black shoes). Most of the boys had crew cuts and all wore jackets and ties to class. In the fall, after class, they donned reindeer sweaters—big bulky wool sweaters with leaping stags on the chest. Nobody in the group was allowed to put on airs because the other boys wouldn't stand for it. "Everybody was certainly an equal down there—if you thought you were a hot shot, they'd take care of you right away," says Sullivan. Lunch periods were spent on the bleachers of the gymnasium balcony, watching the runners below. And though nearly all the boys smoked—Smith didn't quit until the 1980s—they were banned from doing so anywhere near the school; they couldn't light up before they crossed under the railroad bridge two blocks away.

The boys weren't angels. In fact, Smith's 1956 graduating class is still remembered as one of the "frowned-upon" classes of the 1950s, says Sullivan. "The brothers didn't think we performed up to their expectations," he says. For example, if you go to Lane's office looking for Smith's senior class year-book, you won't find one. All you'll get is a Xerox copy of the class "memory book"—sixteen pages with a paper cover. That's because the boys didn't sell enough ads to pay for a yearbook, and the brothers wouldn't let them publish at a deficit. Sullivan defends his pal Smith, who was cochairman of the yearbook. "Smitty was out slugging ice cream cones. He was trying to make a buck," Sullivan says.

But on Sunday nights in the summertime, once they got their driver's licenses, one of the boys' cars would pull up in front of the Smiths' house. Mrs. Smith would call down her greeting and Jack Smith would bound down the steps, some-times dressed in khaki slacks and a plaid sports shirt. He'd grin at his pals and climb in the backseat. Off they'd go, to the movies, to have a sandwich at their hangout, the Levitt's drugstore, to swim at Lake Quinsigamond.[3] Once in a while, they'd end up at a Smithfield's for ice cream, where if Frank Smith was working the boys would get bigger-than-usual scoops. "Billy Petersen [Gordon Petersen, a veteran news anchor in Washington, D.C.] thought Frank Smith was God," laughs Quinlivan.

Maybe the brothers thought these kids could use a little polishing, but they weren't out looking for trouble. There were some crosstown rivalries between public school and Catholic school kids, and sometimes skirmishes would break out be-tween the boys. But "We never had situations where kids would go and kill themselves," says Sullivan. "If somebody got punched in the nose, that was the end of it. Nobody had weapons." There was plenty to do to keep out of trouble— "Either you worked or you played sports. There was not too much in between. School, sports, and work, and homework," he says. Especially classwork, because St. John's was a school that prided itself on the high percentage of its boys who went on to college. Says Lane, "I wouldn't think of going to class without my homework done."

It was tough to drag Smith to a dance and even harder to get him on a date. He had no time for girls—even though plenty of the young women who worked in Smithfield's tried to get his attention. Sally Mahoney says her brother often talked about remaining a bachelor. "He was going to get a room in the Sheraton," she says. But he did go to one party, where he met the girl who became his first wife. Marie Holloway was fifteen and Jack seventeen when they met in his senior year at St. John's. She was a hometown girl, devoted to her family and to Worcester. Frank Smith knew Bob Holloway, Marie's father, but their children had never met, probably because the Holloways lived on the other side of town and she went to Ascension, the girls' Catholic high school. Marie Holloway loved New England; she wanted to be a housewife and settle down near her parents. "This was a very provincial city," says Moran. "We all thought we'd make our livelihoods here."

Two months after they met, Smith and Marie were a couple. Smith tossed aside his plans to go to Cornell and applied at UMass to be closer to her, which disappointed his father, who wanted his children to reach beyond his own accomplishments. But the family liked Marie, who was loyal but unobtrusive, not clinging—the guys with whom Smith palled around say they didn't know too much about her. Smith didn't talk about her, and since they didn't go to school together, they rarely saw her. Sister Sally, ten years old at the time Smith and Marie met, liked seeing her brother in love. "It was great. He became human, like a real person, and he took an interest in other people," she says.

After graduation from St. John's, in 1956, Smith went off to college in his first brand-new car, a little Pontiac. "He was very proud of that car," says Moran. He'd drive up to Amherst on Sunday nights, come back on Friday with his laundry, and call Marie as soon as he got home. At UMass Smith majored in production management, preparing himself to join a big company. (Later on, UMass awarded Smith an honorary degree and asked him to be commencement speaker. That afternoon, names of distinguished alumni were hung on banners around the sides of the stadium where commencement was being held. Along with such notables as Natalie Cole, Bill Cosby, and Julius Irving hung a banner that read, "John Smith." Some of the people in the audience, who hadn't heard of him, buzzed in confusion, turning the pages of the graduation program until they spotted his biography.)

When his senior year at UMass came, Smith went on interviews, hoping to capture a job at his first choice: Raytheon. (He'd given up his idea of joining Hood Milk and Ice Cream by this time.) The big defense contractor was a major Massachusetts employer, and Smith was intrigued by the idea of joining a company that had a foot in the emerging nuclear age. But Raytheon didn't offer him a job, and Smith went off to serve six months in the Air Force in Texas. The experience was dismal—Smith developed a cyst that sapped him of his strength and he was plagued by chronic backaches. He had no affinity for the rigidity of military life or for the Southwest, says Sally.

When his tour ended, he came home and eventually landed a job at General Motors as a payroll clerk at the Framingham, Massachusetts, plant, about a twenty-minute drive up Route 9 from Worcester. Though in the Midwest and even in the Boston suburbs it wasn't unusual for high school and college students to get jobs in car plants during the summer, nobody in his group had gone to work at Framingham. It was an easy commute, but it was also a crossroads: of the eighty-two in Smith's St. John's class, only twenty-one moved away; fifty-three of them still live in or around Worcester. Sullivan says they all felt they could advance in the world, given natural drive and opportunities, although in Smith's case, "You'd think any chance of advancement was ruined by associating with us," he jokes.

None of the men could have guessed that, thirty years hence, Smith would rise so far, or that the fate of the world's largest corporation would one day rest in his hands. "I certainly had no idea," says Moran. Adds Sullivan: "I don't think he ever had any inkling that he'd be president of General Motors. You can think of somebody becoming a policeman or a doctor. But it's such a big position—like president of the United States—the realities are so farfetched that I think it's a dream." Sally Mahoney, visiting Worcester with her husband in the summer of 1994, drove by the Hood plant where her brother once worked for a summer and hoped to begin his business career. "I said to him, if things had been different, I wonder if Jack would be chief executive of Hood Ice Cream now?" Told of his sister's remark, Smith quipped, "Probably not."

What Jack Smith found at the Framingham plant was the apex of General Motors' self-protective corporate culture. The sprawling complex, which GM closed in 1987, was really two big factories—one that built Chevrolets, the other run by Fisher Body, which made key GM car components that were shipped across the country. They may have been part of the same company, but they could have been Ford and Chrysler for all the camaraderie and cooperation that existed. "They had a line down the middle of the floor," Smith recalled in amazement. "And there were times when the plant managers of both sides didn't speak to one another."[4] He saw, early on, that GM had grown so big the idea of an upper crust of management over a vast empire was no longer working. Little turf battles had developed that robbed the company of the economies of scale that it could have benefitted from. The lessons of Sloan were forgotten, and as the years went by, disputes broke out everywhere. "During his time, it was a phenomenal system. But General Motors needed to change," Smith says.[5]

Because of its vastness, GM had become a company that fostered competition among its young managers, figuring the best of the lot would survive to rise and develop. One method was to create special training programs and encourage the young men to vie for them, in an early test of their business and political skills. Shortly after he got there, Smith decided it would help his chances if he went to Boston University at night to earn an MBA. GM, as it often does for promising young employees, paid his way, and he spent long hours in the classrooms on Commonwealth Avenue in Boston, after working all day at the Framingham plant. Smith graduated in 1965.

He was already married by then. Jack and Marie, who'd broken up once during their seven-year courtship, had wed in 1962. Two children followed quickly—Brian in 1963, Kevin in 1964. Marie wanted a girl, but there were no more children. Every weekend, the couple, who'd moved to Shrewsbury to shorten Jack's commute, visited their parents with the babies in tow. By this point Jack Smith's bosses at GM had noticed his abilities and thought he'd be an ideal candidate for a job in Detroit. Smith turned it down. He wanted to work in New York, home to the treasurer's office, the powerful GM financial staff and site of the company's monthly board meetings. Eventually he beat out sixty other young candidates for the New York job and landed on the comptroller's staff. Roger Smith, then on GM's finance staff, took credit for picking him out of the stack of applicants. "I brought him down from Framingham to the treasurer's office," he said.

When Jack Smith got to New York in 1966, he had to camp out in GM's temporary offices at 1775 Broadway for a couple of years. GM was building itself a soaring skyscraper on Fifth Avenue, tearing down an architecturally beloved building, the Savoy Plaza, to do so. Even now, books about New York's architectural past mourn the destruction of the Savoy, which had arched arcades and elegant shops similar to those on the Rue du Rivoli near the Louvre in Paris. Designer Hattie Carnegie, known for her elegant fashions and unique costume jewelry, had a shop there that was patronized by society women and movie stars. Wealthy tourists loved to stay at the 1890s Plaza Hotel across the street, shop at castle-like Bergdorf Goodman, then cross to the Savoy Plaza for a stroll.

But this was now an era of the International style—big boxy buildings that could be put up anywhere, with no hint of cultural identity. GM, whose officers were housed in a 1920s limestone building in Detroit, wanted something ultra-modern. It hired the architect of the John F. Kennedy Center for the Performing Arts, which was then rising on the banks of the Potomac River in Washington. GM picked white marble for the exterior of its new building, which soared straight up more than forty stories, looking like ribs against the sky. It became so widely known as a symbol of 1960s corporate prosperity that tourists sent postcards of the building home to their friends. There was a showroom in the lobby filled with glistening cars—very few of which sold in Manhattan, where most residents didn't drive—and FAO Schwarz's upscale toy store eventually moved into the other end. Elevators would whisk board members directly to the twenty-fifth floor, where GM's teakwood-lined boardroom sat with its dramatic views of Central Park.

The floors below and above went to house members of the financial staff, many of them Harvard or Columbia MBAs, some of the sharpest and most competitive minds in the corporate world. "The treasurer's office was a top-notch re- cruiting post," says Charles Golden, a former GM treasurer who now runs the GM's Vauxhall division in England. "For a high-powered MBA, it was an exciting prospect to see what you'd get involved in."[6] Among them now was Smith. He and Marie settled with the boys in suburban Piscataway, New Jersey, just off the New Jersey Turnpike. She rarely saw him in those early years because then, as now, the hours in the treasurer's office were brutal. It was not unusual for the young MBAs to roll into the office at 6:30 or 7 A.M., spend hours in meetings or writing reports, and remain at their desks until 10 P.M. or even later. Six- and even seven-day weeks were com- mon. Often, the young financial staffers found themselves headed home at midnight, the only traffic on the dark New York City streets. "Let me paint you a bleak tableau," says a graduate of the treasurer's office. "It's Sunday night, 2 A.M. You're riding in a taxi. You can look out the window and there's nobody on the street. And you say to yourself, 'I'm rotting away. What the hell am I doing this for?'" It was even tougher for Smith, who had to travel through the Lincoln Tunnel every night to get home. Even so, Jack and Marie went to Worcester every weekend—a four-hour drive each way—with the boys.

But in the early years of Smith's career, such devotion to the job was a necessary part of climbing higher. Everybody in New York knew they had to put in several years of such long days. The treasurer's office is in charge of many areas at GM, from calculating the cost of new labor contracts, to mergers and acquisitions, to investments, to investigating joint ventures. "It's a good place to get your foot in the door," says Golden. Yet some of the work had little to do with GM's finances. If they weren't crafty or capable, the young MBAs would find themselves glorified clerks—making copies, typing for their bosses, carrying briefcases for visiting executives. Some became "bag men," whose job it was to pull the correct binder out of a case when a question came up, or change transparencies during a top executive's presentation. Time spent as a "bag man" allowed a young finance staffer to rub shoulders with top management, hoping to be noticed by the right executive and invited along on the ride to the top of the corporate ladder. When it came down to it, however, some who served as bag men felt they were merely glorified errand boys. "How mindless some of the stuff was that you had to do—running a copier at two in the morning to get ahead," sighs a former GM manager.

It seemed worth it, though, because GM was the most powerful company in America. Despite the tragedy of the Corvair, and the embarrassment of GM's unscrupulous surveillance of Nader, the carmaker's influence in the corporate world was unchallenged. To rise within GM, even Smith had to put in some time performing mundane chores. But his responsibilities grew and his titles reflected it. Among his jobs was a stint in what is now GM's investor relations department. It fields calls from important shareholders, big institutions that hold GM stock, and from Wall Street analysts seeking to chase down rumors they'd heard about the company or looking for information. It was a guaranteed way to build contacts that could be used in the future. Among the callers that Smith helped was a young number-cruncher named Joseph Phillippi. Now a veteran and respected auto industry analyst at Lehman Brothers, whose pronouncements can send GM stock up or down, Phillippi forged a friendship with the young GM executive that lasts to this day. (Smith marked his first anniversary GM president by lunching with the Wall Street analyst). Nonetheless, the friendliness hasn't dulled Phillippi's sharp criticism of the giant auto company. Running into Phillippi unexpectedly at the 1994 Paris Motor Show, Smith took Phillippi by the arm and grinned, "My God, Joe Phillippi. That garbage I've been seeing from you in the *Detroit Free Press*. What are you, on their payroll?"

Roger Smith, who became treasurer in 1970, was impressed by Jack Smith's grasp of computers. The business world in the early 1970s was entering a transition period from big, bulky mainframes that ran off punchcards to the earliest desktop machines. Personal computers were still in the experimental stages, but Jack Smith figured out that he could use one to monitor government securities trading in Washington. Hearing about the idea, Roger Smith borrowed a suitcase-sized computer from GM's research lab. Jack Smith had a telephone line wired to a coat closet and would regularly sit inside, trading bonds on his jury-rigged PC.

In the 1970s it was a sign of success in the treasurer's office to be asked to give a presentation to the monthly meeting of the board's finance committee—even though the topic might be as unimportant as the latest ten-day sales report or the latest GNP projection. Attendance by senior executives was mandatory; paying attention was not. "People used to snore while they were giving that thing," snorts an executive who attended the sessions. Jack Smith by then was giving these presentations regularly, and they made him a nervous wreck. Often, the only time to rehearse was Saturday or Sunday, and Smith was still making the regular treks to Massachusetts with his wife and boys. One weekend, the family—Jack, Marie, Michael, Sally, their parents and assorted children—gathered in a house on Cape Cod. Smith couldn't concentrate with all the ruckus, so he and Marie climbed into their car and she drove him around the Cape's back roads while he rehearsed. In one office in the GM Building in New York, there hangs a picture of a heavyset Smith, with a 1970s haircut, giving one of these talks. "He went over and over and *over* those notes," says Sally Mahoney. The stress was the worst of Smith's career—even worse than when he became CEO, she says.

But Smith's years in New York were a valuable base for the career that would later take him around the globe. His promotions came quickly, and soon he was in a position to mentor some of the younger men who were starting their own careers.

The young staffers quickly learned that Smith was a valuable asset when they began their own climbs. Twenty years later, the lineup of men who helped Smith with his GM rescue plan included a number of treasury office alumni.

One of the first people to work for him was J. Michael Losh, a graduate of the General Motors Institute in Flint, Michigan. Losh, lanky with a Roman nose, was bright, aggressive, cynical, and ambitious. Over the next twenty-five years Mike Losh would sprint up the GM ladder, landing at Pontiac in the 1980s on the heels of treasury graduate Bill Hoglund, taking the helm of Oldsmobile late in the decade just as its sales were plummeting, and ultimately landing two key jobs under Smith—vice president for sales, service, and marketing, and chief financial officer. Others who came under Smith's wing in the period were Golden; John Smith (no relation), who headed European strategic planning and now runs the Allison division in Indiana; and Robert Hendry, who worked with Smith in GM's joint venture with Toyota as well as at GM's European operations and is now group executive in charge of business support at NAO.

But the most important tie was with Louis Hughes. Known as Lou, he was born in Cleveland and, like Losh, attended GMI as an undergraduate. Hughes, however, didn't want a career as an engineer or a car designer. Like Smith, he recognized that GM's true strength lay in its financial operations. He wanted to be in on the action in New York. As a sign that he was one of the chosen, GM sent Hughes to Harvard to earn his MBA. (One of his classmates was Thomas Plaskett, who eventually would try to save Pan American World Airways from extinction in the 1980s.) In Hughes's second year, 1972, he met with a GM recruiter who was trying to find the right entry-level job for him within the GM system. Hughes had no interest in heading back to Detroit to get lost in a division. "I asked him, do you have a place where all the MBAs go?" Hughes recalls. That place, it turned out, was the treasurer's office, and that's where Hughes landed a job.[7]

Of medium height, stocky, with thinning blond hair, Hughes, born in 1949, reminded his coworkers of the actor Harrison Ford. When he became passionate about something, he shared his enthusiasm with everybody. A student of Abraham Lincoln, he'd quote bits of Lincoln's second inaugural address during philosophical moments. Hughes loved New York with the kind of fervor usually found only in converted Catholics—or Midwesterners who escape to Manhattan. A treasury colleague recalls Hughes vowed to stay in the New York office for life. When he heard in the 1990s that Hughes didn't want to leave Europe for a job in Detroit, the coworker said dryly, "I remember when he wasn't going to leave New York."

Later, when GM named Hughes head of its German Opel division, he plunged into intensive German lessons so he could give his inaugural address to the Opel staff in their own language. Unlike English-speaking GM executives, who'd wait patiently while their words were translated via small headsets, Hughes would charge ahead in his Midwestern-accented *Deutsch*. He became fond of saying, "There's a word for that in German." Kenneth Levy, New York–born director of GM Europe public relations, remembers the morning Hughes walked into his office and gave a directive in German. Levy, a former Berlitz instructor whose grasp of German is flawless, gazed at his boss and replied, "Lou, we're both Americans. Talk English!"[8]

Smith, a little burned out by years of sixteen-hour days, got a kick out of the young executive's energy and his razor-sharp brain. A dozen years apart in age, they became more like brothers; Smith openly sponsored Hughes for GM jobs. When Smith left for Detroit in the late 1970s to become head of GM's worldwide planning office, he tried to convince Hughes to come with him. Hughes refused; his sights were set on the top New York job. "I wanted to be treasurer of General Motors. I burned with desire for the job," Hughes says.[9] The pair were to hook up again in Canada, where GM sent Smith in the mid-1980s to run its operations. Smith offered him the job of CFO for Canada, but Hughes turned him down again, still hoping for the top treasury post.

It never was to be his; the closest shot Hughes had at the position came in the mid-1980s, when GM named Leon Krain, an older financial staffer, to the job. Once again, Smith called to invite Hughes to become Canada's CFO. "He said, 'You turned this job down once before. You'd better take it this time if you know what's good for you,'" Hughes says. So Hughes, his wife Candice, a psychologist, and their children headed for Oshawa, outside Toronto, where Hughes and his mentor began their stellar international careers.

Before Canada, however, came more promotions for Jack Smith and a move to Detroit. F. Alan Smith, no relation, had taken a liking to Smith, and began to put his name in the hopper for key positions. In 1982, GM made Jack Smith its executive director in charge of worldwide product planning. And Roger Smith, on F. Alan Smith's advice, handed Jack a big challenge. He was placed in charge of negotiating a small-car deal with Toyota. In the late 1970s, GM and other U.S. car companies watched their market shares erode thanks to an onslaught of foreign-car sales. Small Toyota Corollas, Datsun B-210s, and Volkswagen Rabbits were snapped up by consumers shocked by skyrocketing oil prices and gasoline shortages. Each company had a small car—GM sold Chevrolet Chevette, Ford the Escort, and Chrysler the Omni and Horizon—but none could match Japanese cars' quality and durability. Nor could the Big Three make any money on the cars because the cost to manufacture a small car was the same as it cost to build a car selling for twice as much. GM lost about $600 on every $6,000 Chevette it sold.

Roger Smith knew GM didn't have the expertise to develop a small car quickly and profitably. But he wanted to know the manufacturing secrets that allowed Toyota to outearn GM on cars half the size of big Chevrolets, Oldsmobiles, and Buicks. So he sent the team to Toyota City, outside Nagoya, Japan, to sign up Toyota for a joint venture in the United States. For Jack Smith it proved to be a turning point. Asian culture, the grace of the buildings and the gardens, the centuries of history, and the very pace of Japan intrigued him. So did the Japanese style of doing business. He saw that his Japanese counterparts placed great store in a person's integrity and inner strength rather than his outward bluster. Japanese executives, Smith learned, felt social occasions were as important as business discussions. An entire three-hour dinner could pass

Mark Hogan, coauthor of the Fundamental Change turnaround plan and now president of GM do Brazil. (*GM*)

G. Richard Wagoner, the baby boomer who shot through GM's executive ranks, takes a break during a 1994 party on the White House lawn.

Peter Hanenberger, GM's international technology wizard. (*GM*)

Louis Hughes, Jack Smith's closest friend and president of GM's international operations, poses with the Opel Tigra, one of the nine variations on the Opel Corsa. (*GM*)

Louis Hughes. (*GM*)

Lydia and Jack Smith enjoy their frequent trips to their Cape Cod home. Sometimes Smith even cooks. (*Courtesy Lydia Smith*)

August 28, 1988: Jack and Lydia Smith's wedding picture.
(*Courtesy Lydia Smith*)

Jack Smith and his family pose for their 1993 Christmas card. *From left:* Brian Smith, Kevin Smith, Kathy Smith, and baby, Sally Smith, Lydia Smith, Nicola Sygrist, Jack Smith.

1995 Chevrolet Lumina, plagued by a sluggish startup. (*GM*)

1995 Oldsmobile Aurora, the car that revived a dying division. (*GM*)

"A car for every purse and purpose," decreed Alfred P. Sloan, GM's legendary chief executive. His memoirs are still a must-read for hints at the strategy that Jack Smith tried to restore. (GM)

John Smale, the mysterious, intimidating chairman of the board and leader of GM's outside directors. (GM)

G. Richard Wagoner Jr., the baby boomer who shot through the ranks to corporate stardom as the first president of NAO. (*GM*)

Chief financial officer J. Michael Losh, Jack Smith's first protégé, who blocked Hogan and his planners from implementing the successor to Fundamental Change. (*GM*)

without any mention of the subject at hand, but that did not mean his hosts were not paying attention to the way he and his peers conducted themselves.

The Toyota officials, whose negotiating team included Tatsuro Toyoda, nephew of Toyota's founder Eji Toyoda and now president of the carmaker, were impressed by Smith. And they knew he had the faith of GM's CEO, which raised his importance in their eyes. Once, Smith was tied up with business in Detroit and sent his negotiators, including Hughes and Hendry, in his place. The group arrived at Toyota headquarters without him, and the Japanese bargainers asked where Smith was. Told he couldn't attend the session, they canceled the meeting rather than deal with his subordinates.

The negotiations resulted in the creation of New United Motor Manufacturing, Inc.; the two companies agreed to build cars for ten years at a closed GM plant in Fremont, California. That factory wasn't Toyota's first choice; it wanted to use a truck plant in Shreveport, Louisiana.[10] But GM insisted on Fremont because it was closer to Japan. The Japanese were concerned because Fremont's workforce was infamously undisciplined. When they worked for GM, Fremont employees had a higher absenteeism rate than their counterparts elsewhere. There was talk of drug use and alcoholism among some of the workers. And Toyota was concerned that the veteran auto workers, angry that GM had closed their plant, might carry their bitterness to the new enterprise.

But a funny thing happened: the Toyota production system, which GM agreed to use at Fremont, calls for workers to be well and frequently trained in methods of building cars. If they don't understand, if there's a problem on the assembly line, they're encouraged to ask for help. The Fremont workers felt they were being treated like humans for the first time in their careers. The Toyota Corolla and Chevrolet Nova cars (later renamed Geo Prizm) built by UAW members at NUMMI turned out to be as good as cars built by Toyota in Japan. At a time when GM cars were derided as of poor quality by *Consumer Reports*, the magazine gave the NUMMI cars its highest recommendation. GM managers who worked at the plant began to talk about teamwork, sharing ideas, and continuous improvement. As they were transferred to other GM jobs, they tried to spread the gospel of NUMMI. Most of their colleagues treated them with scorn and skepticism.

But Smith remembered his experiences in Japan and the success of NUMMI. He began to draw on both in Canada, where Roger Smith sent him as a reward once his work on the NUMMI deal was completed. It was the first time he'd held an operations job, in which he was responsible for manufacturing, marketing, and sales, as well as financial data. He arrived in Oshawa "green as grass," Smith says.[11] He had to spend hours walking the long assembly lines at GM Canada's car and truck plants and days traveling the country, visiting dealers, before he felt up to speed. GM Canada's team of homegrown managers helped him through it. None of them was likely to climb the GM corporate ladder, but they loved the car business and wanted to see GM's operations prosper. They were determined to do their jobs well—a trait Smith had noticed among the Toyota employees whom he'd met in Japan. Though his learning curve was steep, he found the assignment to be a growing experience.

His personal life wasn't keeping pace, however. Marie didn't join her husband in Canada. The marriage began to suffer in the 1970s, most likely due to the long days Smith spent in Manhattan, Detroit, and Tokyo. She hadn't liked being away from her family in Worcester when they were living in New Jersey, and she was unhappy farther away in Detroit. Midwesterners, known for their friendliness, are often puzzled when people from the East Coast express dislike for their part of the country. But the first thing Easterners notice about Detroit is a sense of single-mindedness: this is a company town, and the company is the U.S. auto industry.

Whether they work for GM, Ford, Chrysler, any of the dozens of automotive parts suppliers, or act as consultants, the men of Detroit are focused on cars. In the 1990s a few women infiltrated the management ranks, but in the 1960s and 1970s it was a corporate cave society: The men did the work and brought home big paychecks while the women kept house, raised children, and tended to the couple's social life. Almost as in a caste system, the wives weren't expected to socialize with anybody beneath their husband's rank or outside his company; GM wives might know women whose husbands worked for Ford or Chrysler, but their social events would include only people from their husband's employer. Some of this stemmed from their companies' constant worries about antitrust suits. The government warned that any intra-company chumminess might bring on charges of collusion, so the companies set strict policies that barred all but the most innocuous conversations outside the workplace.

Even the very landscape of northern Detroit was different from other parts of the country. It had little to compare with the breathtaking shore of Cape Cod or the rolling hills of central Massachusetts, with its soaring oak and maple trees. The northern Detroit suburbs where top-flight managers and executives live—Bloomfield Hills at the top of the sphere, followed by Birmingham, Farmington Hills, Rochester, Northville, and Novi for the younger managers—are largely products of post–World War II prosperity. Houses in the Detroit suburbs are large, expensive, and new, set on flat acres of land that were once fields or orchards. Broad highways seem to extend to the horizon, and interchanges curl upon one another in concrete swirls.

The northern suburbs are not a place where speaking a foreign language, keeping up on politics, or reading the latest bestseller or biography is a priority to many people, as it might be in eclectic Ann Arbor, fifty miles to the west. When wealthy suburban Detroiters travel, they go to summer homes on Lake Michigan, to Florida to visit aging parents, to Chicago or Toronto for hotel getaways, and less often to Europe or exotic locales. Family ties aren't quite as deep as in the East, because husbands are constantly being transferred and climbing the social ladder from neighborhood to neighborhood. Few people who have made it still live in the house where they grew up. In fact, ten years in a house is remarkable for some families in parts of town where rising executives live.

By 1978 Marie had moved back east. Her sons, entering high school, stayed with their dad. She visited regularly for holidays, football games, and school plays. "She was a very caring mother," Sally says. But the marriage couldn't be salvaged despite Smith and Marie's best efforts. "They always loved each other. They tried very hard," Smith's sister says. The separation made the decade a dismal one personally for Smith, who in the 1970s also had to deal with the loss of both his parents. Along with his challenges at work, Smith and his sisters had to settle their parents' affairs.

One night in 1974, about a month after his father died, Smith and his sisters were cleaning out their parents' home in Holden, a small town next to Worcester, getting it ready for a real estate agent. One of Sally's friends, a bachelor professor at Quinsigamond Community College, came by to see the house, hoping to put in a bid before it was listed with a realtor. Arthur Krupnik had gotten acquainted with both Smith sisters, who taught at the school. It had once been Assumption College but was sold to the county by the Roman Catholic diocese. Krupnik had never met Smith but had heard about him from Sally and Mary Carroll. Krupnik walked up the steps and rang the bell. Smith came to the door, holding a broom and wearing an apron. He invited Krupnik in, the pair sat down on packing boxes, and Smith listened as the chemistry teacher haltingly explained that he had met Jack's parents and always liked the little Holden house.

"Well, we've got a real estate agent coming over here tonight, and she's going to be plenty upset [not to get the listing]," Smith replied. But he accepted Krupnik's offer—and in time Krupnik was welcomed into the Smith family circle. (In 1993, eight months after Smith became GM's CEO, as a favor to Krupnik he gave tiny Quinsigamond its commencement address—astounding more prestigious schools like the University of Michigan, which also had invited him to speak at its far grander graduation ceremony in Ann Arbor.)

In the early to mid-1980s, Smith and Marie treaded water, living apart but not divorced. Neither wanted to take the final step while their children were still in college. But Brian finished his degree in 1983, joining Procter & Gamble, and Kevin, who would eventually join GM, was working on a law degree. In 1985, after two years in Oshawa, Smith was told he was going to Europe in January 1986. He'd begin as a vice president at Opel, headquartered in Russelsheim, outside Frankfurt, with the understanding that he would eventually succeed Ferdinand Beickler as head of GM Europe when Bieckler retired midway through 1986.

Roger Smith had tried to sell GM Europe but felt the offers he'd received did not reflect the company's value. Now he wanted Jack Smith to halt GM Europe's losses and pull its operations together into a coordinated unit. For most of its life GM had been a North American–focused company with some operations overseas, says Hughes. But Roger Smith had watched how big profits from Ford's international operations propped up its near-bankrupt North American operations. He wanted to see if GM Europe could be revived. It was a daunting job: In the mid-1980s European carmakers' productivity and efficiency was dismal. In the U.S. it took about twenty-eight worker hours to build a car, compared with twenty-two in a typical Japanese factory. In Europe the average was thirty-five hours; Swedish companies, like Saab, took almost 100. Many plants hadn't been overhauled since they were rebuilt after World War II.

GM Europe included two brands—Germany's Opel, whose cars were sold in continental Europe, and Vauxhall, the nameplate for Great Britain. Opel cars were seen as dull, middle-class "farmers' cars" that no BMW or Mercedes owner would be caught dead driving. Vauxhall's operations in England were plagued by quality problems and frequent labor distruptions. The two divisions barely communicated and battled over the designs of the cars and trucks that each sold under different name. Because Opel was in charge of their development, the cars generally were designed with German buyers in mind, and were tough to sell in England. Further, until Smith got there, GM Europe was based at Opel headquarters in Russelsheim, and there was always a perception that it was a "German" company.

While Europe was a stepping-stone at Ford, getting sent to Europe took an executive out of the GM mainstream, which lived and breathed North America. And Smith was being sent to Europe just as GM was about to undergo a changing of the guard. F. James McDonald, the company's president, was scheduled to retire in 1987. By sending Smith to Europe, Roger Smith signaled that the younger man wasn't going to move up in North America in the near future. Buick-Oldsmobile-Cadillac chief Robert Stempel, who'd once run Opel, seemed the clear candidate for the president's job and eventually got it. Jack Smith, wiped out, overweight, chain-smoking, seemed depressed when his sister Sally drove him to the airport to catch his flight to Frankfurt.

"He looked terrible. He was very upset about going over there," she says. "He was totally by himself. His attitude about it was, 'Well, why not.' He'd told me he'd never go to Europe, even if they forced him. Of course, he'd always said he'd never leave Massachusetts," she recalls.

Smith doesn't remember it quite that way. "Oh, I wanted to go to Europe. It was a big opportunity," he contends.[12] Nonetheless the first few months, with Smith stationed at Opel's technical center in Russelsheim, were difficult ones as he searched for solutions to GM Europe's problems. Sally says her brother was so unhappy he'd sometimes call their brother, Michael, in the United States, and simply sit with the phone in his hand, saying nothing, as the long-distance charges mounted.

GM Europe's problems, Smith discovered, were far deeper than even its balance sheet indicated. Smith, with Hughes and Hendry, who soon followed their boss overseas, had to ponder every alternative: "Would it be worthwhile selling bits and pieces of GM Europe to other companies? Would this operation stay viable? When an organization is faced with that moment of truth, you begin to raise fundamental questions about yourself, who you are and what you're trying to achieve," Hughes said.[13] The last time GM Europe had made money was in 1982, when it scraped together a meager $6 million profit. Combined losses the three years before Smith arrived were nearly $900 million, including $372 million in 1985. And GM Europe was set to lose another $343 million in Smith's first year there.

The losses were hard to understand because the company's vehicle sales were actually growing each year. But consulting firm Booz Allen, hired to study the mess, concluded that the company's costs were skyrocketing because so much work was concentrated in Germany, Europe's high-cost manufacturing site. GM Europe sales were erratic: Opel and Vauxhall did well in their home markets but dismally elsewhere. Ford, Volkswagen, and Fiat were trouncing GM in France, Italy, and Spain. It was partly a marketing problem, exacerbated by keeping the headquarters in Russelsheim; GM Europe would never have a continental view if it was based in what was a GM company town, Booz Allen said.

Once Smith began as president of GM Europe, in June 1986, he launched into a flurry of activity. The first job was to create a new headquarters for GM Europe in Zurich. Somewhat akin to moving GM headquarters from Detroit to Atlanta, it was a bow to Switzerland's historic neutrality and a practical move. While one of the world's most expensive cities, Zurich is an easy jumping-off point for travel around Europe. The headquarters Smith picked, in a neighborhood called Glattbrugg, is just five minutes from the Zurich airport. Smith deliberately kept the headquarters staff small—only 200 people, the size of GM's public relations staff in the U.S.

Smith wanted to see more coordination between the executives who ran Opel, Vauxhall, and the manufacturing and technical operations. So he created the European Strategy Board, a kind of governing body that would be in charge of setting corporate goals, with input from everybody who was affected by them. At the first meeting, the executives from all parts of Europe involved sat, warily, in a conference room, wondering what they were supposed to talk about. With Smith and Hughes egging them on, the meeting soon exploded into discussion. And years after that first meeting, the men who took part chuckle over their hesitancy to start talking.

With a structure in place, Smith next attacked the product lineup, with the help of Opel's disciplined chief engineer, Fritz Lohr. Smith wanted vehicles that would work throughout Europe, whether on the continent or in Britain, which was notoriously snooty about embracing cars built outside the United Kingdom. He wanted to focus on the simplest, strongest-selling segments of the car market. Opel was not going to be allowed to dream about a super luxury car that could compete with top-priced BMW and Mercedes models. Vauxhall, meanwhile, was going to have to get its quality act together. Smith wanted to be able to ship cars from Britain to other European markets without fear that consumers would reject the vehicles as poorly made.

In all GM Europe's plants, Smith and his team found inefficiencies that would not be tolerated in the United States— for example, too many steps taken to perform a task and too many workers participating in what should have been simple manufacturing functions. Some job cuts would be necessary. In 1985, GM Europe had 125,000 employees at Opel and Vauxhall. Within two years, that fell to 112,000, a savings of $520 million. Smith thought Europe was ripe for Japanese-style management techniques, so he asked Hughes to put together a team to see if the ideas that had worked at NUMMI could translate to a factory in Europe. Smith didn't have a location in mind yet, but he knew that someday GM Europe would have to diversify away from Germany and into other European countries.

It was clear that GM could comb more savings from its purchasing operations, although Smith was stumped as to how to do it. In those days, European suppliers were almost a cartel. They set prices that each of the continent's seventeen major car companies were forced to pay, without significant negotiations. Just-in-time inventory systems, so vital to Japanese factories and increasingly in use in the United States, were only beginning to appear in Europe. Automakers had to keep big stocks of parts inventory on hand, not knowing if their supply pipeline would be interrupted by a strike or a national holiday.

European automakers inwardly steamed about their cost structures, knowing that their competitors in Japan and the United States paid far less for the same parts. They didn't see a solution. But Smith found one at GM's plant in Zaragosa, Spain. During his travels around GM's operations, he heard about a bright Spanish engineer who was finding ways for GM to save money building its small Corsa. His name was José

Ignacio Lopez de Arriortua, and his friends called him Inaki. Smith and Lohr arrived at the Zaragosa plant to find Lopez's office desk, chair, tables, and floor strewn with Corsa parts. Lopez had taken apart a Corsa, piece by piece, and diagnosed ways GM could cut its costs while ensuring that the quality of the auto remained the same. For hours into the night he walked Smith and Lohr through what he had done. Lopez held his visitors in thrall as he pointed out steps and parts that the car did not need.

Lohr, trying not to seem too upstaged by his underling, walked around the room declaring, "We'll do that. We'll study that. We won't do that," in response to Lopez's suggestions. The trio worked through the night, and by dawn, says Smith, Lopez had found ways to take 600 DM ($428 at 1995 exchange rates) out of the cost of building GM's cheapest model.[14] "It was a defining event," Smith says. Nearly a decade later, his voice and his bright eyes still reflect his awe of what Lopez had accomplished.

Armed with his plans for cutting costs on the Corsa, Lopez segued into another pet project: maximizing production at Zaragosa. Italian automaker Fiat had boasted it would soon have the only plant in the European automobile industry that could run twenty-four hours a day, with three shifts of workers. Lopez thought Zaragosa could do it, too. He devised a plan for the Spanish plant to run at full speed, twenty-eight cars an hour for the first sixteen hours. In the final eight hours, Lopez concluded the factory should not run as fast because machinery would need maintenance. But it could build twenty cars an hour. Lopez got the go-ahead to put the plan into action, beating Fiat, which never managed to launch its twenty-four-hour factory.

The two projects propelled Lopez into a job at Russelsheim, working with Opel's engineers on a new concept: worldwide purchasing. It was a breathtaking challenge to the European suppliers who had held the industry in their grip for so long. To prove to the suppliers that the parts they sold could be made more cheaply, Lopez began conducting workshops dubbed PICOS, or Purchased Input Concept Optimization of

Systems. Although it fed his reputation, Lopez didn't invent PICOS; that came about after consulting firm A. T. Kearney came to GM Europe, at Smith's request, to find ways to cut purchasing costs. But Lopez put his own stamp on the sessions, which involved visits by teams of GM purchasing and manufacturing experts to suppliers' factories.

The GM staffers demanded full access to every step of the production process. As suppliers looked on, sometimes in fear, sometimes in aggravation, the PICOS teams spent hours and sometimes days quizzing factory workers and managers to find out how a production system was set up. Then the teams would prescribe ways to speed things up, steps that could be eliminated, costs that could be slashed. In the late-1980s, when the Lopez teams swept across Europe, the auto industry there hadn't been jolted awake by Japanese competition as had automakers in the United States.

The European industry was by far the least competitive of the three major world production centers. Unlike Japan, which had to rebuild its industry from scratch after World War II, and the U.S., where two oil shocks had caused carmakers to scramble to save money, European companies were protected against heavy-duty competition by government-imposed quotas on sales of imported cars. European auto unions, not yet faced with big job cuts, hadn't had to make major concessions, as the UAW had. And European auto sales were on an upswing that seemed like it wouldn't end soon.

But Smith and Lopez knew GM had to cut costs on its parts in order for Opel to become a big-time player in the European market and a major source of profits for GM. Because there was so much fat that could be cut, Lopez was able to boast of 20 percent and 30 percent cost reductions through his PICOS systems. That translated to hundreds of millions of dollars in savings, and was a key element in the impressive turnaround that Smith was able to bring off so fast. From the $343 million loss that GM Europe had posted in 1986, GM Europe in 1987 earned $1.25 billion—a $1.6 billion improvement. That year, GM Europe even outearned Ford of Europe—"Miracle of miracles," says Smith.[15] And he wanted to make sure the folks back in Detroit knew about it.

GM Europe net income, before and after Jack Smith's turn-around efforts

1982:	$6 million
1983:	− $228 million
1984:	− $291 million
1985:	− $372 million
1986:	− $343 million
1987:	$1,255 million
1988:	$1,819 million
1989:	$1,830 million
1990:	$1,915 million

(Source: General Motors)

Early in 1988, Smith wrote a memo to CEO Roger Smith and president Robert Stempel, touting GM Europe's financial results vis-à-vis those of Ford. He showed the crowing note to Lou Hughes. "Don't send it," Hughes cautioned his boss. But Smith put the memo on the fax machine. Back the next day came a response from Roger Smith: "You did a great job. Now, what are you going to do for us this year?"[16] His bosses were more impressed than they let on. The turnaround, and subsequent prosperity in GM Europe, put Smith on track for a big promotion. But in the meantime, his life had already been transformed in a way he had never expected when he boarded the plane for Europe two short years before.

The GM Europe building hardly looks like a setting for romance. It is a modern low-rise that sits on a service drive amid a new crop of hotels, almost within walking distance of the Zurich airport. There is no neon sign on top that blares GM EUROPE, just a small marker outside the front door. Though some offices have views of the surrounding mountains, others simply look out onto a parking lot and a highway. But that building was where the scene opened on Smith's second shot at happiness.

When he arrived for work in June 1986, he was greeted by a recently hired secretary, a fit-looking blonde woman in her forties named Lydia Gabriele Sygrist. They had met briefly a few weeks earlier, when Smith was in Zurich for a meeting. Lydia had just joined GM Europe, leaving another job in Zurich because she saw greater opportunities at her new company. It wasn't quite love at first sight—but almost. Within three weeks Lydia would quit her job at GM Europe, and a little more than two years later the pair would be married. That first day, however, Lydia was more interested in getting her new charge settled. High on the list: moving the Smith family from suburban Detroit to Zurich. Or so she thought. "I was asking him what kind of arrangements I should make for Mrs. Smith and his family to come over," Lydia says.[17] And he said, very quietly, "Mrs. Smith won't be coming. We're separated and I'm in the process of a divorce."

It took only a few days for Lydia to realize that this was the man she had given up hope of ever meeting. When Smith got to Zurich, she had been divorced from her first husband for nearly ten years. She and her daughter, Nicola, then fourteen, lived in a "tiny" apartment in an old building in the outrageously expensive Swiss business capital, where they'd moved after Lydia's marriage broke up. Unlike many upper-middle-class European women, even now, Lydia had had a career for many years, working in partnership with her first husband in his furniture exporting business. She had lived in North Carolina and traveled extensively through the United States. But the marriage didn't last. "I went home to mother to get a divorce, like all good Swiss girls," she says.[18]

When she got back to Switzerland, she found that her business skills didn't take her as far as she would have liked. Despite her management experience and fluency in English, German, and French, it was hard to get a job higher than that of administrative assistant. At GM Europe she joined a flock of bright, capable women who, even at male-dominated NAO, would easily be considered for higher-level jobs. Despite the company's financial problems, the atmosphere at the newly opened offices was fun. People dressed casually—men in sweaters or shirtsleeves, women in leather jackets and miniskirts or trousers. Staffers bantered easily with their bosses and guests were made to feel at home, with fresh-brewed coffee and cookies on hand for nearly every meeting. It wasn't much of a hunting ground for spouses, since most of the managers who came from Detroit were married with their families nearby. Those who were European-born also were spoken for.

And despite the informal atmosphere, dating between superiors and underlings was officially frowned upon.

In her first years back in Europe, Lydia dated a few men, although, she says, "I told my mother I had given up hope of finding anybody again." Her mother, despairing that her attractive daughter hadn't remarried, told her not to give up. "Somebody will come along, you'll see."[19] So she says she felt something of a shiver after just a few days of working with her new boss; she realized she had fallen for him. "I knew right away" that Smith was the one, she said. Smith, shell-shocked by his move and stumbling onto a new romance before his divorce was final, says it took him a little longer. But late in June, the pair, realizing that their relationship was beginning to catch fire, sat down for a heart-to-heart talk. Smith, trying to keep the conversation light, jokingly reminded his secretary that GM Europe had a rule against fraternization. In what has become one of the most-told Jack Smith stories, he continued, "You can't work for me. If we get involved, one of us will have to quit, and it will have to be you because I have more seniority."[20] So she resigned a few days later. Smith was stunned. "I thought it was a hell of a thing to do," he says with a grin.

Richard Dirkan, the GM Europe executive who had hired her, was surprised too. When she handed in her resignation, not stating the real reason, he urged her to reconsider, offering to reassign her to another executive or transfer her to another department. She refused, saying she didn't think the office was the best place for her to work, and returned to the company where she had been before. (A year later, the then-engaged couple appeared at a GM Europe picnic in their official coming-out, stunning Dirkan and all but a few people sworn to secrecy.)

Smith left the U.S. strained by a workaholic life. Once he met Lydia, that began to change. A natural athlete, she regularly took to the Alps in the winter for downhill and cross-country skiing. In the summer she laced on her hiking boots for family trips. It had been years since Smith had gotten much more exercise than a walk on the beach at Centreville or roughhousing with his boys. But, struck by the beauty of the European terrain and the zeal with which his GM Europe coworkers enjoyed the outdoors, Smith let Lydia lure him out. He quit smoking, and they began taking spring and summer walks in the hills, on trails that are easily hiked by Sunday strollers. They went sailing on Lake Zurich. As winter approached, Lydia convinced him to try cross-country skiing.

She subtly made changes in his diet, too. Smith's eating habits leaned to big, fat-laden breakfasts and multicourse dinners. That was fine when he was traveling in Germany or England, but the Swiss lifestyle tends toward much leaner food and much less reliance on meat. One of the best restaurants in Zurich is a vegetarian café named Hiltl, where students, shoppers, and international bankers all feast happily on a sixty-four-dish item bar and completely flesh-free menu.

In the course of their first eighteen months Smith lost twenty-five pounds. His sisters were thrilled by the romance. Friends from home, seeing him at Christmas in 1987, remarked that Smith seemed revitalized. "You have to give Lydia a lot of credit," says Arthur Krupnik.[21] "A lot of it is due to Lydia," says Smith's sister Mary Carroll.[22] "I thought it was great," adds his sister Sally. "Here he was with a lot of money and no one to spend it on. She opened up a whole new life for him."[23]

As invigorating as their courtship was, the path wasn't as smooth as Lydia would have liked. She had hoped to be married in the spring of 1988, a little less than two years after they met. But there were complications with Smith's divorce. And Lydia wasn't happy when Brian Smith planned a spring wedding of his own. Lydia had wanted to go, figuring it was time she take part in family events. But Smith felt that because of the touchy situation with his soon-to-be-former wife, it would be better if she didn't. Nor did it help that Lydia's daughter, Nicola, hadn't taken immediately to Smith. The teenager hadn't had to share her mother with anyone since she was four years old. Lydia could understand, because Lydia herself had never warmed to her mother's second husband, either. Despite Jack's best efforts to win her over, Nicola, a strikingly pretty girl who resembled Grace Kelly, would sometimes sulk when he was around, vying for her mom's attention by speaking in German. Yet, Lydia said Jack never showed impatience with her daughter.

Ultimately, the impediments were dealt with and the couple picked August 28, 1988, as a wedding date. For their honeymoon they planned a long holiday throughout Europe after which they'd settle in Jack's comfortable home in Zurich. One afternoon late in the spring, Lydia was deep into making wedding plans when her phone rang. Jack told her he'd been called back to Detroit by Roger Smith for a meeting the next day. No, Roger Smith wouldn't say why, just that he had to show up. As everybody at GM knew, it was typical of the way the CEO operated. It could mean the worst or it could mean a big reward.

When he arrived in Detroit, Jack Smith went to the fourteenth floor of the GM building and walked into Roger Smith's southeast corner office, facing downtown Detroit. The CEO grinned, stuck out his hand, and congratulated Jack Smith. He was getting promoted to executive vice president in charge of international operations. Bob Eaton would be his replacement. Roger Smith told Jack to be back in Detroit to start on July 1. The news, delivered in the space of twenty minutes, shook Jack Smith, Lydia, and the GM Europe staff, which had embraced its boss with respect and affection. A mere two years after he arrived in Zurich, Jack Smith delivered his farewell to his colleagues. He seemed close to tears.[24] In his speech he said, "This is as big a surprise to me as it is to you. I certainly hadn't planned this. As you all know, I'm about to be married."

Smith headed back to Detroit alone, leaving Lydia to complete the plans for their wedding. Despite his cajoling, she refused to be married in Detroit or to move up the date for the ceremony. "In Europe, it's considered very bad luck to change your wedding day," she reminded her fiancé. Lydia admits that in the back of her mind she was a little uneasy about her firm stand. "I guess I wondered if he would come back," she says. He did. They were married in Zurich on a beautiful day. The ceremony was quiet. She wore a yellow suit trimmed in black; Smith had on a navy suit with a gardenia in his lapel. Lou Hughes gave the wedding toast, and the newly married couple posed for their wedding portrait on a boat in the middle of Lake Zurich. Then the pair headed off for a two-week honeymoon—"Shorter than I would have liked," Lydia says—on the island of Sardinia, off the coast of Italy.

As in many marriages, that honeymoon trip was a brief spell of calm and serenity. In moving back from Europe to the U.S., Lydia faced a culture shock as deep as the one Marie had encountered when she arrived at Smith's home in Bloomfield Hills. Gone was the dramatic scenery of Zurich, where weather can change from snow to showers to clear blue sky in five minutes' time. Gone were the ragged mountain peaks and sparkling waters of alpine lakes. In their place was the expensive enclave of ambitious men and their socially focused wives. Smith's manicured neighborhood was among the most exclusive in the Motor City. But compared to the grandeur of Switzerland, it might as well have been Nebraska. And she was living in the house where Smith had spent many years alone. Lydia often jokes that she moved to Detroit "only for love." Even after spending most of a decade there, she is still a bit of a curiosity. If Lydia had moved to Manhattan, or Greenwich, Connecticut, or Chicago's Gold Coast, she would have been just one of a group of accomplished "trophy wives" with careers and interests equally as varied as those of their husbands. There, a second wife fluent in several languages with a keen business sense and an interest in sports would be a subject of interest, but hardly a novelty. New York's large community of Europeans would have welcomed her.

But in Detroit Lydia landed in one of America's golden pockets, an enclave where even the wives of executives in their thirties are expected to remain at home with their children and then busy themselves with organizations like the Detroit Symphony Orchestra, the Junior League (if they're young enough), and the Detroit Institute of Arts. Almost as unchanged as it was when Smith moved there in the 1970s, Detroit is a place where executives frequently joke in interviews and at press conferences about their wives' spending habits—jokes that tend to fall flat on the ears of female journalists trying to juggle their own careers and families.

It was a shock, Lydia recalls, to leave her small apartment in Zurich and move to Smith's rambling house with its cathedral ceilings, expansive glass windows, and huge kitchen with a cooking island almost as long as the room. "My mother used to come and visit and say, 'Two people don't need this much room.' She didn't like this house at all," Lydia said.[25] And there is no telling what Lydia's mother, who died in 1991, would have thought of the Smith's spacious new house, finished in 1994, that sits on a Bloomfield Hills lake.

Even more startling than the house was her discovery that nobody went for walks in Bloomfield Hills. Her neighborhood, dotted with homes worth in the high six figures, didn't have sidewalks. Because the subdivision had short streets, she found it hard to go for bicycle rides, and sometimes had to strap her bike onto the roof of her car and drive to an area with bike trails before she could get her daily workout. Getting Smith to exercise wasn't the simple thing it was in Europe. Sometimes, very early on winter mornings, she'd drive him to nearby Birmingham and they'd go for short cross-country ski jaunts in a park.

Paternalistic GM didn't let Lydia flounder when she arrived in Detroit. Jim Farmer, now vice president of corporate communications at Saturn, was working in GM's Washington office when Lydia called him, panic-stricken, soon after her arrival. An invitation to a White House state dinner had arrived. "What do I wear to the White House? What do I say to Mrs. Reagan?" Lydia asked. "I said, 'You wear something formal and you say, Good evening, Mrs. Reagan,'" Farmer said.[26] In Bloomfield Hills there were plenty of invitations to lunch from other GM wives. But Lydia found the conversations tended to center on husbands, charities, and children. Her closest pal was the wife of a Ford executive who'd lived overseas. The pair liked to joke that a few decades earlier, when carmakers were constantly under scrutiny for possible antitrust violations, they wouldn't have been allowed to be friends.

To European-born Lydia, life among Smith's family in Massachusetts was downright puzzling. When they were first married, Smith brought Lydia to Worcester for a tour of the landmarks of his boyhood. She was a little startled when one of the stops was a sprawling discount department store, Spags, in Shrewsbury, where bagels are stacked next to car batteries along with maple syrup—and the parking lot is so full on a weekday that customers have to wait for spaces. He showed her

St. John's, his old neighborhood, and took her to Elm Park, where he'd played with his friends as a boy.

The summers on Cape Cod were tough at first, Lydia says, because of the closeness of Jack's family and the childhood memories that they constantly shared. Classmates from St. John's or UMass sometimes dropped in on Saturday afternoons and the conversation would turn to events that took place in the forties and fifties, long before Jack and Lydia had ever met.[28] "I didn't know who a lot of the people were, and they all go so far back," she mused. But she quickly grew more comfortable. And, as it has with countless other people, the Cape began to capture Lydia's heart. She took up gardening— something she never did at Smith's first Bloomfield Hills home, whose grounds were tended weekly by the same lawn service that everyone else in the neighborhood used. The Smiths went sailing and boating and hosted big family dinners where he would be in charge of steaming the lobsters.

Marriage to Smith brought Lydia untapped social influence, adventuresome trips to Peru and Moscow and the Carribean, visits with world leaders like the emperor of Japan and the chancellor of Germany. Still, even now Lydia misses the stillness and the grandeur of her native Alps. Standing in the early-evening twilight on the South Lawn of the White House in September 1994, as Hillary and Bill Clinton talked with friends nearby, she spoke about the peace she felt when she was in Switzerland and how much she missed her native country. Her visit to Telluride, Colorado, that summer only reinforced her homesickness. "It's the closest thing I've seen yet in the States to Switzerland," she confided. Yes, a friend reminded her, but there aren't many people like Jack Smith in the world.

Almost as if on cue, her husband appeared, beaming at her affectionately as he joined the conversation. And she smiled back at him, glowing softly in the warm Washington evening. It was clear to the handful of people watching that this was a real love story—one that proved to be Smith's strongest support as he climbed to the pinnacle at GM.

CHAPTER ▪ 4

Revolution From Within

The Roger Smith era finally ended when Bob Stempel took over as GM's CEO on August 1, 1990. A few weeks earlier, he held a press conference to introduce his new team—Lloyd Reuss as president, Robert Schultz as vice chairman in charge of Hughes and EDS, and Jack Smith as vice chairman in addition to keeping his job as head of international operations. There hadn't been a new CEO of GM in a decade, and Stempel wanted the focus not to be on him, but on the executives as a group. He stressed they would be running GM as a team and used the word over and over and over, twenty-six times in all. At the conference end, Stempel, Roger Smith, Jack Smith, Reuss, and Shultz posed for a hokey "all for one, one for all" photo, forming a semicircle, their arms thrust to inward, their hands stacked on top of Stempel's in the center. Jack Smith, standing on the outside, had to stretch the farthest to get his hand in the stack. At a signal, the five grinned at the clicking cameras. The new executives didn't know that two years later, only one of them would still be in a top management job.

The smiles died on August 2, when Americans woke to the news that Iraq had invaded Kuwait, a source of valuable petroleum for the United States. Consumer confidence nosedived. Car and truck sales, already in a four-year decline, began grinding to a halt. Stempel, who'd so hoped he could preside over a prosperous company, stunned the auto industry on the last day of November 1990, when he announced a shattering 111,000-unit cut in fourth-quarter North American production of cars and trucks. The news, coming so late in the quarter, triggered massive layoffs throughout the carmaker. GM's factories, scheduled to run through Christmas, basically shut down the second week of the month. The way the news broke was another surprise: Instead of letting reporters discover GM's plans during their weekly calls to get production numbers, Stempel announced it in a speech in Indianapolis. He knew why car sales had dried up. "People were expecting peace after forty years of the Cold War," Stempel said. "They were even talking about a peace dividend, and now they're concerned about the possibility of conflict in the Middle East." In another stunner, that same day GM gave hints that shareholders should be ready for a dividend cut, which ultimately came early the next year. Stempel knew the disclosures would start the rumor mill swirling about the need to address GM's dire condition—and that's what he wanted. "I chose my words very deliberately and carefully," he says.[1]

It was just the beginning of the bad economic news. Vehicle sales stalled out that winter, when worries over the war in the Persian Gulf kept everyone at home, glued to television sets and radios for news of the conflict. It was the worst possible atmosphere in which to start a new era at the world's biggest carmaker. But Stempel hoped to use it to his advantage by focusing the company on reorganizing its operations in the U.S. and Canada. Of the Big Three, GM was last to tackle its structure with any kind of sincerity. Ford had slimmed down a decade before (though it began bulking up again in the late 1980s, having lost the urgency to keep fixing itself in the wake of hot-selling vehicles and record earnings). In 1989, Chrysler completely reorganized itself around teams of people who engineered, designed, and manufactured its new cars. The savings were impressive: $4 billion over three years. And Chrysler was beginning to crow about new Jeeps and a lineup of full-sized cars it planned to introduce in the next few years. Stempel knew Chrysler was perilously close to bankruptcy when it announced its reorganization. He doubted GM was in nearly so much trouble, but he could see benefits for GM in streamlining.

So fifteen staffers were detached to work up some ideas under Reuss. In the spring months just after the Persian Gulf war, they proposed creating the North American Vehicle Organization, or NAVO. Known later as "the twenty-six strategies" or just "that pyramid thing of Lloyd's," the idea was to set down nine basic goals that GM should concentrate upon, then come up with ways to accomplish them. It was shaped like a pyramid—a mission statement at the top, with the nine areas of concentration beneath and the twenty-six strategies fanning out as the base. It was unveiled to GM's top management at a meeting in August. Reading the agenda and the notebook of material each participant received, one can almost experience the meeting without having been there. Everything was scripted, with speeches scheduled to the half hour, and even a seating chart for executives attending the session. A few weeks after the meeting, Reuss started explaining the plan to visitors in his fourteenth-floor office on the Gold Coast—the long corridor of offices on the eastern-most end of the GM building. On the farthest southeast end, in the coveted "corner office," sat Stempel. Next door was Reuss. Across the hall was O'Connell. Upstairs was GM's legal staff, downstairs was the financial staff. Jack Smith's office, often empty, was at the farthest end of the fourteenth floor, opposite Stempel, with big windows that faced Detroit's northern city limits.

Reuss, usually clad in a crisp white shirt and one of his custom-made black gabardine weskits, flipped the pages of a black binder as he outlined the plan for NAVO, pausing once in a while so that dazed listeners could scratch down some of the information that came flooding at them. Laughingly refusing requests for copies of the complex charts, Reuss admitted the plan wasn't all that simple. But GM was a big company. It would take a big job to get it streamlined so that its factories could reach full capacity when vehicle sales picked up again in a year or two. Reuss was confident that GM, whose market share had been plunging steadily since the early 1980s, was going to bounce back from its mediocre 35 to 40 percent within three years.

And he adamantly insisted that GM wouldn't discuss any plant closings that summer. Wall Street was saying GM had to close four or five assembly plants and perhaps ten more parts plants in order to make a profit in the next few years. But Reuss told visitors that GM wasn't going to be pushed into anything. The market was going to bounce back from the shock of the war—and when it did, GM was going to need all the capacity it could get so it would have plenty of new cars for buyers whose old ones, bought during the mid-1980s, were wearing out. Meanwhile, GM wasn't shying away from sales to fleet customers—even though analysts were screaming that GM was losing $2,000 per car on these cut-rate sales.

With consumers fleeing its outdated cars and trucks, GM saw a potential market in rental cars, corporate fleets, and sales to the government. It decided to offer bulk sales of these cars at prices cheaper than dealers paid for them, in special programs that encouraged customers to buy new vehicles every quarter. GM promised to buy them back if the companies would purchase new ones. When these fleet customers turned in these "program cars" with just a few thousand miles on their odometers, dealers snapped them up at steep discounts at auto-auction houses. The savvy retailers figured GM's stupidity could work to their advantage. Some dealers liked program cars so much they put them on sale right inside their showrooms, next to brand-new models. Even by selling them at bargain rates—say, $5,000 off on a $25,000 Buick Park Avenue—the dealers made more money on program cars than GM let them earn on new ones.

Eventually, fleet sales would turn out to be the most destructive sales strategy in GM's history, far worse than the incentive plans that ran rampant in the late 1980s and early 1990s. The cheap prices on program cars ruined the value of many used cars as well as new ones. Customers didn't want to pay full price once they realized they merely had to wait for three-month-old used models. Eventually, fleets were the only place GM could unload some models, like the Chevrolet Corsica, Beretta, and Lumina, because consumers refused to buy them new. They knew they could get used ones for 25 percent off. *Automotive Fleet* magazine estimated that 82 percent of the Berettas sold in 1991 went to fleet customers. Less than one in five were sold to individuals.

Reuss ignored the grumbling over the $2,000-a-unit losses. "We want to serve all our customers," Reuss said, including fleets. He insisted the cars weren't draining GM's profits, because the more cars GM could build the more money it could save on production costs. And GM, under the terms of a new contract with the UAW signed that fall, had to pay its veteran workers even if plants weren't operating. The contract stipulated workers could spend only thirty-six weeks, or nine months, on temporary layoff. After that, they went into a "jobs bank." GM had to find the laid-off workers a job or pay them wages and benefits. Since GM had to pay workers anyway, why not keep them busy building cars and trucks?

Reuss didn't put much stock in the danger signals being sent by prewar jitters. He was a true believer in the ability of the car market to solve GM's problems. "Lloyd's favorite saying was, 'The market will come back and save us,'" says a young GM manager. "If I heard it once, I heard it fifty times. 'Don't worry about it. We're in great shape. The market will come back and save us.'" Visitors left Reuss's office wondering if anybody at GM was getting the message from Wall Street.[2]

Clearly he wasn't, but two crucial groups of people knew something had to be done: a group of GM board members from outside the company and GM's strategic planners. If anybody inside the company deserves credit for sounding the alarm bell, it is the strategic planners. Each major section of GM, such as the Buick-Oldsmobile-Cadillac and Chevrolet-Pontiac-Canada groups and the ACG parts operation and the powertrain division that built engines and transmissions, had a small staff of people in charge of keeping abreast with industry trends and coming up with possible strategies for dealing with business issues that might arise in the next few years. The planners were in the first tier of the management ranks, generally younger men in their thirties, often people whose mentors thought they'd benefit from exposure to the big picture.

Like posts in the treasurer's office, these were stepping-stone jobs, important in that the planners had access to top management, yet rarely did any of them have enough authority to order something be done to head off a problem. Before embarking on his international career, Smith had served as head of worldwide product planning, a job he received with the backing of F. Alan Smith, once GM's top finance official. Senior executives often accused the planners of overreacting to outside trends and underestimating the clout of the mighty GM. Later, after the planners had carved out the scheme that would ultimately become GM's turnaround road map, a senior executive snarled, "You know we're in trouble when you have the planners telling us what to do."

The unofficial leader of the planners was Mark Hogan, in charge of planning duties for GM's truck operations. Jack Smith had taken Hogan under his wing years before. Like a number of Smith fans at GM, Hogan was disappointed when the board, at Stempel's insistence, named Reuss GM president in 1990. He thought Smith's international experience and his big-picture view would have been the right thing for GM as the new era of international competition approached. And when Stempel became GM's chief executive, Hogan was hopeful that he'd take the kind of action that was needed to turn GM in the right direction.

But fairly early in the CEO's administration it became clear to Hogan that Stempel was not going to be a man to take dramatic steps. "Bob Stempel is just a super-nice guy. Probably too nice. His personality is such that he didn't have the meanness to be more forceful with certain people who needed it," says Hogan.[3] Knowing that Reuss's pyramid, with its endless categories and strategies, was not the answer to GM's problems, Hogan and his fellow planners started to hold some informal meetings through the spring and early summer of 1991. "A lot of people were feeling frustrated," says Hogan, a ruggedly handsome man, built like a linebacker, with pre-maturely gray hair and mustache. "I just don't think [senior management] fathomed how precarious it was. I feel like they should have acted with more decisiveness."[4]

Working with Hogan that early summer were Purcell, head of planning at the powertrain group, Don Sullivan, who eventually became head of GM's Asian operations, Isuzu, and another planner, Don Sharp. They knew many of their bosses needed to be convinced that GM's problems weren't just the result of a bad economy and couldn't be solved by a strong car market. The men agreed that Reuss's plan for NAVO "didn't have the teeth or the specific road map and dates and accountability that we would have liked," says Hogan. The strategies "were too much for anybody to remember."

Just to be sure Reuss wasn't right, the planners fed numbers into their computers to predict what might happen at GM if a quick industry recovery ensued. They wrote a best-case scenario that had GM climbing back to 40 percent of the car market (a level it hadn't seen since 1985). The results showed that even with five more percentage points of share than it had in 1991, GM needed to shut several assembly plants, as well as a dozen parts plants and to cut its costs dramatically in order to simply break even. Seeing this, the planners decided to face the brutal reality of GM's financial problems, the pressure of outside competition, and the threat that the recession might last another two years. By midsummer they'd come up with a broad outline of a turnaround plan that they all agreed could be the starting point for a formal program setting out GM's goals for the next few years. Plant closings, spending cuts, sales of unprofitable divisions, and a complete reorganization of GM were among the actions the planners prescribed. The planners decided to show it to their bosses, who were all group executives, one notch below top management. Without their support, the plan would die; with their support, Reuss might listen to the idea.

But the planners, realizing how revolutionary their grassroots movement was, didn't want to hold the meeting on GM turf. It was safer to go off-campus to a neutral site. So, in August 1991, the group rented a meeting room at the Ritz-Carlton Hotel in Dearborn. Just across the Southfield Freeway from Ford's world headquarters, it was hardly a GM hangout. When GM used a hotel for a meeting, it was either the modern Marriott in Troy (partly because J. Willard Marriott sat on GM's board) or the small St. Regis Hotel across from the GM building. Ford's Land Development company built the Ritz, and its own vice presidents often went there for cocktails in the wood-paneled grill with its big fireplace, English furniture, and horse-and-dog paintings on the walls. Had any Ford executives wandered by that August day, they could have seen the seeds of an incipient rebellion.

The group executives—Mike Mutchler, head of CPC, J. T. Battenberg III, who ran BOC, Clifford Vaughn from GM's Truck and Bus division, and Bill Hoglund, then running the ACG parts division—listened with deepening concern as Hogan and Purcell outlined the proposal. The group already had Battenberg on its side. Early that month, Battenberg had addressed the University of Michigan's annual automotive-management seminar, held in Traverse City, near the shores of Lake Michigan. Aside from the event's prestige, executives love to attend because they can play golf on one of two Jack Nicklaus–designed courses during the afternoon. On the final day of the 1991 seminar, Battenberg was asked if GM would meet its goal to be at full capacity in 1994, as Reuss had promised. Battenberg replied GM would not. If that was true, he was asked, did it mean GM would not be profitable in North America by 1994, as Reuss had vowed? Battenberg carefully reiterated his first answer, trying to not to be quoted as saying GM couldn't make money in North America in the next few years.

But the veteran automotive reporters at the seminar knew just what he'd meant: GM's losing streak in North America had no end in sight, and analysts were right in saying the company had to close factories. GM stock plunged and Reuss was furious, and sent out the word that no one should repeat Battenberg's faux pas. In the coming weeks, senior executives (who were nowhere in sight when Battenberg talked with the media) would take turns insisting his words had been taken out of context—often to the same journalists who'd heard Battenberg's original remarks. It was a stinging episode for the executive, who'd been known up until then as one of GM's least controversial. "He got tattooed with it," says Hogan. "Those of us who tried to be open were often misinterpreted as disloyal. He was one of the best guys at GM."

Knowing how Battenberg had been shunned, the senior managers were caught in a political bind. They knew that GM was officially backing the twenty-six strategies and that Reuss was sure the market would be GM's savior. Yet the executives also knew that GM was on precarious financial footing and that something had to be done, even at the risk of corporate suicide by supporting the planners. They decided to take the chance. Battenberg and Mutchler joined forces with Hoglund to convince their colleagues to support the planners' bid, Hogan says. Ultimately the group executives voted to endorse the plan and to have it presented it to Reuss.

Unknown to many in the room, that same month outside members of the board asked New York attorney Ira Millstein to help them draft their own study of just how bad things were at GM. Millstein was a longtime friend of Elmer Johnson, the Kirkland & Ellis senior partner whom Roger Smith had brought into GM in the 1980s. Hoping Stemple would sense their seriousness, the outside board members told him what they were doing. Secure in the belief that Reuss's plan was good enough, and not yet knowing what the corporate planners were concocting, Stempel thanked the board members for filling him in. He had just missed the first signal from the board that his job was about to be put in jeopardy.

The 1992 model year brought one of the biggest waves of new and restyled products in GM's history. Their success was critical if the company was to rebound from the market-share slide in which it had been stalled for years. The new model year also meant the planners had to cool their heels for two months. Reuss's calendar was clogged until October with meetings and events related to the model-year launch. Finally, one morning early that month, the group executives reserved Dining Room No. 2 on the fourteenth floor so that the planners could give Reuss their presentation. It was customary at carefully scripted GM to send over an agenda and material summarizing the issues to be discussed a day or two before a meeting. The information came in a gray folder, and the whole package was called a "gray cover." So the planners put together a gray cover of their proposal—"pretty clear, not too abridged"—for Reuss to review before the meeting, Hogan says.

The planners hoped that the result of the meeting would be a letter sent to the GM board saying, "We've got to change. The situation is desperate," according to one of the group. In hindsight such a move might have stopped the board's management shakeup before it began. But that dream was dashed when the gray cover landed on Reuss's desk before the meeting. The GM president, leafing through the report, was outraged at the mini-mutiny. He called the group executives into his office before the meeting and chewed them out. The executives backed down. The planners, who got the message from their bosses, half-heartedly went ahead and presented a watered-down version of their survival plan at the meeting, knowing it had no chance now of being adopted as GM policy. Hogan says simply, "Lloyd took the advice [into account], but he didn't move on it as fast as we would have liked."

At any other point in history, an executive as powerful as Reuss could have punished the participants by reassigning some, shunning others, and refusing to act on projects that needed attention. But in the fall of 1991, GM's crisis was close to the boiling point. As the group executives tried to forge their own mini-revolution, outside members of GM's board, the results of their own study in hand, were beginning to grumble uneasily about the mess in which the giant automaker was mired.

Hoping to reverse its market-share slide, for months GM had been hyping the 1992 model cars and trucks as breakthrough vehicles. Nearly every size of car had undergone an overhaul or a transformation. Some, like the Cadillac Eldorado and Seville, seemed to be standouts. But nearly all the rest got off to sluggish starts. Almost the entire wave had been introduced without air bags, even though Chrysler's cars had been equipped with them since 1989. Consumers were rebelling at the cars' average price, which was close to $20,000. Competition was even stiffer that fall than GM expected. Toyota introduced a swoopy new mid-sized Camry, bigger than anything it had ever sold, while Ford made 200 changes in its flagship Taurus. GM's sales were stalling, and the losses on fleet cars were mounting. And outside GM board members, led by former Procter & Gamble CEO John Smale, now were demanding reasons why.

For the past year, almost since the day he took charge of the company, Stempel and Smale had held a series of Sunday-night dinners prior to the monthly Monday board meetings, generally in the twenty-fifth floor boardroom in the GM building on Fifth Avenue in New York. The boardroom, which overlooked the Sherry-Netherland Hotel and the tony Upper East Side, was paneled with gleaming golden teakwood. Former director H. Ross Perot once cracked that a forest had been felled to line the walls of GM's New York offices. Smale had not had regular meetings with Roger Smith, who'd packed the board with enough GM executives to assure approval of any scheme he wanted to try. (Staffers in the treasurer's office still snicker when they recall the way Smith railroaded those meetings. They'd hear Smith say in a rapid-fire tone, "Ladies and gentlemen, I have an item for which I'd like your approval. Is there any discussion? No? All in favor, say aye. Thank you very much, next item, please.")

Stempel quickly learned that Smale was taking a far keener interest in GM's business than he had in his previous years as a GM director. Tall, solidly built, with a far younger face than his mid-sixties would indicate, Smale had been a tough boss at P&G. He started his P&G career as a salesman in Oklahoma City and he was known in the consumer-products world as the man who got the American Dental Association to endorse Crest as a cavity fighter. He knew how to put on a successful marketing campaign, he prized the value of brands, he admired Sloan and the tenets he'd tried to instill in GM, and his famous impatience was starting to build when he went to GM board meetings and saw that the managers had little idea about how to fix the company.

As the months of Stempel's tenure wore on and things grew graver, the Sunday-night sessions got longer and more pointed. Ultimately, GM's bond ratings agencies played a pivotal role in triggering an atmosphere for change. That November, Standard & Poor's notified GM it was placing the company on CreditWatch for a possible downgrade of its long-term and short-term debt, and it cut its top rating on GM's preferred stock. Moody's, another ratings agency, quickly followed suit. The move sparked a crisis, for without top ratings GM's financing arm, GMAC, would surely have trouble raising the $20 billion it needed each year to fund loans for GM car and truck sales. And institutional investors, such as large banks and pension funds, might abandon GM's stock as too shaky for their conservative customers.

In Detroit, the downgrade threats triggered the first "Lloyd is out" rumors within GM. The speculation made its way to Wall Street, where analysts repeated it hopefully. GM officials did their best to stamp out the fire, insisting at every turn that Reuss was safe—just as they'd insisted Battenberg had been misinterpreted. Finally, in early December, before the monthly board meeting the outside directors, led by Smale, demanded that Stempel take action. The group, which included Dennis Weatherstone of J. P. Morgan, GM's investment banker, Edmund Pratt, retired chairman of Pfizer, Marriott Corporation CEO J. Willard Marriott, former GOP chairwoman Anne Armstrong, and former Labor Secretary Ann McLaughlin said they wanted to see immediate and drastic steps. "Stempel came back [from talking to the group], and he was going nuts," says a GM manager who met with the CEO shortly afterward. "He said we've got to have a plan to mollify the board and make it look like we're taking decisive action."

The board was demanding that GM finally name the assembly plants and parts plants that would be sacrificed to its slimmer market share. Stempel says he knew the day would eventually come when he would have to get GM's production capacity in line with its sagging sales. One day in May 1991 he looked at GM's latest sales figures and saw the company had no chance to ever fill up its plants again. Stempel picked up a yellow legal pad and a blue felt-tip pen. Working from what he knew about the manufacturing capacity of each assembly plant, the products each built, and the future products GM planned, Stempel came up with a list of factories he thought would have to close. When he was finished, he folded the piece of paper into a square and stuck it in the inside pocket of his suit coat.

From that day on, each morning, rising before 6 A.M., Stempel would shift the list from the suit he'd worn the day before to the one he planned to wear that day. In time, the yellow sheet grew soft, the writing blurred, and the paper filled with scribbles as Stempel made adjustments in his estimates. He crossed off names of plants, filled in others, and made changes periodically as sales rose and fell. Eventually his secretary transferred the scribblings to a plain white piece of stationery, which, in its turn, would become dog-eared and scribbled upon. Only the two of them ever knew about the list, which Stempel now keeps folded away among his papers in the drawer of his desk in his office in Southfield, Michigan. Stempel says he deliberately kept the list in his suit coat to remind him what would have to happen if things at GM did not improve.[5]

When he began calculating what each plant could build at full steam with two shifts of workers working forty hours a week, Stempel was shocked at the discrepancy between production capacity and GM's plant utilization. "The capacity thing was overwhelming," he says.[6] Publicly, GM had always acknowledged it could build 7.5 million cars and trucks in North America. But Stempel figured out GM really could build 9 million vehicles if its factories were filled. In 1991, the entire auto industry—GM, Ford, Chrysler, and Japanese and European carmakers—sold a combined 12.6 million vehicles. So GM, though it had less than 40 percent of the market, had the ability to build three quarters of the cars sold in the U.S. that year. In 1990 GM sold 5 million vehicles in the U.S.; in 1991 GM was destined to sell 4.3 million, or less than half what it was capable of producing.

Part of the problem, Stempel says, was GM's wave of plant-building in the 1980s. Midway through the decade, Roger Smith opened what he thought would be three state-of-the-art factories able to build more than 1.5 million vehicles a year. Among them was a sprawling car factory straddling the border between Detroit and Hamtramck, an enclave of blue-collar Polish-Americans, in a neighborhood nicknamed "Poletown." To build the plant, GM asked the city of Detroit to bulldoze dozens of houses. It indemnified homeowners for their losses at prices far higher than their rickety wooden inner-city houses would have brought on the market. And GM promised five thousand jobs would result (a figure that was at least double the factory's typical employment). But hundreds protested the destruction of the neighborhood, one of the saddest episodes in a sad decade for the city.

Smith's trio of new factories—in Wentzville, Missouri, and Lake Orion, Michigan, as well as Detroit-Hamtramck— were constructed just before the industry turned to more judiciously designed plants that required half as many people. Loaded with expensive high-tech robots that sometimes went haywire, shattering windshields and sending parts racing down assembly lines faster than workers could deal with them, they became white elephants within the GM system. Though as technologically advanced as GM could make them, they were able to build just one type of car in a market that was increasingly becoming split into segments. If buyers' tastes changed overnight, GM couldn't shift production at the factories without tearing out machinery and tooling. "Building the new factories was the right thing to do. I would have built them not so big. But as we built the new plants, we should have shut down the old ones. That was mistake number one," says Stempel.[7] His calculations showed GM cut 29,000 jobs in the 1980s but added 38,000 through the three plants and other facilities. When the board members warned him to act on December 9, it was clear Stempel had to move from list to reality. He tried to stall for a decision in January, arguing it wasn't fair to frighten workers during the Christmas holidays. No, the board members said. Get it done. So the fourteenth and fifteenth floors of the GM building became a crisis center. In Reuss's office, planners began taping up sheets of paper outlining all of GM's options. In a conference room upstairs, sheets detailing the capacity, products, future products, and efficiency of each of GM's assembly plants and many of its parts plants were propped up on easels.

Over the next week, Stempel and Reuss, and many of the planners, cobbled together the plan. The goal was to cut production almost in half, to 5.4 million cars and trucks by mid-decade. All that mattered was hitting the number, which the GM executives based on plants operating on two regular eight-hour shifts a day, with no overtime, no special work agreements that could squeeze more cars or trucks out of a factory. By necessity, it was a broad-brushed program, not a detailed one. The important thing, Stempel kept saying, was to carve enough plants to hit the target; GM would fill in details at some later date. As the work progressed, courtly GM vice president Alfred Warren, the company's chief bargainer with the UAW, tried to tip Stephen Yokich, then head of the union's GM department, about the extent of the job cuts Stempel was planning.

The rush left no time to do any kind of serious analysis. Some nights, the planners slept on beds in a suite at the end of the fourteenth floor so they could be back on the job at 6 A.M. "Basically, Lloyd and Stempel said, 'Just give us what you can do. Come in with what plants you can shut down. Put it all up on the wall,'" says a participant. Although Stempel knew GM eventually was going to have to tell the nation the number of plants it planned to close, he firmly refused to name any of the factories before Christmas. He thought he was sparing workers undue worry. But this intentional vagueness would cause many autoworkers as well as GM employees and family members to have the worst holiday season in recent memory.

Things were even more tragic for people in two factories. Everybody in the company knew GM would have to shut one of the two plants building its boatlike Chevrolet Caprice and Buick Roadmaster sedans. Both factories—Willow Run, outside Ypsilanti, Michigan, about thirty-five miles from GM headquarters, and Arlington, Texas, ten miles from Dallas— had suffered rounds of temporary shutdowns because sales of the cars were nowhere near enough to keep one factory full, let alone two. Stempel, knowing it was inevitable that one of the factories would close, set up a rivalry that would tear two communities in two states apart. "They lived in an unreal world. Stempel thought he was doing everybody a favor. He believed it," sighs a GM official.

At 2 P.M. on Monday, December 18, Stempel, accompanied by senior members of his management team, including Jack

Smith, strode into the press conference room on the fifth floor of the GM building. In the preceding days speculation had swirled that the announcement would be huge. GM's stock skidded below $27 a share, a four-year low. But nobody expected what Stempel unveiled. Over the next four years, he said, GM planned to eliminate 74,000 jobs in the U.S. and Canada, including 54,000 hourly workers. GM would close twenty-five factories, including five assembly plants. Among them would be either Willow Run or Arlington—the only plants named in the press release. GM would take a $2.8 billion charge to pay for the factory shutdowns, bringing the total of its restructuring charges over the past ten years to $9 billion. There would be no executive bonuses, no holiday bonuses for workers, no profit sharing. GM would start looking at operations it could sell—shaking out its parts subsidiaries, whose bosses knew they were not competitive with outside companies. GM would cut capital spending by $1.1 billion, meaning more delays at a time when new cars slated for the mid-1990s, such as a long-needed replacement for the Chevrolet Lumina and a new Monte Carlo, were already behind schedule.

Reaction was immediate from all corners of the nation. Though they'd been warned in advance, Yokich says he and UAW President Owen Bieber "had a shit fit in the meeting" they had with Stempel on December 17 to officially learn of the cuts. "Obviously there wasn't a lot of preparation put into it. We had questions that they didn't answer properly or avoided answering," Yokich said. "I know it breaks their hearts to do this, but they really have no choice," said Perot, who six years before had harped on his fellow GM directors to take action. "They are facing reality." Filmmaker Michael Moore, who'd lampooned Roger Smith in his cult movie, *Roger & Me*, was appalled at Stempel's decision not to name the plants. "It's like putting six people in a room and saying, 'Well, one of you has AIDS,' but not telling them right away. Why would you do that to somebody?"

Scores of reporters stood outside the limestone building as snow fell and the words GENERAL MOTORS glowed in blue neon. Nearby, a homeless man named Jerry Brown walked on

West Grand Boulevard with a sign that read, WILL WORK FOR FOOD. The television reporters told their viewers the GM moves were sweeping, unprecedented, and as dire as anything that had ever happened to the giant auto company. But they were wrong. The curtain was just lifting on the most tumultuous year in GM history, one that would claim Stempel as its victim and elevate Jack Smith to a job he'd never sought.

Bob Stempel wanted to start 1992 focused on fixing General Motors. Instead, the year began with him halfway around the globe, in Japan. The month before, President Bush had invited the Big Three CEOs to join him on a state visit that quickly turned into disaster for the president's image and that of the U.S. auto industry. Stempel, Ford's Harold Poling, and Chrysler's Lee Iacocca thought they could use the trip as an occasion to demand greater access to Japan's car markets, where they sold less than 16,000 vehicles in 1991. But, when they arrived at Narita Airport, they had to face their own accusations. How could the U.S. carmakers expect Japan to help them when none shipped cars with the steering wheel on the right-hand side of the car? All over Tokyo, as the trio participated in dull, official meetings at the elegant Okura Hotel, Japanese consumers were trashing the quality of U.S. autos to the world's press corps. The models were too big to fit in tiny Japanese parking spaces. They consumed too much fuel. They broke down too frequently and were too difficult to repair. It certainly wasn't what the three CEOs needed to hear. By the time Bush, woozy from the flu and the sleeping drug Halcion, vomited and fainted at the farewell banquet, the trip had already been a disaster for the auto leaders.

No more so than for Stempel. As he was stuck in Japan, support for a move to oust his management team was building among the outside GM board members. Attorney Millstein, seeking answers to their questions, asked for a meeting with Stempel, who was puzzled why the session was necessary. It took two tries for the pair to hook up—Millstein's original flight was canceled because of bad weather and he was forced to hop on another Northwest Airlines jet a few days later. To suit Millstein's schedule, Stempel and Millstein met in GM's private aviation terminal at Detroit's Metropolitan Airport. As Millstein was expressing the board members' concerns to Stempel, Smale decided he wanted to talk with GM's top executives individually and in private. He wanted to see who understood the challenges the company faced, who bought into the need for a turnaround plan, and who would be in the way.

As the outside directors were acting, the planners were stuck trying to fill in the blanks with the hastily conceived cutback plan. Stempel had promised GM would come up with more specifics on plants to be closed by the end of the first quarter, and the biggest decision GM faced was whether to shut Arlington or Willow Run. On paper everything tipped toward keeping Willow Run and closing the factory in Texas. It cost $400 more per car to ship vehicles from Arlington across the country. Willow Run, which could build more cars, sat in the middle of GM's supply system, just a fast half-hour's drive from the GM building. It was filled with history: The factory was the centerpiece of the World War II arsenal of democracy, cranking out hundreds of thousands of bombers. The plant's workforce included children and grandchildren of men and women who had come north to Michigan during the Depression and the war for well-paying jobs.

But Stempel was weighing other factors. A few months before, workers at the plant rejected a request by GM to make changes in their schedules so cars could be built more quickly and cheaply. He felt the Willow Run workers were too confident GM would never shut their plant to try to help save it. "They were so cocksure they had the shipping advantage, and they didn't have to change a damn thing," he says.[7] Arlington workers, on the other hand, panicked when they heard their jobs were on the line. They appealed to Texas governor Ann Richards, who offered GM an incentive plan to keep the plant open. The workers presented GM with a proposal to streamline their job classifications and pointed out places where the plant's efficiency could be improved despite its distance from Detroit. Stempel insisted publicly GM wouldn't cut a deal. But privately he was impressed at the Texas workers' willingness to negotiate. "The Arlington people committed to a plan. And the amazing thing is that since everybody in the plant bought into it, they did it," he says. The decision to pit the plants against each other infuriated the UAW, which for years had denounced the practice of "whipsawing," or making factories bid to get work.

The Willow Run–Arlington battle turned into a news story of national melodramatic proportions. It brought up the worst North-versus-South stereotypes. Countless stories claimed that closing one of the plants would spell economic devastation for the town that housed it (which was not true in either case: Willow Run lay outside the city of Ypsilanti, which relied heavily on Eastern Michigan University for revenue and employment, and Arlington was a prosperous suburb of Dallas). And few mentioned that the workers who lost their jobs at either plant likely would be taken care of by the company for the next few years. Some would be able to transfer elsewhere in the GM system. All would get tuition assitance to learn a new trade. If they were eligible to retire, they could have lifetime health care and virtually all their wages for the next few years under special plant-closing provisions of the GM-UAW contract.

Countless times that winter, Stempel scheduled the closing of one plant only to change his mind again the following week. Stempel finally settled on February 24, a Monday, as the date when he would give the next set of details about the plant closings. The decision about Willow Run versus Arlington went down to the night before the press conference. When Stempel took a break to pick up his wife at Detroit Metropolitan Airport on Saturday afternoon, he had not yet made up his mind. Clad in an old plaid jacket and khaki slacks, Stempel looked like any other prosperous husband as he greeted his wife at the gate. "Hello, dear," Stempel said, taking her case. The pair walked toward the baggage carousel to wait for her suitcase, and Pat asked her husband to wait while she made a quick stop to freshen up.

On the flight back from visiting her parents in Arizona, which had stopped in Chicago to pick up passengers for Detroit, Pat Stempel struck up a long conversation about feminist author Gloria Steinem's latest book with the passenger next to her in the comfortable first-class chairs. Pat Stempel had never had the easiest time in Detroit; her starkly simple, chic style went against the chiffoned and sequined sort that other auto wives embraced. During the plane ride, she asked her fellow passenger where she lived. "Washington," came the reply. "Oh, I love Washington," Pat Stempel replied. "I would love to live there, but my husband's business keeps him in Detroit." She did not mention her husband was the CEO of the most embattled company in the United States.

She also didn't realize that the person next to her was this author, sent from an assignment in Chicago to cover Stempel's press conference that following Monday. But Stempel, spotting the reporter in the airport corridor, looked startled. Greeting Stempel, the journalist realized there was no point in asking Stempel about the plant-closing program because he was unlikely to say anything—and might storm off in anger. So the reporter simply wished Stempel luck, went to wait for her bag, and watched as Stempel picked up his wife's suitcase and loaded it and her into a waiting Chevrolet Blazer. The following Monday, calling on the reporter at the crowded, brightly lit, tension-filled press conference, Stempel said, "I'm glad to see that there are some human beings left in this world."

The few minutes in the airport may have been Stempel's last moments of peace as GM's chief executive, for the decisions announced at the February 24 press conference were the start of a fast downward slide for Stempel. Almost eight months later to the day, the victim of events that were snowballing out of control, he would announce his resignation. The move that got the most attention on February 24 was, of course, GM's decision to close Willow Run. "It was a last-second call. We didn't decide until Saturday night or Sunday morning. It went back and forth many times," says one of the planners. Stempel wouldn't let the public relations department write his speech. He spoke from notecards he'd scribbled himself that morning. (He still keeps them in his desk.) In the end it was Stempel's call; more than a little miffed that the Willow Run workers hadn't lifted a finger to save their jobs, he decided that it should be the plant to close. The decision touched off a legal battle in which Ypsilanti officials charged that GM had promised to keep the factory open at least fifteen years when it approached the township for tax incentives in the 1980s. GM ultimately won and the factory shut within a year.

Stempel may have had eight months more, but Reuss had less than two. The plant closings and cutbacks outlined that day were clearly a repudiation of his insistence that GM could get back to 40 percent market share and full capacity by 1994. Seeing this, veteran *Detroit News* columnist James V. Higgins put up his hand. There had been constant rumors, Higgins said, that Reuss was on his way out. What was his future at GM? Stempel uttered words that were to come back to haunt him. "Lloyd's my man," Stempel responded as some in the room shivered at the endorsement. He insisted the GM president was firmly in his job and was the man who would implement the carmaker's second major reorganization in eight years.

Lost in the uproar over Willow Run and the other plant closings that day was the outline for the new North American Operations, to be known as NAO. And hidden deep in the presentation were the first inklings of the turnaround plan that would come to be known as Fundamental Change.

NAO was the key element. For years Ford had had a separate organization responsible for its operations in the U.S. and Canada. Running NAAO—North American Automotive Operations, as Ford called it—was a key stepping-stone to becoming CEO at Ford. Harold Poling had held the job in the early 1980s before taking charge of the carmaker at the end of the decade. Alexander Trotman ran NAAO before he succeeded Poling in the mid-1990s. The move meant Ford could clearly see how its North American operations were performing in contrast to the rest of the corporation and leave the vital NAAO decisions up to the people running the operation. Now GM would finally consolidate all its crucial functions in North America under one heading. No longer would there be duplicative staffs at each car group who never got the opportunity to share knowledge or expertise. The chart Stempel revealed which described the first version of NAO seemed to be the final repudiation of the 1984 reorganization that created BOC and CPC. When asked about it, Stempel denied that the move was any criticism of Roger Smith's efforts to fix the company.

But Stempel now says he'd long felt that GM should have created one big automotive operating group in 1984, when Roger Smith attempted to break down the walls of the General Motors Assembly Division and Fisher Body division, whose executives could delay and even cancel car programs by their refusal to design the factory floor layouts and craft the car bodies. Roger Smith wanted to bring the talented, single-minded specialists closer to creating whole cars. Instead he scattered them throughout BOC and CPC, causing confusion, duplication, and even further delays.

"If we made a mistake, it was in keeping the two car groups. Nobody had the courage to do one," Stempel says. "It can be argued that you could have done it, but I think the culture of Fisher Body and GMAD wouldn't have allowed it. You had too many internal conflicts, and people couldn't see themselves winding up with anything."[8] Because GM hadn't taken that step, he chuckles, "Fisher Body is alive and well today." Roger Smith, surprisingly, agrees. "Bob is right. I wish we could have snapped our fingers and said, 'There! It's done'"[9]

The creation of NAO was supposed to shift the focus where it belonged: on North America. Hogan and the other planners had used the structure Jack Smith had created in Europe for their model. Smale and the outside board members liked the concept of a strategy board for North America and told Reuss to start implementing the idea. Barely two weeks after the Febuary 24 announcement, Smale sent Hogan and group executive Gary Dickinson to Europe to investigate how the European strategy board concept worked. Smale wanted to see ways to pull it off in North America. They were to give him a proposal by the middle of March. It seems absurd, in hindsight, that Reuss never had any conversations about the idea with the strategy board's architect, Jack Smith, who worked a few feet down the hall from him. But Smith's schedule as vice chairman in charge of international operations was hectic. He made at least a dozen trips outside the

United States each year, usually coming back to Detroit a few days before monthly board meetings. He wasn't scheduled to be back in Detroit until late in March for the April 6 meeting that would change his life for good.

While the planners were in Europe, Smale was doing his own investigation. Since Millstein's meeting with Stempel in January, Smale had been conducting interviews with GM executives. He worked his way through the management committee and the group executives. He asked them to rate, on a scale of one to ten, the seriousness of GM's problems and the chances of success in fixing them.[10] The interviews became kind of a loyalty test. Many of the executives who were chummy with Reuss and Stempel got on the phone to them after their sessions, filling them in on the questions Smale had asked and the answers they'd given. Smale was soon able to tell who the loyalists were by the answers they'd give to his questions. Like a judge in the Miss America beauty pageant, who can detect which contestants have rehearsed a bit too well for the interview portion of the evening, Smale grew to recognize who was just spouting the official spin.

His round of interviews included Smith, who says he didn't get any inkling of what was to come from the session. Indeed, the interviews caused only some of the executives to wonder what the board was planning. It wasn't that unusual for board members to occasionally chat with GM executives, although they were supposed to go to Stempel, who was supposed to pass a request for information down to the executive involved. Few ever expected that Smale would start toppling people. Nobody got fired at General Motors. They got promoted out of the way, were given special retirement deals, or at least were rewarded with car dealerships in Florida, as John De Lorean had been when he resigned in 1972. After all, Stempel had only been in office eighteen months by that point—and Roger Smith had run into trouble his first couple of years, only to ride it out for the rest of the decade. There was no reason to think the interviews were any signal of what was about to transpire.

Hogan, off in Europe, was aware that Smale was talking to the bosses. He knew Smale wanted to spend some time with him, too. But he was too busy to worry about it: "I don't remember speculating too much," he says.[11] He was more puzzled by the reaction he and Dickinson had gotten when they went to see Robert Eaton, who'd replaced Smith as chairman of GM Europe. The men spent some time together in Eaton's office on March 13, and agreed to meet for dinner that weekend to continue their talk. Unexpectedly, Eaton's secretary called to cancel. Wondering why Eaton would scrap the session when they expressly were in Europe at the direction of the GM board, the planners instead filled up their time by meeting with John Smith, head of GM Europe planning, European technology chief Peter Hanenberger, and Louis Hughes, then head of GM's German Opel division.

By the time the weekend ended, the planners knew why Eaton couldn't see them. On Monday, March 18, Chrysler CEO Lee Iacocca named Eaton the number-three automaker's new vice chairman and his eventual successor. Eaton had canceled their dinner so he could fly to New York to be interviewed by the Chrysler board for the post. The news provoked a smile among people close to Jack Smith, who remembered the sparks of tension that occasionally flew when Eaton would bypass his superior to call Stempel to lobby for a program or get advice on a change he wanted to make. "Somebody ought to remind him who his boss is," Smith once muttered to one of his colleagues.

Leaving behind the turmoil in Europe, the planners headed back to Detroit, where they pulled together a detailed proposal for a North American Strategy Board that would, in effect, displace Reuss as the key decision-making power in GM's U.S. and Canadian car and truck operations. Their model was GM Europe, whose strategy board included the head of GM Europe, its chief financial officer, and the heads of key departments such as engineering, manufacturing, marketing, and powertrains. The structure's main purpose was to guarantee communication, speed up decisions, and give people in charge of each area more of a say in their fate rather than waiting for issues to get to the top for a ruling.

When he was running GM Europe, Smith felt it was far more efficient to give the department heads the power to approve minor-league financial moves rather than take up his time with them. He would leave all but the most expensive decisions up to those who would be spending the money. That didn't mean free rein; on the contrary, they'd be held strictly accountable for meeting financial targets and project timetables. And if they missed a target, they had to explain why in reports that were not kept hidden but circulated to everyone involved. Members of the board would meet whenever it was necessary to discuss a crucial issue, take stock in a project, or simply make decisions. That meant weekly if necessary, or even every few days.

Reuss knew he had no choice but to accept the NAO strategy board plan, but he thought the frequent meetings were ridiculous. There was no need for top executives to gather that often. Once a month was enough—or even once every six months, he told Hogan. (Later, when the strategy board was meeting every few hours during one hectic summer week, members would recall what Reuss had said and chuckle darkly.) Reuss told the planners he'd give a capsule presentation on the NAO strategy board idea to the directors at their next meeting, and make his own recommendations. But he never got to do so. After the next meeting of the board, Reuss was out on his ear and Stempel's hold on the CEO's job was dangerously weak.

Despite the constant rumors that Reuss's job was in trouble, there was virtually no speculation outside GM that a wholesale shift in management was in the works. To the contrary: With Stempel's announcement of the plant closings, and the outline for the new NAO organization, it seemed that he had beat back the rumors of any troubles. It was far from the truth. Compiling the results of his interviews with GM's senior management, the planners, and other executives, Smale found that a high proportion of Stempel's team did not seem to think there was a crisis at hand. Meeting with Millstein and other outside members of the GM board, the directors decided it was time to act. There is a perception that nobody within GM knew what the directors were planning until the Sunday night before the Monday board meeting in Dallas.

Perhaps some people didn't know, but Stempel's top cadre

of officers were aware the week before that their jobs were in deep jeopardy. It is traditional in GM for the top officers to work on the agenda for the board meeting the following week. (That is why GM executives generally spend little time at the Detroit Auto Show, held the first week of January each year. GM's board always meets the following Monday, tying up the executives' time in the days before. The meeting is always preceded by a visit to the auto show, where directors ride golf carts down the aisles of Cobo Center to view the cars and trucks.) On Thursday, April 2, chief financial officer Robert O'Connell, who played a direct role in crafting the agenda, noticed that the list of topics included personnel changes. From that moment, the fourteenth floor began to reverberate with rumors, speculation, and fear.

The weekend before, Stempel had been summoned by the outside directors to a meeting at the Marriott Suites hotel near Chicago's O'Hare airport.[12] He was told by the directors that he was going to have to make management changes, beginning with dumping Reuss. This was not the first time Stempel had heard that the directors were unhappy; on March 25 Stempel met with Smale in Cincinnati to talk about the recovery plan that had been announced on February 24. The directors felt that it did not go far enough. Smale told Stempel that Reuss would have to go and that more changes probably were going to be needed. Smale did not tell Stempel that his job was in jeopardy, but he wanted him to prove that he would be the agent for change that the directors were seeking.

Meeting with the outside directors in Chicago, Stempel insisted that the plan for the NAO organization, coupled with Reuss's pyramid of ideas for fixing GM, was sound. He castigated the directors for their impatience. But the directors had already decided to act. They would replace Reuss with Jack Smith. Smale would replace Stempel as head of the GM board's executive committee, a crucial decision-making body that had historically been run by the CEO. Smale would formally operate as GM's "lead director," speaking for the outsiders on corporate issues. And the board members wanted Stempel to reassign O'Connell, EDS and Hughes chief Robert Schultz, and executive vice president F. Alan Smith, who was a mentor to Jack Smith and had served as a board member for eleven years.

When he got back from Chicago, Stempel spoke with members of his management committee—the two Smiths, O'Connell, Schultz, and Bill Hoglund. He told them the board was being unreasonable and that he was enormously frustrated with the uppity outside directors. But it was not until the end of the week that the group knew the shakeup was coming. On Friday Stempel tried to reassure them that none would be fired, and he kept arguing through the weekend for the board to keep Reuss and O'Connell in place. On Sunday night Stempel and the board members held their customary dinner at the Marriott Quorum Hotel near EDS headquarters. Afterward Stempel met with the directors to plead for Reuss to be kept on as an executive vice president. He did not think O'Connell should be dumped, despite the financial crisis that faced the car company. The directors listened to his suggestions, convened among themselves, and then called him back to deliver some news: Jack Smith would be named GM president and chief operating officer. Reuss would allowed to remain, but he and Alan Smith would have to leave the GM board. At that point the board hadn't decided what to do with O'Connell.[13]

In typical GM fashion, word of the biggest management coup since William Crapo Durant was ousted in 1920 drifted out an hour and forty-five minutes after the New York stock market had closed for the day, and right on the edge of most East Coast newspapers' deadlines. At quarter to six, a news release with the ordinary headline "GM Management Changes" appeared, startling automotive and management journalists who thought their day was about to end. Alan Smith, whose responsibilities included GM's public relations department, had written the release, which disclosed Jack Smith's promotion, Reuss's demotion, Smale's acension to the top of the executive committee, O'Connell's banishment to GMAC, GM's dealer-financing arm, and Hoglund's selection as GM's new chief financial officer. What the release did not disclose was that Alan Smith was no longer a member of the GM board on which he had served for nearly a dozen years.

Jack Smith, stunned by the day's events, tried to call Lydia from Dallas to tell her the official news. He was unable to connect with her until he was on the GM jet flying home. It was the start of a journey that he had never planned to take, and whose destination, like the island of Ithaca in Greek myths, he could not tell when he had reached.[14]

CHAPTER · 5

Boardroom Coup

Jack Smith is often praised as the creator of GM's turnaround plan, but he's probably the first such artist who had a sketched-in canvas thrust in his hand on the first day of work. That's exactly what happened on April 7, when Smith arrived back at his fourteenth-floor office to begin his new job as GM president. Eventually he'd move down the hall to the suite where Reuss, now banished to the GM Tech Center, once worked. But he was still in the northeast corner when Hogan showed up, his first appointment of the day.

The afternoon before, Hogan, like every other employee at GM, was stunned by the board's announcement. He'd been among those whom Smale interviewed, but, he says, "I was caught very flatfooted, most of us were, with the speed at which it moved." At 5:45 P.M. he was sitting in his office with fellow planner Don Sullivan when the fax machine, quiet for the past hour, flicked on. "I'll never forget this: The fax rolled in from Dallas, and it said Lloyd was removed and Jack was installed. Right then and there I knew that we'd be moving on the concept [of Fundamental Change] at a much faster pace," says Hogan. One of Hogan's colleagues, sitting in his office in Europe at the same time, remembers getting ready to leave after a long evening of meetings and stopping by his fax machine. He picked up the release, which a friend in the New York treasurer's office had sent him. "Surprise!" the pal had scrawled across the top. Not everybody in GM was fortunate enough to get the news firsthand that night. Some vice presidents got the news when reporters called them for com-

129

ment. Others learned about the shakeup from friends who called because they'd heard reports on radio and television.

As Hogan stood in the doorway, Smith looked up, grinned, and said, "Woooo. We've got a lot of work to do. Man, let's go."[1] That moment, Hogan says, Fundamental Change went from a document the planners doubted would ever get fully implemented under Reuss to a living, breathing blueprint to fix General Motors. Smith, who knew something of the turnaround effort but had never been fully briefed on it, appeared delighted and relieved when Hogan took him step-by-step through the outline of the plan he and the planners hoped would be implemented quickly. Just how quickly, they had no idea: Stempel had told them he didn't think even the basic elements could be implemented much before the end of 1994, possibly into 1995.

With Smith, says Purcell, "We went from two years to two months. We used to talk a lot about that—what was going to take a period of years instead took just months."[2] Smith is quick to give the planners credit for the outline of the turn-around plan that awaited him. "It was luck" that Fundamental Change was under way, Smith says. "Luck has a lot to do with everything."[3]

The board's management shakeup had given Smith and his new team of managers a sense of urgency no one at GM had ever felt before. Action came breathtakingly fast. The week kicked off months of eighteen-to-twenty-hour days, and six- and seven-day workweeks as the managers tackled the challenge of fixing the company. The same day that Smith met with Hogan, he telephoned Lopez at his office in Russelsheim, Germany, and asked him to take a new job as vice president for worldwide purchasing. Lopez accepted. Then Smith summoned the members of the new North American Operations strategy board to his office Friday for their first meeting.

Atop the agenda, prepared by the planners, was discussion of the role that the strategy board would fill. Smith agreed with the planners' idea that it should be the decision-making body for North America. No longer would all the power for NAO be vested in the president, as it had been with Reuss. "This sounds pretty fundamental, but the key was that nobody at the corporation was going to be second-guessing what NAO was doing," says Purcell. As William McWhirter later wrote in *Time* magazine, "They have broken a chain of command that once rattled as slowly and creakily as castle plumbing."

Further, members of the strategy board would be encouraged to actively discuss any and all topics on the agenda. This spelled the end of meetings in which no executive dared speak up in an area in which they had no direct responsibility. There would never be another instance like the one Hoglund experienced, in which he received the deep-freeze for daring to make a comment.

In the first four hours of the very first meeting, the board took more action on GM's future than in any such meeting in recent history. The members were setting the philosophy for what they hoped would be a new GM. The actual nuts-and-bolts work would follow; right now Smith wanted to get the strategy board members to buy into one direction for the company. The top priority, they all knew, was for NAO to stay within tight financial boundaries. In 1990 and 1991 NAO had lost $13 billion, its third straight year of losses. In 1992, NAO would lose another $4 billion. The combined two years of losses wiped out nearly all the record profits Roger Smith had boasted about during his decade.

Jack Smith told them the bleeding had to stop—a phrase he would repeat many, many more times as the year went on. Heidi Kunz, GM's treasurer, used to groan when she heard someone intone, "Stop the Bleeding," but the motto got the executives focused on the job that needed to be done. Next, the board members agreed that all sections of GM had to meet their annual budgets—a sharp contrast to the past, when budgets were missed almost routinely and with the permission of top management. Back then, when a project was headed above its target, all it took was a call to Reuss, who'd usually accept the excuse and approve the extra funds.

In defense of the practice, GM officials insist they weren't blatantly disregarding the figures they said they'd meet, but they contend that GM's forecasting ability was not very good. GM's economists would routinely overestimate the strength of the car market, meaning GM wouldn't take in as much money as it expected on new cars and trucks. GM's product planners would routinely underestimate how long it would take for a new model to get to the market, which sent product development budgets out the window. And every year manufacturing plants would take longer than planned to retool for model changeovers, meaning higher launch costs.

Nobody knew what it really cost to bring a new car or truck to market because there were no real financial controls. One year in the 1980s, GM's purchasing department figured it spent about $60 million on paint for its cars. But it couldn't give an accurate number because nobody had the computer printout that summarized paint spending. All these factors played havoc with GM budgets and ultimately destroyed its North American profitability. In the new GM such sloppiness would be unforgivable, the planners vowed. There would always be unexpected reverses, but the organization was going to be lean and flexible enough to absorb them and move on without spending months determining why what happened had happened.

The second priority, the board agreed, was to make NAO profitable in 1993. It seemed a daunting task even to the most optimistic members of the strategy board. NAO was expected to lose at least $4 billion in 1992, and probably couldn't cut those losses completely in 1993, no matter how deep it slashed. And so the planners suggested that GM pick a more arcane measurement, called EBIT, as their target. EBIT—earnings before interest and taxes—is meant to reflect how much a company takes in on its core operations after expenses but before it has paid interest on borrowed money and government taxes. Privately, the financial staff thought EBIT was a Mickey Mouse target that GM could easily meet. They favored declaring flat out that GM would be profitable in 1993. But Smith ruled the idea out, saying it was too ambitious and could result in daredevil cost-cutting ideas that could hurt the company more than help it.

Purcell says the board wanted everyone in the company to concentrate on becoming profitable. EBIT was a way to show it could happen soon. "Remember, we'd had staggering losses and people were starting to believe it was never going to be possible," he says. The planners knew that if GM as a corporation was going to be solidly profitable in good years and bad, NAO had to be get back in the black. Thus they wanted to make sure that no executive could make their profit center—whether engines and powertrains, a car division, or the research department—profitable to the detriment of the corporation. That happened more than anybody at GM liked to admit. It was a holdover from the prereorganization days, when GM's assembly and body divisions were eager to prove how profitable they could be. They'd cut corners to turn out cars that they would then sell to GM divisions at inflated prices. That would make the manufacturing operations look efficient—but the car divisions weren't able to make a profit on the vehicles because they couldn't charge customers more than their competition. And they'd have to shoulder the warranty costs for fixing anything that went wrong with the vehicles. The problem continued even after the 1984 reorganization: In 1988, when GM posted a then-record $4.5 billion corporate profit, the CPC group lost $2 billion.

Those tenets would go a long way toward reshaping the slack financial attitudes that had been prevalent for so long throughout the company. But even when the financial crisis was solved, the planners weren't going to let NAO relax. It had to set aggressive, achievable goals. Every year, General Electric CEO Jack Welch urges his employees to stretch and set goals beyond what they think they can do. Welch isn't trying to encourage recklessness, but his philosophy is that his divisions must push with deliberateness to keep ahead of the competition. He is well known for his decree that GE should be number one or a competitive number two in every business sector. That's what the strategy board wanted for GM. It would not be enough for NAO to simply break even someday, or make a few hundred million dollars. The actual financial goals would take time to develop, but the planners wanted an atmosphere in which GM wouldn't just coast but truly compete.

With the basis in place, Smith and his team demanded quick action. The plant closings and job cuts eventually would yield significant savings by making GM much cheaper to operate. That wouldn't happen immediately, and in the short term would in fact be expensive, as the $2.1 billion charge against earnings to pay for the plant closings reflected. "Get me something now," Smith told the group. The planners, working with members of the finance staff and the strategy board, saw three immediate targets where GM would get fast results.

First, GM would cut its platform organizations from twelve to seven. The move would officially dismantle the two car groups created in the 1984 reorganization. The planners knew that platforms, best described as a car's architecture, were major expenses. In technical terms, a platform is a car or truck chassis, the underpinnings on which a vehicle is built. By adding sheet metal, an engine, a transmission, and interior features, one creates a car. Each size of car generally needs a different platform, and a rear-wheel-drive car is built from a different platform than a front-wheel-drive car.

Ideally, a carmaker wants as few platforms as possible because of the high cost of creating each one. In the 1990s a facelift for a car—called a "minor"—usually runs $750 million to $1 billion. A completely new platform costs upward of $2 billion, depending on how many variations it will yield. (The $6 billion Ford spent in the early 1990s to develop a new family of cars, sold as the Mondeo in Europe and the Ford Contour and Mercury Mystique in the U.S., is believed to be an industry record.) But some of GM's platforms were barely different, although it had spent billions of dollars to engineer each one separately. GM simply was not earning enough money to fund the dozen platforms that it had in existence in North America. In turn, the cars that came out of each platform weren't selling in big enough numbers to cover the expense of creating each platform. By reducing platforms, GM could phase out some of the vehicles that were not moving and make more models off fewer platforms, leveraging the expense of creating a new platform.

Meanwhile, the planners attacked another area that was costing GM tremendous capital: fleet sales, Lloyd Reuss's expensive pet project. By 1992 GM was selling 775,000 cars to fleets—two assembly plants' worth of cars each year. That was the equivalent, in a normal car market of 15 million cars and trucks, of nearly five points of market share sold at an average loss of $2,000 a vehicle. "We're supposed to sell cars, not give them away," Smith quipped.[4] The planners emphatically demanded that GM cut back these sales dramatically, to no more than 500,000 a year or fewer if it could afford it. It was a much-debated issue, Hogan recalls, in part because the cars were a source of cash that GM so badly needed. The company got paid for cars as soon as they were delivered to the fleet customers; the real expenses came later, when GM bought the cars back from the rental car companies.

Nonetheless, the strategy board agreed with the planners—and GM's quest for market share, so destructive during the Stempel and Reuss era, emphatically came to a close with the blessing of senior managers who once were charged with hitting the phantom 40 percent target. "It was a really key, really important move," says Smith. "It seems like a no-brainer now. But I'm proud that we did it."[5]

Purchasing was more of a challenge. For years GM had tried to cut the cost of buying parts from outside suppliers while in most cases ignoring the high cost of building its own parts. Now Smith and the strategy board wanted to see the issue addressed. When he placed J. T. Battenberg in charge of the ACG components group, Smith asked him to conduct a thorough review of every parts-making section of GM and decide whether the carmaker needed to continue in the business, whether it could be made profitable, or whether it should be sold or shut down.

Moreover, Smith wanted to see if ACG was a place where GM could not just cut operations, but grow the business. He knew that Ford and Chrysler purchased key components from GM; why not look for other customers? Meanwhile, he left to Lopez the job of attacking GM's purchasing organizations. That would be handled once Lopez arrived in Detroit. No one was sure yet, but based on the savings he'd found in Europe, it seemed that reforms in purchasing could yield billions of dollars, enough to help stem the red-ink tide.

Even in those early days of Fundamental Change, word

was leaking out within GM's operations of the dynamic pace the strategy board was setting. Far from the "every six months" schedule that Reuss had envisioned, the strategy board was meeting daily, sometimes several times a day, the most time any of the senior executives had spent with one another in their careers. Hoglund, whose spirit had been so battered during his years in the GM doghouse, was re-energized. He'd grab visitors by the arm and take them to the door of the conference room, where Hogan or one of the other planners was tacking a new idea up to the corkboard wall, covered with sheets of white paper with Magic Marker lettering. "Look at what these guys are up to!" Hoglund would declare. Smith loved the planners' enthusiasm. "They had so much emotion," he says. "But they saw that we had a need to do it."

Smith wanted some of that excitement to spread throughout the new NAO organization, which set up its headquarters at the Tech Center. So he went there. Just days after the management shakeup, GM disclosed that Smith would be spending most of his time in Warren, which led to the belief that he was leaving the fourteenth floor for good. That wasn't true; he held many meetings there and liked to work out in the building's executive gym. His secretary, Terry Miller, preferred her GM building office. Yet as the months went by Smith came to spend most of his hours at NAO, meeting into the night with the planners and members of the strategy board. The activity at the Tech Center gave rise to the idea that Stempel was isolated in the GM building while the work was going on beneath him, which in some sense was true.

The planners did not just stop when they had the basic framework of Fundamental Change in place. They were looking to fill in the blanks beneath the new concepts. Among them was one of the phrases that would become a Smith watchword: common systems and common processes. Smith made consistency a priority, the planners knew. Unwavering in his own personal beliefs and values, he wanted to see how that discipline could be instilled throughout GM. The key place for this to happen was in product development.

At GM, there were as many ways to develop a car as there were cars. There was no single checklist of procedures to follow, and no way to measure one program against another. If a strong project manager assembled a particularly talented team of designers, engineers, and manufacturing staffers, a car could reach the market in as little as three years—about the time the Japanese needed to launch a new vehicle. That is, if funding for the vehicle wasn't interrupted. If it was, the stops and starts played havoc with the development process, forcing the same jobs to be done two and three times just to get the project up to current technology. It was a guaranteed way to bleed money—and it led to vehicles that missed their market target.

Reforms had already been under way when Smith took charge. GM in Europe had begun developing its cars according to a four-phase process (it actually had five steps: bubble up, phase zero, one, two, and three). It broke down the car's development into a well-defined protocol that developers had to follow, or their projects would not be allowed to continue. The process was about to bear fruit with the introduction of the 1993 Corsa, Opel's smallest car. And the four-phase process was being tried by the developers of a pair of luxury cars that Oldsmobile and Buick were set to launch midway through the 1990s.

Smith wanted to see more of these common processes applied across the company. But before that could happen, the planners wanted the strategy board members to focus on the cars and trucks that were important to GM's future. For too long GM's product lineups had overlapped. Everybody, from Chevrolet to Cadillac, had a big car that chased after almost the same buyers. Everybody except Buick and Cadillac had a minivan. Everybody had slow-selling niche products like the Toronado, which sold in far too few numbers to justify keeping it in the lineup. GM had more than 60 models, and the model options were endless. John Rock, whose Oldsmobile division had long been rumored to be endangered, corralled every variation of every Oldsmobile one day in a courtyard. Dozens of cars were packed together, some different only because of their wheel covers or engines sizes. Then he asked his number-crunchers to tell him how many each vehicle sold. Out of the half-a-million cars Oldsmobile sold that year, the slowest-selling auto was purchased by just twenty-six customers.

In the 1950s, nearly all the cars GM sold were large or luxury models. In the 1990s, due to the failure of the mid-sized GM-10 cars and GM's lack of a toehold in the small-car market, the situation was virtually the same. The planners knew GM could not be a successful car company by ignoring the middle of the car market, which was dominated by the Ford Taurus, the Honda Accord, and the Toyota Camry. The planners pushed to make Chevrolet Lumina the centerpiece of a sales comeback strategy, but it was a little too much of a stretch for the entire board to accept. Instead, the strategy board members decided to focus on four core product areas: large and luxury cars; full-sized trucks and sport utilities; mid-sized cars; medium-sized trucks and sport utilities. In picking the four core products, the idea was to keep the organization concentrated on the types of vehicles that were important. No one was saying that small cars or sports cars were not important, but they were less important than other vehicles.

With the core products settled upon, the planners wanted GM to align its operations according to its new focus: NAO. On April 24, just three weeks after Smith took charge, GM announced that the Chevrolet-Oldsmobile-Pontiac and Buick-Oldsmobile-Canada car groups would be combined into a single engineering and manufacturing organization, a move approved by the strategy board that first week. It was a step that Stempel thought would take at least two years to accomplish. Meanwhile, with the center of action moving to Warren and the creation of NAO, GM's central office staff was a clear target for reduction. Once one of the corporate seats of power, the central staff—personnel, public relations, accounting—numbered 13,000 in 1992. Smith called them "the checkers checking the checkers."[6] He cut the number of headquarters jobs to 2,000. Some of the people simply transferred to the NAO payroll; others took early retirement offers and packed brown cardboard boxes full of belongings. There were many complaints about the job cuts; salaried staffers argued they shouldn't have to be the ones to pay for a problem that they felt was really seated in GM's obsolete manufacturing operations. But Smith, who'd operated with just 200 people at GM Europe headquarters, felt the cuts were necessary to make GM leaner at the top. "You can lose so fast in this business," Purcell says. "I think that message was starting to be understood across the organization. We have to keep the staff sizes down."

One task was too important for anyone but Smith to tackle. He knew GM had been hobbled for generations by its bitter relationship with the UAW. The December plant closing announcements and the battle between Willow Run and Arlington had only aggravated the tension between the two sides. So had GM's decision, a year earlier, to send production of the Camaro and Firebird sports cars to a GM plant in Canada. Smith, out of the country most of the time since 1986, did not have much recent experience dealing with the union. But he did have deep respect for the talents and abilities of the union members, whose contributions at NUMMI had made the joint venture a success. Quietly, without any fanfare, he met with members of the union leadership, including Steve Yokich, feisty vice president in charge of the GM department. Many people at GM privately thought Smith was wasting his time with Yokich. Born in Detroit in 1935, Yokich had literally grown up in the union. His parents and grandparents, who emigrated from Lebanon, were union officers. In 1936, his mother marched in a picket line pushing a stroller that bore her infant son. Yokich quit high school to go to work in a tool and die plant in Detroit. After a quick stint in the Air Force, where he earned enough credits for a diploma, Yokich came back to Detroit and ran for union office. He won, launching a swift and steady rise through the UAW's leadership ranks. In 1977, he was elected director of UAW Region 1, which had represented workers in car plants in Detroit. In 1980, he became a UAW vice president in charge of the Agricultural Implement department. It wasn't until 1983, when Yokich became head of the UAW's Ford division, that he began to attract wider attention. Yokich gained a reputation as a hothead; he seemed profane, short-tempered, and unyielding in his defense of union ideals. Coming on the heels of conciliatory Donald Ephlin, who ran the Ford department before taking charge of the GM department, Yokich seemed a throwback to the past. That was true only on the surface. Said Peter Pestillo, Ford's chief bargainer in the 1980s, "We cried when he came and we cried when he left."

For Yokich turned out to be far more cooperative than Ford could have suspected. Pestillo learned that as long as UAW members' interests were protected, Yokich was willing to discuss ways to improve the company's efficiency. Pestillo also noticed that the mercurial union leader had sharp political skills and knew when to balance his sometimes ascerbic personality with just the right note of disarming charm. As he had socialized with Ephlin, Pestillo soon invited Yokich and his wife to company events. Guests at Ford's lavish dinner after Luciano Pavarotti's 1988 concert in Detroit were stunned to spot Yokich in a tuxedo, and his petite wife, clad, in a gown of black lace she'd bought in Hong Kong.

Yokich's first years leading the GM department, starting in 1989, were far different. During sometimes rancorous negotiations with GM in 1990, he and UAW president Owen Bieber insisted that workers' pay and benefits be protected even when they were laid off. Yokich knew that GM, whose market share was plummeting, was going to have to make deep cuts. "They quit hiring [hourly workers] in 1985," said Yokich. "Their market share had gone to hell. By 1989, you could see the signals. Why couldn't they be honest with themselves? You didn't have to be a mental giant to figure that stuff out."

Yokich didn't think much of the teamwork philosophy that Stempel espoused. He smirked when the CEO quoted quality expert W. Edwards Deming, who visited GM many times during the 1980s. In his seminars, Deming, who died in 1994, urged GM to break down barriers between management and workers. "Deming was [Stempel's] hero as long as he could pick and choose what he wanted to use," Yokich said. "I used to remind him, 'Deming says you have to be part of decision making.' It doesn't happen in GM, it doesn't even happen in Saturn. They're a part, to a certain extent, but the last decision is up to the corporation."

The UAW leader fumed when company officials boasted that the 1990 contract led to a new level of cooperation between the two sides. "Even though they like to pat themselves on the back, and go around the whole United States, and say, 'GM and the UAW like to work together,' that was just bullshit," he said. Beneath the platitudes, GM's attitude toward the UAW was fundamentally different from that of Ford or Chrysler, Yokich contends. "I really believe the UAW's been a second thought [at GM]. That's why they have problems that the other companies don't have," he said. "The other companies will discuss with you where they're going, and why they're going there. And if you had any ideas, they wanted your input. I always think we're the last to know at GM."

The union leader didn't feel much sympathy when he heard about the board's management changes. If anything, he was curious about the new GM president, whom he had never met before the week of April 13, when he went to see Smith, accompanied by aide-de-camp Cal Rapson. Joining Smith at the session was GM's vice president for personnel issues, Dick O'Brien. After guarded pleasantries, Smith quickly got to the point. Recalls Yokich, "He asked me why GM and the UAW couldn't get along. I told them they cheat, lie, and steal." Smith was taken aback: "He got kind of red when I told him that," says Yokich with a smile.

Even so, Smith asked him to elaborate. Yokich explained that GM's bargainers, who worked on the Central Office staff, often made promises during contract negotiations that plant managers, responsible for following through, did not keep. He loaded Smith down with instances where plant managers were borrowing from training funds, intended to be used to educate laid-off workers, and from jobs funds intended to contribute to laid-off workers' pay, to keep their budgets from falling into the red. Yokich charged that was the same as stealing from GM. "It isn't in the formal sense what you read in the newspapers about gangsters," Yokich explained. "It's [plant managers] who turn in a [balanced] plant budget. They get a pat on the back, a gold star, a blue star, a red star. But he's taking the money out of the jobs fund, he's taking the money out of the training budget. He's not helping the company, he's still costing the company money."

Yokich also used the meeting to lobby Smith to get behind

his favorite project: planned maintenance at GM plants. Other carmakers had long ago set aside time for machinery in their factories to be repaired. For years, Ford had an annual two-week vacation shutdown during which adjustments could be made. Yokich argued that regular, planned repairs would mean better-quality cars and, in the long term, preserve jobs. "Quality is our job security," he said. But GM did not set aside specific time, arguing repairs could be made while the work-force was on the job.

Smith promised to study the issue, the first time, says Yokich, any GM CEO had paid attention to his hammering. A warm relationship between the new GM president and the UAW vice president began to develop in the weeks that followed, but there were resentments against GM that were too deep to heal in the short amount of time Smith could devote to the matter that spring.

With a basic outline of the concepts of Fundamental Change in hand, Smith sent out an edict to every vice president, every department head, every division general manager, every administrator in GM: If you think of ways to save money, do it. Across GM, a frenzy of cost-saving ideas broke out. Some of them were as simple as employees sharing rental cars on business trips instead of renting a car for everyone in a group; others saved the company millions of dollars. As the suggestions came in, the planners kept a running total of the savings that the managers came up with—kind of like Uncle Billy in the movie *It's a Wonderful Life* adding up the dollar bills that neighbors contributed to help George Bailey avoid bankruptcy.

There was a self-imposed deadline in all the frenzy: For their June 29 meeting the GM board members wanted a report on all the actions Smith and the strategy board had taken to get the company back on track. The planners admit that they didn't know how they were going to implement some of the ideas, like reducing the number of car platforms from twelve to seven. But the board members were impressed by the speed, depth, and the breadth of the changes that Smith and his team were planning to make. They told Smith to get moving and present a more detailed report in the fall.

The work done in those first hectic months was not all

only financial, philosophical, or strategic in scope. Smith started to get rid of some of the trappings that made GM so rigid. One of his first changes was instituting casual Fridays. Now commonplace in many corporations, casual dress days were nearly unheard of at GM. "Casual day? At GM? My God!" quipped UAW vice president Yokich. Men wore suits and jackets even at long meetings, and the few women managers still clung to stuffy ensembles with little silk bow ties that had been out of fashion for years. The exception, and the source of the idea, was Saturn, where every day was casual day. Over the months to come, GM internally dropped its suits for a new uniform: khaki slacks, a polo collar or open-neck shirt, and a cardigan or V-neck sweater. In public and at important meetings GM's conservative dress code remained, but it became far more frequent to see staffers arrive for work dressed as if for a golf game.

Smith quickly banished another GM tradition: gray cover reports. He didn't want a detailed rundown of every proposal and every meeting agenda. A one-page memo was good enough for him, and in any case he preferred to listen to all sides of a debate in a strategy board meeting rather than read about it. If he needed to make a decision, he'd scrawl, "Go ahead. JFS" on a memo and shoot it back to its author. (Among the planners and members of the NAO staff, Smith began to be known by his initials.) But one suggestion did not get acted upon: banishing the executive garages where top brass parked their cars, which were then washed and gassed up while they were at work. Downtown at the GM building, executives dropped off their cars and shot up elevators directly to the fourteenth floor. Even at democratic NAO, executives drove to below-ground garages and scooted up escalators or short flights of stairs to their offices. That perk remains in place.

Despite his dislike of paperwork, Smith was deluged by it that spring and into the summer. Time and again it brought bad financial news, detailed information he was getting for the first time, even though he had been in the highest tier of GM's executive ranks since 1990. Smith would mutter to colleagues, "I was a member of the management committee and I never knew about this." That was the way GM was run. Only

Stempel and Reuss had regular access to information from every part of GM. The financial staff could get its hands on the numbers for a particular project at any given time, but lacked the product and market savvy to tell if GM was in good shape relative to its competitors, or, as was more often the case, falling far behind. And if the numbers were particularly bad, more likely than not the finance staff would filter the data. In the event that they spotted a big screwup, like the GM-10 mid-sized car project, the staffers kept their mouths shut if it was a powerful executive's pet program. This "don't bring me no bad news today" practice meant top management usually heard only good news, or bad news spun somehow to sound good.

As Smith was discovering, the amount of sheer decision-making that went to the top of GM was staggering. "Bob Stempel would make decisions on $250 incentives for Chevrolet Corsica and Beretta," says a GM manager. George Borst, now head of strategic planning at Toyota, shakes his head in disbelief remembering the time wasted waiting for the CEO to sign off on the simplest program. While a marketing manager at Chevy in the 1980s, Borst one winter dreamed up the idea of offering special financing to spring college graduates to help them buy new cars. He wanted to send a mailing in April to 75,000 college seniors who'd be leaving school in May and June. The cost would be minimal—maybe $75,000. Borst put together a plan that his marketing bosses and Chevy's division general manager quickly approved.

Under Jack Smith's strategy board, the program could have gone into action right away. But under Roger Smith, a signature from the man at the top was necessary. Only once a month did Smith hold the management committee meeting where such decisions were made. Borst's idea got on the March schedule, but the meeting was canceled. In April and May, other things took precedent. Borst's idea was finally approved in June, meaning the plan couldn't be cranked up until midsummer, when all the graduates were long gone from campus.

Things barely changed under Stempel. A simple change like a different headlight on a small pickup truck couldn't just be made by the design team that worked on the vehicle. It had to go from design to engineering to marketing. Then it needed car group approval, from Chevrolet if it was a Chevy vehicle, followed by CPC approval. Then the idea went to a pre–work group meeting, followed by a work group meeting. If it made it that far, it would go to a plan review, followed by a business review (the first time the finance staff played a role). After this, the idea for a headlight staggered its way up to corporate level. Once it got to the corporate marketing staff, then it went to preproduct program review, then to program review, then to pre-executive staff, to the executive committee, and finally, fifteen meetings after the idea for the headlight was born, to the management committee. Reuss, while he was president, would attend the last five rounds of meetings. "Why would you waste the time of Lloyd Reuss on a headlight?" a GM manager sighs.

Such examples were repeated hundreds upon hundreds of times, making GM the least-efficient product developer and manufacturer among the Big Three automakers. When Roger Smith left office in 1990, GM earned a tiny $12 per vehicle, according to the automotive consulting firm Harbour and Associates. With the damage done by fleet sales, that tiny profit turned into deep losses, compounded by the fact that GM's vast 1992 model year introduction had been pretty much a disaster. Despite the best efforts of the strategy board and the planners to stop the bleeding, it continued that summer and into the early fall, putting the company's health in peril and ultimately claiming Stempel as its victim.

Earlier in the spring of 1992, GM posted a $179 million first-quarter profit, its first quarter in the black since 1990. In May GM convinced investors to buy $2.2 billion in new common stock, the first time GM had gone to the market with a common stock sale since 1955. The brainchild of treasurer Charlie Golden, it was one of the largest offerings in corporate history. Combined with a preferred stock sale that Golden had overseen the year before, GM now had $4.7 billion in cash to fund its operations. Among the most relieved were GM's product developers, who were trying to put together a lineup of the cars and trucks GM would be introducing five years hence. Without the seed money, those vehicles would be delayed as so many of their predecessors had been time and again because of NAO's malaise.

But the summer brought more signs of trouble. GM's suppliers, who'd gotten their first taste of Lopez's cost-cutting ideas, were ready to revolt. On June 1, just a month after he landed at NAO. Lopez convened a meeting of GM's major suppliers in the Design Dome at the GM Tech Center. Speaking in his Basque-accented English, Lopez delivered a thunderbolt: All contracts for the 1993 model year, about to begin in three months' time, were under review. Lopez and his team would look at each agreement to see whether the company could meet new standards for quality, delivery time, and cost. The Spanish executive emphasized this was a three-legged stool, with each criterion as important as the next. But then Lopez let loose with a stunning pronouncement: GM wanted to cut its costs not by 2 percent, as suppliers expected, but by 20 percent or even more. Ultimately, the carmaker wanted to save $4 billion on its annual $35 billion purchasing bill over the next four years.

That wasn't all, Lopez told the murmuring group. As he'd done in Europe, he was assembling PICOS teams to visit factories in the United States. GM expected access to all aspects of part development and production. And suppliers would have to follow the teams' prescriptions for improving efficiency or risk losing their GM business. They might lose it anyway. GM was launching deeply into global sourcing, and if it could find a part as good overseas, it would have no hesitation handing out the contract to a foreign supplier if the U.S. company making the component couldn't match the price.

Suppliers were furious. Phone calls protesting Lopez's move flooded Stempel's office. "I had guys calling me day and night asking me, Bob, can't you do something about this guy?" Stempel recalled.[7] GM board members also were deluged with letters, enough that they decided to ask Lopez to appear before the board in September to defend himself. In the meantime, Smith had given Lopez his full support, which, given the way things stood with the GM board, appeared to outweigh any qualms Stempel had about him. Things quieted down in

August, when Lopez went back to Europe for a prearranged month's vacation in his homeland. But almost as soon as his plane left the ground, GM's labor situation blew up.

It seemed to be an inconsequential event: As part of its vast job-slashing and plant-closing program, GM planned to eliminate 240 jobs at a tool and die shop at Lordstown, Ohio. Workers there made the molds that the Lordstown stamping plant used to stamp sheet metal parts that it shipped to other GM factories. Lordstown was one of the most militant of GM plants; short strikes occurred there on a regular basis, as the UAW used the best weapon it had to wring concessions out of GM. Smith had hoped his overtures to Yokich would help avoid any walkouts while Fundamental Change was taking shape. But Yokich, still seething with anger over the way the union had been left out of Stempel's hasty plant closing deliberations, allowed the Lordstown workers to go out on strike. The walkout quickly triggered shutdowns as other GM plants ran out of the parts made at Lordstown. Among the factories that closed first was Saturn, which was selling every car it could build that dark summer.

It took nine days for negotiators to end the strike. By then GM had lost $70 million in production, and had to give away far too much. It agreed to keep the tool and die shop open for another year. And it agreed that Lordstown would be the first plant to build the restyled Chevrolet Cavalier and Pontiac Sunfire compacts that GM hoped to introduce in spring 1994. Stempel couldn't have known it then, but it was a decision that ultimately would cost GM far more than the $70 million that was drained away by the walkout.

Worries about future products were far from the top priority when the fall began. Treasurer Golden, who had raised GM's badly needed cash, was fearful that it was being burned away far too quickly. Certainly Wall Street was worried, too. In the spring GM's stock was trading at $39 and didn't plummet even though the new shares joined the pool. But in the fall GM's stock was trading in the low $30 range. An even bigger alarm bell sounded when Moody's Investors Services put GM's debt on CreditWatch once more for a possible review. More frightening, it was threatening to cut off GM's access to the commercial paper market by lowering its credit rating abruptly.

Car buyers probably don't realize it, but commercial paper basically helps GMAC keep dealers afloat until they can sell the cars and trucks on their showroom lots. Dealers borrow money from the automaker's financing arms to pay for the vehicles they order from the company. They get favorable loan rates that allow them to keep a healthy supply of vehicles so that customers can have a selection to choose from. GMAC, in turn, gets its money by selling commercial paper—short-term debt to lenders who expect to be repaid quickly. It is a key financial tool that keeps factories rolling and dealers in business. Without it, things get grave, as Chrysler discovered in the early 1990s. Close to bankruptcy for the second time, it lost its ability to sell commercial paper because no creditor would take on its debt, fearful it would not be repaid. Chrysler was forced to seek a line of credit from a consortium of banks at a higher rate than it would have paid had it been able to issue commercial paper.

Now Golden could see that GM's ability to go to the commercial paper markets was in danger. He and other financial staffers wrote a report that detailed the commercial paper crisis and other financial threats that GM faced. Meant for the eyes of GM's top management, the report found its way to Smale and the outside directors. There the reaction was swift and outraged. Stempel had not seen the report until he was briefed on it by attorney Harry Pearce at Smale's request. At the board's October 4 meeting he was asked whether he had a contingency plan to keep GM's finances from sinking further. Puzzled, Stempel replied that one was not needed. He thought the directors were overreacting at a time when calm was vital.[8] It was the last board meeting that Stempel would attend as GM's CEO. Within three weeks, under fire from the board, increasingly angry investors, and disgruntled GM employees, he would resign. First, however, he would see his world nearly disintegrate.

When it was all over, people in Detroit who admired Stempel said that what had happened to him was a disgrace.

They would use words like "cowardly" and "heartless" to describe the way GM's board sent him the bitter message that they wanted him to leave. More than a few tears were shed over the way the rug was pulled out from under a man whom his colleagues genuinely respected and liked. More than a few executives spent sleepless nights wondering if what happened to Stempel would happen to them some day. Underneath all the mourning that occurred, however, was the chilling realization throughout corporate America that GM was in even more dire straits than anyone could have imagined.

The week of October 12 was going to be an important one for Jack Smith, the strategy board, and the planners. They had called a meeting of GM's top 100 managers in the Styling Dome to hear a detailed explanation of Fundamental Change and what it would mean for each of them. Keeping with GM tradition, the strategy board members would brief the managers, who were each expected to take the information back to their departments to meetings of their own. In past times the information chain usually broke down about halfway down the organization, meaning there were thousands of people walking around GM who had not gotten the details of plans their bosses' bosses had gotten secondhand. The planners were hoping that by making Fundamental Change concise and easy to communicate, the elements of the turnaround plan would spread even more quickly.

Smith and the planners expected to spend the week honing the presentation, which they were supposed to have given in a similar form to the GM board at the same October 4 meeting where Stempel was put on the spot. Their slot on the board's agenda got pushed back to the November 2 board meeting, two weeks away. Most of the planners were too busy to read any newspapers that day or to pick up the photocopied clip sheet of newspaper articles on the auto industry that GM's public relations staff prepared each morning. So some of them missed the *Wall Street Journal* "Heard on the Street" column that hinted GM's outside board members were once again stepping up their role in directing the company.

But the next morning the clip sheet was required reading, for it contained a front-page story from the *Washington Post*.

Writers Frank Swoboda and Warren Brown declared that outside directors had told Stempel to get tough with the UAW or risk losing his job by the end of the year. Stempel didn't have to read the story on GM clip sheet. He could see it, full-sized, in person. He was in Washington that Tuesday for a meeting of the Conference Board. Stempel didn't mention the story to anybody in the meeting room at the Willard Hotel. But just before noon, he felt as if he had a bad case of the flu; he was nauseous and fainting. He asked for a doctor and was quickly rushed to George Washington University Hospital. Admitted in serious condition, he was alert while doctors performed a round of tests. He phoned his wife, Pat, and told her there was no need to rush to Washington, though GM would have put her on a company jet and flown her down. Despite efforts to keep his attack quiet, news of Stempel's illness traveled like a flash. In Detroit, GM's public relations office tried to dampen any panic by issuing a statement saying he was resting comfortably and wanted to return to work quickly.

Against his doctors' advice, that is what he did. He was back in Detroit by Thursday, and made a brief appearance Friday afternoon at the leadership meeting that Smith and the planners had called to discuss the details of the turnaround plan. Smith, who didn't like to speak in front of groups, was nervous for much of the session and even more rattled by the glances he saw people giving each other when Stempel came in the room. Toward the end of the session, when it was time for questions, one of the managers in the audience asked a question about compensation.

It looked like 1992 would be the third straight year without executive bonuses, the manager said. Although there had been raises for top-tier people, some as much as 20 percent, many of them were starting to leave GM. Lewis Campbell, general manager of the GMC Truck division, had recently departed to become CEO at Textron. And everybody knew about Bob Eaton's move to Chrysler. What could the managers expect? Considering the financial straits GM was in, it seemed like kind of a selfish question. But Stempel, nodding at Smith, took the microphone. "We're going to make sure we take care of our executives," he said.

That was the last time many of the people in the room saw Stempel in his capacity as CEO. The following Wednesday, October 21, the *Washington Post* struck again, with an even stronger story that said the outside directors wanted Stempel to step down within thirty days, though they hadn't decided who would replace him. Bruce MacDonald, GM's vice president for public relations, put out a statement that declared there was "absolutely no substance to reports that Bob Stempel will be asked to step down as chairman." And any time a reporter called for comment, MacDonald insisted vehemently that Stempel was in charge. "Mr. Stempel is very much in his office. He is very much running the firm," MacDonald said.[9] Stempel, however, knew it would take more to stop the deluge of speculation. He wanted Smale to issue a statement that expressed his full support.

Before he could make the request, Smale, from his office in Cincinnati, issued his own statement. And from that moment all was finished except for the formalities. Stempel resigned the following Monday, October 26, leaving GM's future in the hands of the outside board members and the management team they had put in place six months before. "The fundamental question is, 'What's best for the corporation?'" Stempel said nearly three years later.[10] "You can play it like Jim Robinson [at American Express] and say, 'We're going to win this one.' Or you can play it like Bill Agee [at Morrison Knudson] just did." In early 1995, Agee fought his ouster by the board, which forced him to resign after a long and bitter debate.

"I could have fought this thing out. I really thought we could pull this thing around. But there would have been a constant bloodbath back and forth. That is not my style." Stempel was distressed by the paralysis that gripped GM during his last few weeks in office. "We had people standing around water coolers saying, 'What's going to happen?'" They should have been working on cars. They should have been doing their jobs and not messing around," Stempel said, his usually measured voice rising in volume.

Stempel's farewell statement was eloquent and sad, like an address from a soldier about to fall upon his sword:

Today, I informed the General Motors Board of Directors that I was resigning as chairman and chief executive officer, effective immediately, and that I would serve at the pleasure of the Board until a successor could be named.

I made this decision in the best interest of the corporation and its fine, dedicated employees at all levels of the organization. I could not in good conscience continue to watch the effects of rumors and speculation that have undermined and slowed the efforts of General Motors people to make this a stronger, more efficient, effective organization.

I sincerely hope that my decision to resign will end the chaos of the past several weeks and allow the management team to again focus on the critical task of assuring the future competitiveness of the greatest manufacturing organization in the world. The management team can only lead in this battle. The future success of GM really lies in the hundreds of thousands of employees who have been striving diligently to provide our customers with leading edge, high quality, high value, satisfying products.

I am leaving after 34 years, confident that the people of GM will continue to be the corporation's most important asset, and that they will give their total support to the new management team as it accelerates the action plan that will continue to improve General Motors' competitive position worldwide.

John Smale's response was gracious but terse:

The Board of Directors of General Motors has accepted Mr. Stempel's resignation and asked that he continue as chairman until a successor is named. We understand Bob's decision and extend to him our gratitude for his contributions throughout his distinguished career at General Motors.

We have, of course, been closely monitoring GM's strategic business programs and studying the critical issues it faces for some time now. We will now concentrate on what must be done in light of Mr. Stempel's resignation and will announce our management changes as soon as practicable.

After just two years as chairman and CEO, Stempel's disappointing tenure had come to an end.

CHAPTER · 6

Stop the Bleeding

Breakfast was over early on Monday, October 26, after Smith came back to his planners with the news that Stempel had quit. Almost immediately, Smith left for a long series of meetings with Smale and outside directors to discuss the next management team—GM's second changing of the guard in six months. There was never any question that Smith would become GM's next CEO. But he would not become chairman. Smale would take that role, splitting duties that had traditionally been held by the top executive at GM. It was an arrangement that was unusual in corporate America, but after the GM management shakeup it would become a way of governing that other boards embraced so they could play a role in the way companies were run.

The board, which just six months before had imposed its choices on Stempel, was willing to let Smith select the other members of his management team. But some of the directors were not sure that Hoglund should stay. Because he was CFO at a time when GM's finances were on perilous ground, some board members argued Hoglund ought to be broomed as a signal that the traces of the old GM were to be banished. Their opposition to keeping him was so strong that Smith feared he would lose his most valuable source of institutional knowledge. "I couldn't save Bill," he confided to one of the planners on Monday afternoon. But Smith persuaded Smale and the other board members that Hoglund was committed to change and that his understanding of what GM had done wrong in the past would make him a precious resource. The board members

154

agreed he could stay, and by Wednesday Hoglund was safe. He would become number two to Smith and assume many of the responsibilities for running NAO on a day-to-day basis. He would remain an executive vice president. Hoglund would also keep his seat on the GM board, the only insider apart from Smith.

Smith's promotion meant he would finally give up his responsibilities for GM's international operations. Picking a replacement was easy. Lou Hughes, who'd become head of GM Europe when Eaton left for Chrysler, was the only candidate. Smith, remembering his sadness and Lydia's consternation when he was yanked from Europe to assume the international post, agreed Hughes could stay in Zurich. He'd keep the GM Europe job as well, at least for now. David Herman, who'd replaced Hughes at Opel the prior spring, had been in the job for only six months. Moving Herman up meant finding another candidate for Opel. He didn't have one in mind, and Smith didn't want that much turmoil at a time when NAO was roiling.

To replace Hoglund, Smith made a surprise choice: G. Richard Wagoner, thirty-nine-year-old head of GM do Brazil. Wagoner was sitting in his office when he received an urgent message to call his boss, Latin American vice president Richard Nerod, now a group executive, who was in a restaurant in Chile. "I just wanted to let you know, you're going to get a call from Jack," Nerod told Wagoner conspiratorially. The young executive was floored, as were many on Wall Street, when Smith offered him the job as CFO. "Wow, this is really surprising," Wagoner told Smith. "I guess I've got to talk to my wife." She quickly told him to take it.[1] It was just the latest in a series of rapid promotions that the tall Virginian had racked up during his fifteen-year GM career. He was a Duke graduate who, like Hughes, joined GM after Harvard Business School. In almost a mirror of Smith's career, Wagoner had worked on the New York finance staff, served as CFO in Canada, Europe, and Brazil, spent six months in Detroit as a planner, and returned to Brazil to run the operations there. Along the way he'd drawn praise for implementing the seeds of GM's global production strategy. Smith was intrigued with the idea of building the Opel Corsa in markets outside Europe. Brazil needed a new small car, but in the past it had never demonstrated the quality and efficiency that were necessary to build Opel's latest products. Usually, GM kept building cars in its Latin American plants for years after they were out of date. Now Smith wondered if the Corsa could work in Brazil. Wagoner, with help from European technology chief Peter Hanenberger and from Lopez, came up with a proposal. It would be slightly more costly to build Corsa in Brazil than Smith had hoped, but Wagoner showed the project would be able to reduce its costs over the next few years. GM's board approved the plan and Corsa went to Brazil. Said Smith, "That was a defining moment"—both for GM in Brazil and for Wagoner's career.

Wagoner, a rabid basketball fan who now boasts a photo of himself with Detroit Piston Grant Hill on his office wall, was one of the youngest men to ever join GM's management committee. (The average age of the five men on what was now called the President's Council—Smith, Hoglund, Hughes, Wagoner, and Pearce—was one year less than that of the Rolling Stones.) Even in the stodgy old GM, Wagoner had risen because of his quick intelligence, poise, and willingness to try new ideas. "This guy is a quick study. This guy is brilliant," says GMC general manager Roy Roberts. "Rick has the intellect. Rick has the understanding. Rick has the ability. Rick understands what he does not understand and he will seek out the right people." Unlike Hughes, he had not worked directly for Smith in New York, but had met up with the senior executive early in his career. Wagoner says his selection as CFO was a sign that Smith placed a high value on broad international experience. "Clearly, I think one of the things that Jack was on to was that he was looking for people with business capabilities beyond just a functional area," Wagoner says.

On the Sunday night before the board meeting Stempel would normally have dined with Smale to discuss issues at GM. Not this Sunday. Rain was strafing Fifth Avenue and it was dark and muggy as the directors gathered for their usual premeeting dinner. Nobody was looking outside, however. The directors were discussing the agenda for the day to come.

Downstairs, in the GM showroom off the lobby, technicians were setting up huge bars of television lights and putting cameras in place for the press conference that GM's management team would hold in the afternoon. Another camera was being installed in the twenty-fifth-floor boardroom for the telecast that GM planned to beam to its employees in the morning. The meeting broke up late, and some of the directors went off for a walk to clear their heads before going to their rooms in the Plaza Hotel. Hoglund, running into a pair of reporters near the elevators on the south side of the lobby, shrugged and grinned when they asked him what was going to transpire. "We'll know tomorrow," he said, darting into an elevator.

On Monday, November 2, the boardroom was packed with directors, attorneys, public relations officials, GM executives, and members of the camera crew. "I can't remember when there were so many people at one meeting," says a participant. The board quickly approved Smith's new management team and made some other appointments. Harry Pearce, the lawyer who had attended nearly every NAO strategy board meeting and every board meeting, was to become an executive vice president and take charge of GM Hughes Electronics and EDS. Golden, who'd risked his career to bring the commercial paper crisis to the board's attention, was named a vice president, as was Gary Dickinson, who'd helped Hogan develop the NAO strategy board. Richard Donnelly, head of GM's powertrain group, was named a group executive, while Herman and Hanenberger became vice presidents, more evidence of the importance GM's European operations were going to assume.

There were resignations, too, beginning with Stempel's. Under the terms of his departure Stempel would remain a technical adviser to Smith for two years, at $500,000 a year; he would keep an office at GM for four months, until he moved to a gleaming blue-glass tower in suburban Southfield and opened a consulting firm. UAW leader Yokich did not think Stempel deserved the cushy package. He felt the board could have acted sooner. "I watched the so-called revolution at the board. Only one board member was new [under Stempel]," he said. "These people were a part of it. How could they point their fingers at management and not look in the mirror? They were a part of all this fiasco." Reuss, dumped as GM president in April, also resigned, although he continues to work from quarters at the GM Tech Center. Alan Smith, who'd played such an important role in grooming Jack Smith, quit, as did Robert Schultz, who'd held the responsibilities that Pearce assumed. Except for Jack Smith, who ascended to the top, every other member of Stempel's original management group resigned that Monday.

Most of the attention focused on the personnel moves. But the board took one action to address the financial mess that faced them: It halved the common stock dividend to 20 cents, which saved $550 million but didn't rattle GM stock, which rose 1⅛ that day to 31⅞. The action cut the annual dividend to 80 cents; just two years before, it had been $3 a year. Investors seemed to take the news in stride. "It's trying to get its act together, so people are looking past all the bad news and into tomorrow," said Ralph Blair, an analyst with Montgomery Securities.

GM employees got their look at the new management team in an eerie national satellite telecast. The camera panned down the group of men as each was introduced. Smith, looking stricken by the day's events, explained the board had to act because GM's losses were so big even the mighty auto company had bent under their weight. But, he said, "We have acted in time. We do have a plan." And he assured the audience that "John Smale will not run the company. I will." It was a line he had not wanted to utter, but the planners encouraged him to do so in order to battle the speculation that Smale would be second-guessing his every move.

As the broadcast ended, Smale, who had been standing next to Smith, shook his hand and patted him on the shoulder, telling the GM audience, "We are confident this team is the right leadership to take the reins at this crucial juncture."

Smith tried hard to deal with some of the uncertainty about GM's future at the press conference that followed the board meeting. It got off to a rocky start as he was pelted with questions about rumors GM might have to file for Chapter 11 bankruptcy. "We're nowhere near Chapter Eleven. This is a very strong company from an asset point of view," Smith said. In fact, members of the finance staff had calculated what GM would face if it had to seek bankruptcy protection. They concluded that the lawsuits brought against GM would be so costly that the company would end up in the courts for years, lose customers, and perhaps risk being broken up. It was far better for GM to attack its financial problems with force and vigor than let the courts run the company. The UAW's Yokich agreed bankruptcy wasn't an option. "The case would last my lifetime, my son's lifetime, my grandson's lifetime, and maybe my great-grandson's lifetime," he said. "The country couldn't allow it. We would have made 10 million lawyers $10 million apiece."

Smith seemed more at ease when asked about speculation that GM planned a shakeup among its division general managers, and might dump one of its brands. A few weeks before Stempel resigned, the *Washington Post* reported that GM might ditch its Oldsmobile division, one of the original companies that formed GM in 1908. GM officials vehemently denied the report, while Oldsmobile general manager John Rock stormed into a press conference to slash the subject to ribbons. "I'm one pissed-off cowboy," the Texan declared. "I feel like somebody just shot my horse." Nonetheless, the issue had come up during one of the planners' brainstorming sessions, when they were looking for ways to eliminate slow-selling cars. The planners talked about combining Oldsmobile and Saturn to give Saturn customers someplace to go once they'd outgrown their small cars and to provide Oldsmobile with a source of buyers that it could not attract on its own. The idea was rejected in part because Rock launched into a rapid and energetic plan to save his division from the junkpile.

Gripping the podium, as Lydia watched from among the packed showroom full of journalists, Smith made it clear that none of GM's car or truck divisions would be eliminated. "We need all the horses in GM's stables," he said. There may have been some silent groaning on the planners' part, but the statement reassured nervous divisional employees. They also saw that despite the pressure, their boss had a sense of humor. Introducing Hughes, he mistakenly said he was forty-four years old. "Wait, I'm only forty-three," Hughes protested. Shot back Smith: "It must be your hairline."

The press conference was the first Smith had held since becoming GM's president in April and the first time many of the automotive journalists had even seen him in person, let alone heard his mid-Massachusetts accent. Along with his voice, the first thing that many people noticed that day was his hairstyle. He'd had a fresh haircut, and his widow's peak ended in a sharp point on his forehead, making him look a little bit like a matinee Dracula. Glancing at the photos from the press conference, impish *Detroit Free Press* writers were inspired. Later that week, the *Free Press* ran a series of six of Smith's publicity photos taken over the years. In some he looked young, others a bit plump. The second-to-last photo was one taken that Monday. Next to it: Eddie Munster.

After the press conference concluded, Smale and a group of directors invited a handful of reporters from national newspapers upstairs to the twenty-fifth floor for an off-the-record chat. They were anxious to get across the idea that they were not going to take control of GM. Sitting in the boardroom where the second management coup in six months had taken place that morning, gazing down at the group from the chair at the end of the long table that he usually occupied, Smale insisted that the board would do what it could to make sure GM employees knew management was in charge. Other directors joined in. "Jack will speak for the corporation. John Smale will not," said Charles T. "Chick" Fisher, chairman of NBD Corporation, Detroit's biggest bank and a primary GM lender.

Their insistence didn't help much. "There is some feeling that Smale is Big Brother," said David Cole, director of the University of Michigan's Office for the Study of Automotive Transportation. Just a few days before, Cole had maintained to the dozens of reporters who regularly picked his brain that Stempel would not be forced to resign. Now, said Cole, "There is a lot of uncertainty about the role the board is going to be playing." Smith may have been unsure as well at that point. But even so, he looked relieved as he ran into a knot of reporters leaving the boardroom that Monday afternoon. Standing in his shirtsleeves, his palm was sweaty as he shook hands with several, who wished him good luck in his new job. "Thanks. I'll need it," he replied.

Smith needed every shred of luck that he could get his arms around. Through the fall and into the winter the planners were implementing the tenets of Fundamental Change with lightning speed. GM, once likened to the Queen Mary, was zipping around like a Cigarette boat. There was a true sense of urgency in almost every part of the company, as executives, product planners, GM's marketing divisions, and even its dealers put their faith behind the newly named CEO and his team of young but seasoned managers. Spurring the company on was the realization that the tide of red ink would only keep rising if something was not done. As if to drive home the point, GM's finance staff decided to book a humungous bookkeeping charge, called SFAS 106, that reflected the costs GM expected to incur in the future for current and retired employees' health care expenses. Companies were required by the Financial Accounting Standards Board to give an estimate of their future costs by the end of 1993. GM's amount was staggering: $20.8 billion, the largest of any company in America. It made GM's loss for the year, which would have been huge anyway, downright breathtaking: $23.5 billion. Though it was mostly theoretical, the writeoff created an immediate shortfall of $700 million in GM's fourth quarter. Hogan remembers that Smith, who easily would have been forgiven had his temper frayed, instead turned the latest crisis into a challenge for the planners. Walking into a meeting with a grin on his face, Smith said, "Okay, guys, we've got to come up with $700 million somehow. Let's roll up our sleeves."[2]

Financially, however, the worst seemed to be over. In February 1993, Wagoner, beginning what was seen as a symbol of GM's new openness, held a news briefing to explain GM's fourth-quarter and year-end results. It was in a sense his debut with the press and with GM employees, who watched the news conference via satellite hookup. For years, Ford had held quarterly news briefings, hosted by unflappable treasurer

David McCammon, who seemed able to handle any question journalists might throw at him. Chrysler traditionally made its top executives available at the end of the year and provided financial analysis during other quarters. GM, by contrast, issued its complex, multiple-page press release and counted on its PR staff to field the flood of phone calls. At the session Wagoner disclosed that NAO lost $4 billion in 1992, but that in the fourth quarter NAO's loss narrowed significantly from the prior year. Not counting the huge writeoff, GM actually earned $92 million in 1992. Wagoner reiterated NAO's break-even EBIT target for 1993. It would be difficult to get there, especially in the third quarter, which is always the toughest in the auto industry because of the high cost of changing plants over to produce new models. But Wagoner said NAO would not let up.

At least there was one bright spot: Saturn. Early on that might have been hard to expect. Despite the hype and the hope, Saturn's start in 1990 was shaky. Because of early quality glitches, cars barely trickled out of Spring Hill. There were two early recalls—one for broken seats, another for faulty coolant that could ruin an engine. Saturn turned them into mini-triumphs by giving customers new cars. It sent mechanics as far away as Alaska to fix them. And the trip to the north country even became a feature of one of Saturn's quirky ads, created by San Francisco's Hal Riney, whose deep voice became the voice of Saturn.

The owners of those early Saturns were as excited about their cars as fans of the 1965 Ford Mustang or the 1954 Corvette. That enthusiasm became Saturn's strongest selling tool. It took about a year, but around Christmas 1991 Saturn went into orbit. As Robert Stempel was announcing layoffs of 74,000 auto workers and GM's plans to close twenty-three plants, Saturns started to show up everywhere, from Midwest country roads to the Pennsylvania Turnpike. Skip LeFauve's mom, who'd once worried about her son's future, called again to ask if he'd hired drivers to zip around in the cars. By spring 1992 GM's top management was in turmoil, but there were waiting lists for Saturn small cars. At the end of the model year, in late summer, Saturn dealers were sold out and customers were forced to wait for two months to get their cars. A survey by marketing gurus J. D. Power and Associates seemed to validate everything that Saturn had reached for. The survey, not surprisingly, showed the most satisfied car owners were those who'd bought Lexus and Infiniti luxury cars. But right behind them were the owners of small Saturn models that cost one third as much.

For dealer Huddy Hyman, success was sweet. Six years after he'd mailed that first application, he owned four Saturn dealerships, was named to a seat on Saturn's governing board, and converted his Buick, Porsche, Audi, and Range Rover dealerships to Saturn's no-haggle policy. And his zest for Saturn endured. As he sipped café au lait at a sidewalk café in New Orleans in 1993, during the annual auto dealers' convention, Hyman's slightly bloodshot eyes sparkled when he talked about the changes Saturn had made in his life as a dealer. "I had always wanted to find a company that had that commitment to pleasing customers," Hyman said. "It's been enriching for me to see it work. People believed in it. They focused on it. And they made it work."

The glow from Saturn seemed to be little consolation, though, when GM was smacked with a pair of crises early in 1993 that would have rattled even the soundest auto company. The carmaker was able to successfully, even triumphantly, rebound from the first. But the second sent Smith and GM down an emotional rollercoaster and resulted in ramifications that still reverberate within GM to this day.

Only six weeks after Smith became CEO, the National Highway Traffic Safety Administration, the government's chief safety arm, said it would investigate whether GM put gasoline tanks in a potentially perilous place on 1973–1987 pickup trucks sold by Chevrolet and GMC dealers. NHTSA's action applied to 5 million trucks with gasoline tanks placed outside the frame beneath the truck. The pickup trucks were among GM's most popular and profitable vehicles. It could earn up to $5,000 on a fully loaded truck. And surveys showed that 61 percent of Chevrolet owners who owned pickups would buy them again, second only to the loyalty of Chrysler minivan owners.

The issue had its roots in the early 1970s, when the

government ordered carmakers to move trucks' gas tanks. Until then, the tanks were installed behind the passenger compartment, and drivers could often hear gallons of fuel sloshing around as they drove. Ford and Chrysler decided to put a single thirty-gallon gas tank at the rear of the truck, inside the frame. But GM decided to install two twenty-gallon tanks on either side of the metal frame beneath the truck. GM felt its owners wanted to be able to travel long distances without stopping to refuel. Its crash tests showed the tanks could withstand a collision at 50 mph without damage. The government didn't perform its own side crash tests then, so it accepted GM's data.

But safety advocates charged that the placement of the sidesaddle gas tanks made the trucks more prone to catch fire in side crashes than trucks built by Chevrolet and Ford, which had single gas tanks inside the frame. They alleged GM knew the tanks were unsafe but kept building the trucks anyway. Between 1973 and 1992, the Insurance Institute for Highway Safety charged that 295 people had died in fire-related crashes involving the trucks, including sixty-eight who perished when their trucks were hit from the side in high-speed collisions.

GM's safety officials were perplexed by the recall demands. Although GM's trucks used a different design from those built by Chrysler and Ford, the trucks had met federal safety guidelines in effect during the 1970s and early 1980s. "These trucks are absolutely safe to drive," said Robert Sinke, Jr., GM's director of engineering analysis. "This whole situation has been blown out of proportion." But the safety advocates circulated documents from NHTSA that showed GM changed the gas tanks' design in 1983, and in 1984 began to encase the gasoline tanks in hard plastic. By 1987, GM switched to a single thirty-seven-gallon gas tank when it redesigned the full-sized pickups for the 1988 model year. Sinke said the improvements were normal and not an admission of guilt. "Just because you've learned how to improve does not say the previous product was defective," he said.

The story, which began to surface during the summer, gathered steam and quickly became the most publicized auto safety case since allegations in the late 1970s that Ford Pintos could catch fire in rear-end collisions. On November 17, just two weeks after Smith had become CEO, the television news program *Dateline NBC*, hosted by Jane Pauley and Stone Phillips, aired a report that showed a truck catching fire in an "unscientific" test that the network paid to perform. Meanwhile, GM faced more than 100 liability lawsuits charging that the automaker was partly responsible for deaths and injuries that had taken place in accidents involving the trucks.

The demands for a recall began to escalate, fueled by the publicity-savvy Center for Auto Safety, founded by Nader after the Corvair case twenty-five years before. Clarence Ditlow, the center's director, publicly demanded that GM fix every single truck on the road. The cheapest estimate was that the repair would cost $250 million; with legal fees, the bill might reach $1 billion. It was another headache for Smith, up to his ears in implementing Fundamental Change. "GM just can't get a break," said auto analyst John Casesa of Wertheim Schroder. The pending lawsuits simply compounded the problem; each time a suit went to court, a GM executive had to testify about the actions the company had taken. A particularly poignant example occurred in January 1993, when a Georgia court heard a case involving the death of eighteen-year-old Shannon Moseley, who died when his 1985 pickup truck was hit from the side at an intersection by a drunk driver traveling 68 mph. Stempel, who'd kept out of sight since his resignation as CEO, was called to testify on GM's behalf. The sight of the former CEO defending the company that had forced him from office was painful for many to watch. And far more people saw the case than GM would have liked, because it was featured on the fledgling cable television channel Court TV. Despite Stempel's attempts to reinforce the assertion of the trucks' inherent safety, the jury in the case sided with the Moseleys' attorney and awarded the family $105 million—$101 million of it in punitive damages. It was the third-largest automotive product liability award in history.

The controversy might have swirled beyond GM's control, blackening its public image, had it not been for a stroke of luck. Pete Pesterre, a writer with *Popular Hot Rodding* magazine in California, heard from a pal who had heard from a friend in

Indiana that there was something fishy about the *Dateline NBC* segment. The *Dateline* crew had been spotted in a Hendricks County, Indiana, field that summer, filming some footage that was used during the report. Producers had hired local firefighters to be on hand so they could put out any truck fire. The firefighters had set up the video camera they used in taping fires that broke out in the area. Also on hand was a sheriff's deputy, whose girlfriend, excited by the presence of network people in a small town outside Indianapolis, brought along her still camera. Pesterre, who died in 1994, didn't know what to make of it, but placed a call to a friend in GM's public relations department. The message found its way to Bill O'Neill, newly named head of GM's North American public relations department. O'Neill launched an investigation that introduced the world to lawyer Harry Pearce.

In early February, as more than 400 journalists from around the country gathered in Chicago for the Chicago Auto Show, there began to be rumblings that GM was going to sue the network over the *Dateline* report. GM CEO Jack Smith wouldn't talk about it at GM's annual media lunch but said he hoped GM would have something to say on the subject "very soon."[3] That weekend, with many of the same journalists now in New Orleans for the National Automobile Dealers' Association convention, GM sent out an announcement of a media briefing it was going to hold on Monday afternoon, February 8, in its showroom in the GM building. That was a departure, because GM usually had press conferences in a small auditorium on the fifth floor. GM public relations officials promised the reporters in New Orleans that it would broadcast the briefing on satellite. They were advised that it was something they would not want to miss.

Joined by Ford president Alexander Trotman, a pack of journalists gathered around a TV set in New Orleans at the same time as reporters filed into the GM showroom, where a big, unidentifiable object was sitting under a tarpaulin up on the stage. Also watching the telecast, from her office in New York, was Pauley. She could not believe her eyes as Pearce's presentation proceeded. "It was like theater," she told public television interviewer Charlie Rose a year later. Speaking in his deep voice, in tones that could alternately intrigue and indict, Pearce in two hours laid out a story that was every bit as good as any episode of Perry Mason. "This is nothing more than a search for the truth. We are entitled to that. Our employees are entitled to that. Our customers are entitled to that."

First, Pearce played the original NBC report, which had lasted about ten minutes, for the audience. At one point he told the crowd, "Watch that corner of the screen, because we're going to go back to it." Then Pearce revealed that GM, tipped by the Indiana journalist, had obtained videotape shot by the firefighters of the NBC crew, correspondent Michele Gillen, and the team of safety "consultants" staging accidents on a dirt road near a plowed field. The voices of the firefighters watching the afternoon's events could clearly be heard on the videotape, which showed that in both accidents a car was pushed down the field by a truck into the GM pickup. In the first accident, the car and the truck collided and nothing happened. In the second accident, the car and the truck collided, fuel spilled, and a fire broke out. At a distance, and at a glance, it seemed as though the fire had been the result of the car smashing into the truck.

But, slowing the tape down, Pearce pointed out two small plumes of smoke in the lower left corner of the screen that flumed *before* the car and the truck collided. It turned out to be the ignition of a model rocket that the safety consultants had attached to the truck to simulate flames just in case none occurred when the vehicles collided. As a teenager in North Dakota, Pearce had fooled around with model rockets, even building a two-stage missile that won a U.S. Navy award. "I got to know a lot about model rocketry," he said.[4] Punctuating what the *oooing* reporters had just seen, Pearce displayed one of the spent ignition cartridges. The explosion that NBC had blamed on the GM pickup truck was ignited by remote control. Further, it looked like the trucks' fuel tanks were deliberately overfilled so that any gas that spilled would easily ignite. The fire was a grass fire, not a truck fire. The gas cap on the truck didn't fit properly, causing it to pop off when the car hit the truck. The explosion, Pearce said, had been caused by "gunpowder. Good old saltpeter, charcoal, and sulphur." By clocking the tape, GM discovered that the car and truck collided at a significantly higher speed than NBC had indicated in its report. Gillen, in her report, said the two vehicles collided at 30 mph; GM figured out that one accident was at 39 mph, the other at 47 mph or more. "Both of these fuel tanks did just fine," Pearce said, even though the speed was higher than in government crash tests.

The afternoon press conference was filled with comic relief, punctuated by Pearce's deadpan delivery. On the fire-fighters' video two officers are heard discussing the fire. "It didn't do what they wanted it to do," one says. As the flames flicker, the other firefighter replies, "Are we going to go stomp it out?" They don't move, and the wind blows out the flames. "So much for that theory," the first firefighter says. And there was more drama. In a flurry of letters between *Dateline* producer Robert Read and O'Neill after the report had aired, NBC had told the carmaker that the two pickups used during the simulated crashes had been junked, and no trace of them remained. That wasn't true, as Pearce showed his audience. He swept aside the cover behind him and revealed a crumpled red pickup that had been displayed in the firefighter's videotape minutes before. GM found the truck, and its cousin, in junkyards within ten miles of the Indiana field. The spent rocket was in the truck bed, and duct tape used to hold the rocket was still in place beneath the truck.

Pearce ended his presentation with a threat: GM planned to sue NBC for defamation of character, seeking significant monetary damages for ruining its reputation and that of its pickup trucks. In the meantime, GM was pulling its ads from NBC news shows and would rethink the other advertisements it placed on the network. "If it's a betrayal, it's a betrayal of the American people," Pearce declared. The explosion of criticism that followed Pearce's press conference shook the media world to its foundation. At first NBC stood behind the report. But in New York, attorneys for General Electric, NBC's parent, and GM held intense negotiations aimed at heading off GM's suit. The carmaker was one of NBC's biggest advertisers and a major customer for GE's automotive products.

Another episode of *Dateline* was set to air on Tuesday,

February 9, the night after Pearce's press conference. All day long the lawyers worked on a settlement. And when the program went on the air, at 10 P.M., Pauley and her cohost did not know what they were going to say. Only at the end of the program did the carefully negotiated statement appear on the teleprompters in front of her and Phillips. They were seeing the words for the first time as they read a long list of points retracting the claims the report had made about the trucks' safety. "First, and most importantly, we want to emphasize that what we characterized in the November *Dateline* segment as an unscientific demonstration was inappropriate and does not support the position that GM's C/K trucks are defective."

The statement concluded, "We acknowledge and take responsibility for the problems GM has identified in the demonstration crash. We believe we present in the balance of the segment all sides of the controversy over the safety of the GM trucks. We deeply regret we included the inappropriate demonstrations in our *Dateline* report. We apologize to our viewers and to General Motors. We have also concluded that unscientific demonstrations should have no place in hard news stories at NBC. That's our new policy."

GM, in response, said it would drop its defamation suit. Under terms of the deal, NBC reimbursed GM for the costs of its investigation. Michael Gartner, NBC News president, resigned, and Michele Gillen, who had vehemently protested using the rigged test, was sent to NBC's affiliate in Miami. At GM, people were exchanging high fives and hugging each other in glee over what Pearce had pulled off. Even Smith, in an unexpected call to the author, gave Pearce high praise for his actions. "That was a real shot in the arm for us," Smith said.[5] The episode raised the profile of the attorney, already a power within GM, and seemed to make television reporters, at least for a time, a little more careful about staging events. "I think a pretty strong signal was sent, interestingly by journalists themselves," Pearce said. A lot of very responsible journalists stood with us and made similar indictments of what NBC had done. It was a pretty good cleansing process for the professional journalism world. And in that respect I think it absolutely has caused those kinds of titillating television programs to draw back and think about their responsibilities."[6] Today, a picture of Pauley and her coanchor, Stone Phillips, smiles out from a paperweight on Pearce's desk. It was a gift from his former colleagues at Kirkland & Ellis.

GM still had a government investigation to deal with, but the victory over NBC made many euphorically certain the company could best any challenger. Unfortunately, the glow lasted only a few short weeks. GM was brutally brought back to reality by the betrayal of a man whom Smith had relied on in his darkest hours to help guide the foundering NAO to safety.

CHAPTER · 7

Lopez: The Man Who Broke Jack Smith's Heart

José Ignacio Lopez de Arriortua's star at General Motors soared with the spectacle and glory of a comet seen just once in a century. Then it exploded with the flash of a nuclear bomb, leaving devastation, disbelief, and despair in its wake. What GM hoped would be a triumph of efficiency by the Spanish-born executive in charge of its purchasing operations turned into a tragedy of Shakespearean proportions and the toughest test of Smith's first twelve months on the job. Yet as scandal erupted, long-time relationships were torn asunder, and Smith's own credibility was called into question, the GM leader never uttered a criticism of Lopez, who once vowed to "cut off my right arm for Jack Smith." Years after the tumultuous months that rocked the U.S. auto industry, Smith contended that bringing Lopez to the United States from Europe was the most important thing he had done in his first days as GM president.[1] And others agree. "He was the most brilliant executive who ever worked here in the whole eighty-some-year history of the company," says a GM manager. The Lopez affair became the defining moment of Smith's first year, and may yet prove to be the single most remembered event of his tenure.

It would take a 500-page book to do the story justice, Lopez himself declared in the midst of the bicontinental uproar over allegations that he masterminded the theft of 10,000 GM documents, computer discs, and plans for new plants and cars.[2] That supreme confidence—on a scale that put even the most arrogant executives who preceded him to shame—became one of his many hallmarks. "We are in a war!" he would declare to listeners at press conferences, dinners, and private meetings. His dark eyes would light up and his hands would gesticulate as he spoke. "We are fighting to save the auto industry and our lives. If we lose the battle for the auto industry, our sons and daughters will become second-class citizens and the U.S. will have a second-class economy."[3]

His appointment as GM's vice president for the new post of worldwide purchasing, assigned to GM's North American Operations, was made on April 7, 1992, when GM was still in shock from the management shakeup the day before. It was the first move Smith made, which should have signaled its importance. But purchasing was one of those cobwebbed tickets to nowhere in the auto industry. GM spent $35 billion a year on the 10,000 components used on each of its cars and trucks, but purchasing ranked far below design, engineering, and even manufacturing on the GM status ladder. Each model year, GM's twenty-seven purchasing managers and their buying agents would conduct the same negotiations with 5,000 or more small, medium, and large companies. GM preached quality and longterm relationships but made deals based on who could come up with parts when GM needed them—or, even worse, on who went to church with Reuss or joined him for golf at the Bloomfield Hills Country Club.

Because of those friendships, GM might pay three times as much for a part as its competitors, or suffer with poor quality and slow delivery even when it was clear another company could supply better materials. Antoinette Simonetti, now director of GM's New York public relations office, recalls that some of her colleagues felt it was punishment when she was assigned PR duties for GM's purchasing department the December before Lopez arrived. The national news media, more interested in GM's precarious financial position, rarely paid attention to purchasing except in the spring, when the *Wall Street Journal* did its inevitable story on what GM had agreed to pay for steel that year. Otherwise, GM's purchasing operations made news only when bosses said they wanted to reduce the thousands of suppliers they did business with, or sought larger than usual price cuts.

Lopez would change all that.

Ignacio "Inaki" Lopez was born in 1941 in Amorebieta, a town in the Basque region of Spain. His home territory was best known for two things: St. Ignatius of Loyola and the zealous separatist movement that fought to break the Basques away from the mother country. Trained as an industrial engineer, he came to Opel in 1980, after he was discovered by an Opel executive, Hans Huskes. Named manager of Opel's industrial engineering, he was working at GM's new plant in Zaragosa, Spain, when Smith first encountered him in 1986 during his visit with Fritz Lohr. From there it was a quick jump to Opel's operations in Russelsheim, Germany, where Lopez was based when a call from Smith came on April 7.

It wasn't really a surprise to him. A year earlier some GM managers had suggested to Stempel that Lopez come to the United States. Stempel didn't see the need, even though Lopez had developed something of a reputation as a cost-cutting, efficiency-seeking purchasing boss. This gained him a certain notoriety inside the automotive world. But, recalls James Taylor, who worked with Lopez in Europe and later became one of his senior aides in the U.S., Lopez was just a member of the Opel management team. His title was executive director of central purchasing, not the step-higher job of vice president. "He certainly wasn't this huge star that he became in the States," said Canadian-born Taylor, now head of truck parts purchasing at NAO. Also, Opel staffers say the discipline of the German development center where Lopez worked did not allow the Spaniard to become a cult figure.

To stall bringing Lopez to the U.S., Stempel approved a plan that would become known as "3-2-2," the numbers coming from the percentage price cuts he wanted to make over three years. (In reality, GM insiders smirked, the cuts turned out to be 2.1, 1.8, and 0.8 percent.) Animosity was thick between Lopez and Reuss, who was loyal to his pals in the supplier community. "As long as Lloyd was around, Lopez wasn't coming over," says a GM manager. By the time Smith was named president, Stempel couldn't do anything to block Lopez from coming to Detroit.

Later, people would say that Lopez left Europe reluctantly, promising his wife, Margarita, and his daughters that they would return as soon as he could arrange it. In fact Lopez was eager to come now that Reuss was gone and his friend was in charge of NAO. "I did not think about it for one minute," he confided.[4] Taylor contends that Lopez thirsted for the arena that the American auto industry could provide, and Margarita, ambitious for her husband's success, was in favor of the move. Lydia Smith recalls that as confident as Lopez was in himself, Margarita was even more self-assured. "My husband deserves everything that comes to him," Lydia says Lopez's wife told her.[5]

Though GM Europe was the second-biggest car company in its market, everybody at Opel knew that the real focus at GM—and the real source of crisis—was Detroit. The move was a second chance for Lopez at real influence in GM. Just a few weeks before Smith's phone call, Opel and GM Europe were shaken when GM Europe chairman Robert Eaton suddenly jumped ship to become CEO at Chrysler, skipping the Saturday dinner he had scheduled with the planners sent to Europe by the GM board to discuss the European strategy board.

Eaton's departure left Stempel with a vital personnel appointment to make just as outside board members were preparing to dump his management team in the U.S. In those turmoil-torn days Lopez's name was floated for a top job, but Lou Hughes, president of Opel and Smith's close friend, quickly was named the new GM Europe chairman. A few weeks later, Saab boss David Herman replaced Hughes at Opel. People at Opel say it was fairly well understood that Lopez, though passed over once, would be back in Europe within a year or two and in line for Hughes or Herman's job when one or the other moved to his next post.

Lopez arrived in Detroit at the end of Smith's first week, as the crisis team was putting into place the structure for NAO.

On Saturday night the Smiths hosted a small group of people at their Bloomfield Hills home to welcome Lopez to the neighborhood (he would eventually lease a house just doors away.) That evening, Lopez made a gesture that became his trademark. As the group gathered around the Smiths' modern white dining room table, Lopez stripped his wristwatch from his left wrist. Hooking it onto his right wrist, he told the GM executives and their wives that he wouldn't move the watch until GM again posted record profits in North America.

Smith, amid some chuckling, did the same. So did Bill Hoglund, who that week was named as GM's new chief financial officer. Lopez admitted it was irritating to make a change in a lifelong habit.[6] But there was a reason: For weeks afterward, every time executives looked at their wrist, they found their watches missing from the usual place. Then they'd remember the task ahead and persevere. As word of the watch switch spread across the company, executives seemed eager to stick out their wrists and show they'd jumped onto the bandwagon. All except Hoglund. The lanky executive admitted months later that he'd planned to join his colleagues in moving his watch. But early that Sunday morning, Hoglund woke up to find his right wrist chafing from the unaccustomed watch strap. Hoglund turned on his bedside light, stripped off the watch, and put it back on his left wrist. "Damn thing kept me awake. I couldn't sleep. It's been there [on his left wrist] ever since," he laughed.[7]

Lopez hardly needed a gimmick like switching his watch to remind him of the huge challenge he had to tackle. GM's bloated purchasing operations epitomized the competitive headaches that the company faced. During the 1980s, carmakers had been pushed by Wall Street and industry experts to farm out the production of automotive components, like seats, seatbelts, and headlights, to companies that didn't have to pay high UAW wage rates. By the early 1990s, the Big Three paid around $18 an hour—plus generous benefits such as fully paid health care—to unionized workers at parts plants. By contrast, workers at nonunion plants averaged about $8 to $9 an hour, and few had anything approaching UAW-style benefits. And plants based in Mexico or Asia paid workers just a fraction of nonunion U.S.

wages. Workers there took home in a week what UAW members earned in a day.

Manufacturing experts argued that the automakers should be worrying about designing, developing, and producing the final product, not spending valuable engineering time and resources developing sprockets and seats. When they could get away with it, the carmakers moved work to outside suppliers. The practice, called "outsourcing," was anathema to the union, which was locked in a losing battle to preserve jobs. Chrysler, and to some extent Ford, didn't have the problems GM faced because they were far less vertically integrated. The smallest of the Big Three, Chrysler had long relied on outsiders to do its components work simply because it couldn't afford to do otherwise. Chrysler built just 30 percent of the parts used on its cars—mainly engines and transmissions. During its second brush with bankruptcy in the late 1980s, The number-three car company set up programs to involve suppliers in cutting costs and invited them to help in automotive design. Ford, although it still made its own steel and automotive glass, produced in total about half its auto parts and bought the rest. In the 1980s, it had weeded out those who couldn't meet quality and cost targets.

But GM built 70 percent of the components it used to produce cars and trucks, which meant more GM workers built parts than finished vehicles. One reason was GM's buying spree during the 1920s and 30s. At the time GM's managers felt the corporation, with its far-flung operations across the United States, needed the most dependable suppliers of components. Instead of relying on outsiders, GM officials had long felt that keeping the parts in-house meant it could keep closer control. But this was an astounding level of integration for the lean 1990s. And all of those people were earning UAW wages and benefits.

During the late 1980s GM had tried to slim its parts operations by ranking each one "red, yellow, green." The colors signified which it wanted to dump, which it would constantly review, and which it would keep. And it kept pressure on the companies that built the 30 percent of parts GM didn't make itself. But dealing with the giant car company was never simple. When Lopez got to Detroit, the purchasing offices were miniature centers of power. Each purchasing manager could grant and refuse contracts and make changes in parts specifications at will. Even when cars were built from the same platforms, like the compact J-cars sold as Chevrolet Cavalier and Pontiac Sunbird (now Sunfire), suppliers still had to deal with the purchasing managers for each separate vehicle. Virtually none of the parts used on cars in the U.S. could be installed on cars overseas. This astounded GM's disciplined European engineers. "Why should their bolt have a dimension of eleven millimeters while we and everybody else use [a measurement of] ten?" wondered European technology chief Peter Hanenberger.[8]

Although GM had preached its willingness to involve suppliers more clearly in product design, to give them help in making investments in new equipment to produce auto parts, and pledged to award longterm contracts, GM suppliers often complained they were left out of crucial decisions and didn't get paid enough by the company to build the kind of quality parts GM needed so its cars could hold up as long as Japanese models. And suppliers who did business with GM overseas still had to keep bidding for the company's contracts in the U.S. There was no coordination within those twenty-seven offices in the U.S., let alone between GM's North American operations and those in Europe.

It was clear to the planners that purchasing was one area that could yield quick savings—and dramatic savings as well. "Get me something now," Smith had told GM number-crunchers, who were pointing out future savings once NAO's tangled product development operations were straightened out. Smith made it clear he was giving Lopez his full backing. So the minute Lopez started work at GM's Tech Center in Warren, Michigan, the changes began. Immediately, the twenty-seven offices were abolished and Lopez set up a single, centralized purchasing office. He quickly assembled a team of managers, including Taylor and Australian-born Alan Perriton, both of whom had worked at GM's Saturn Corporation, and brought a group of aides over from GM Europe, many of them Spanish as well. With many of these people by his side, Lopez faced

Detroit's supplier community on June 1, 1992, when he unveiled his plans for transforming GM's purchasing operations.

Far from being intimidated by the suppliers' outraged reaction, Lopez seemed to relish the attention. Stories about the newcomer began to circulate, launching the Lopez lore. Some people in Detroit were convulsed with giggles when they heard that Lopez dubbed his team of managers his "warriors" and quickly established a weekly ritual at the department's Friday purchasing meeting. Lopez shipped to Detroit a long, antique refectory table that he claimed was once used at meals by European monks. Seated at the table, the purchasing managers would review suppliers' bids for car part contracts. When the group approved the bid, they'd pound their fists on the table. (Though it seems slightly barbaric, it was the agents' variation on a Bavarian custom called *stammtisch*. When a visitor joins a communal table in an inn's pub, the people already seated pound on the table to welcome the newcomer to their midst.)

Auto industry veterans, raised on liquid lunches and prime rib dinners, smirked when they heard that Lopez had prescribed a "warrior diet" for the group to follow so they'd have the energy for long, tension-filled days. First, Lopez banned French fries and Hostess Twinkies and all junk food. Warriors were to eat only fruit for breakfast, no oatmeal, toast, eggs, or bacon. They could have as much as they wanted— "nine or twelve pieces"—because the water from the fruit, together with natural saliva, he explained, cleaned toxins out of the body. Warriors couldn't imbibe alcohol. Lopez allowed only wine and it had to be good wine. Carbohydrates and protein couldn't be mixed. If an executive had a steak—and the lean Lopez frowned on most meat—he couldn't accompany it with a salad. Mineral water was okay, but caffeine was an enemy. Starches were fine, but not potatoes, only whole-grain products like rice and whole-wheat bread.

Lopez was serious about the diet, recalls Hogan, who met with him just two weeks after Lopez arrived in Detroit. Hogan wanted to brief Lopez and Taylor on Fundamental Change and find out more about PICOS. The planner expected the meeting to go through lunch and he ordered box lunches with ham sandwiches and potato chips. "So Taylor comes in with Inaki, and he sees the lunch, and right away he launches into the Warrior Diet," recalls Hogan. "We ended up hustling around to get him fruit and yogurt. He ate a little bit of it but I remember he wasn't very pleased." Still, Lopez admitted that the diet was only semisuccessful. "When I walk through the cafeteria, [employees] throw their napkins over their plates to hide the cake!" he chuckled.[9]

Early on, when people were still sizing him up, it was hard not to laugh when Lopez expounded. He spoke in heavily accented English that brought to mind the worst stereotypes of Latin characters on 1950s television. "I laugh at this question!" Lopez scoffed, Zorro-like, at his first American press con-ference, held in the drab surroundings of a Saginaw, Michigan, college classroom.[10] In Lopez's mouth Buick became "Booo-ick," Cadillac was transformed into "Cad-DEE-Lock," and Oldsmobile into "Olds-mo-Bee-lay," which reporter Keith Naughton of the *Detroit News* promptly set to the operatic refrain of "La Donna e mobile." Unlike other company officials who avoided the press or barely hid their disdain for reporters' pestering, Lopez seemed to like the men and women who were dogging his steps. Journalists tried hard not to be charmed the first time Lopez confided his admiration of the press. He would always be grateful to reporters because members of the press in Spain defended the country's right to a democracy. "The journalists of Spain [he pronounced it 'yourna-leests'] saved our country!" Lopez would assert.

Like many of the tales in Lopez's arsenal, the journalists of Spain story became one Lopez would repeat whenever a reporter was within earshot. In a year's time, Detroit scribes had heard it six or seven times and PR woman Simonetti finally had to ask Lopez not to tell the story so often. But he was still telling it in Europe months after he'd defected to Volkswagen and was trying to deflect charges involving the stolen GM documents.

Lopez's own charisma was another weapon. Anyone seated next to him at a dinner, male or female, soon found his hand on their arm or around their shoulders as he gazed into their eyes and made a point. Lopez would grab any nearby prop—a pencil, a fork, a dessert plate—to help illustrate his cost-cutting ideas. Holding a fork at eye level, Lopez would explain that was the price GM was willing to pay for a part. Lowering his coffee cup, the executive said it was his goal to reduce the cost that suppliers incurred to develop and sell the component. It wasn't GM's intention to have the fork come any lower but the coffee cup had to drop, he claimed.

Suppliers said otherwise, and loudly. During the summer of 1992, as Lopez's PICOS efficiency teams began fanning out across GM's operations, some of GM's biggest customers balked at being forced to cut prices and costs. Rockwell International's automotive division, which had worked closely with Stempel and others on development of GM's electric car, the Impact, announced it was withdrawing from the effort because it couldn't afford to make the kinds of cuts Lopez's teams were demanding. Just a few months later, GM, which had planned to build Impacts in Lansing, Michigan, at a workshop that had once produced Buick Reatta two-seaters, scrapped the Impact program. It was simply too expensive for GM to take on all the development costs now that Rockwell had pulled out.

Rumors began to circulate that Lopez teams were taking confidential information the companies were forced to supply to the PICOS teams and sharing it with suppliers bidding for the same contract. GM's goal was to get the lowest possible prices for parts, angry suppliers charged, and delivery and quality were playing little part. Lopez and other GM officials strongly denied the allegations, and still do so. Taylor says that competing suppliers know what their competitors charge, and heatedly denies GM ever shared confidential information with competitors. But Stempel contends Lopez's tactics did tremendous damage. "He took a lot of heat and he deserved to take a lot of heat," Stempel says.[11] Long after Lopez had left Detroit, GM was still plagued by the shattered relationships that complicated its efforts to get vehicles developed and launched on time.

None of this mattered, because Lopez had Smith's support. And his tactics were paying off, big time. In just eight months, Lopez and his warriors had found ways for GM to save $2 billion over 1993 and 1994, and seemed to be well on their way to finding the target $4 billion in savings. It was the "something, now!" that Smith had demanded of his young cost-cutters and it was the kind of good news GM desperately needed in light of threats by Wall Street ratings agencies to downgrade GM bonds. By creating such a furor, and by seeming to revel in the attention he'd drawn, Lopez was taking heat off Smith, who was working sixteen- to eighteen-hour days trying to get the rest of GM's North American operations in shape. GM's board, alarmed by angry letters from the heads of GM's major suppliers, also had given Lopez the green light at a fall board meeting. He had been summoned to explain himself, and speculation ran that he might even be fired. Instead of cowering, Lopez turned his presentation into a triumph. Members of the board gave him a standing ovation when he was through. Even UAW leader Yokich fell under Lopez's spell, in part because Lopez sympathized with Yokich's demands that GM set aside regular repair time in its factories. "We get a Spanish guy, who [doesn't] know shit about the United States, and number one on his list is planned maintenance," Yokich said. "I said to him, 'Come on our side of the world,' because he knew what needed to be done."

Thus Lopez had never seemed more firmly in place by the time Smith became GM's CEO on November 2. A week later, Lopez mounted a podium in front of a Plaza Hotel ballroom filled with Wall Street auto industry analysts and outlined the savings he expected to find in coming months, a performance he repeated across Fifth Avenue in the GM building's automotive showroom for a crowd of reporters. As he held forth at dinner that night with a small crowd of financial journalists, Lopez seemed to radiate confidence and determination. He merely shrugged when reminded that a few weeks before, legendary quality guru W. Edwards Deming had blasted Lopez's tactics for creating fear and unsettlement among GM's supplier ranks. Lopez, Deming told top GM managers, was the antithesis of Deming's exhortation to "drive out fear" from an organization. It would be nice if things were more comfortable at GM, and if there could be more teamwork. But Lopez said, "We do not have time to waste."

Neither, as it turned out, did Lopez. His words that night,

and his constant insistence on other occasions that there was little time to accomplish his task, could have been his own way of warning what was just ahead. By the time Smith became GM's chief executive officer, and Lopez delivered his cost-cutting forecast to the Wall Street analysts, the Spanish executive already was thinking about his future.

In October a call came from Europe, from an intermediary. Volkswagen, Europe's biggest car company, was in deep trouble. A new chairman, Austrian-born Ferdinand Piech, had been appointed to wrench the inefficient auto giant into the future. Piech had watched, admiringly, as Lopez had transformed GM Europe's purchasing operations and taken hold of GM's troubles in the U.S. He wanted to know if Lopez would help him, not just in purchasing but across VW's worldwide manufacturing operations. On a global scale, VW was the fourth-largest automaker behind GM, Ford, and Toyota. But it dominated Europe. In Germany, where VW was based in Wolfsburg and Opel in Russelsheim, competition between the two car companies was part of German culture. (Piech's first choice had actually been GM Europe boss Hughes, who wanted nothing to do with VW.) Plunged in his GM duties, Lopez was intrigued but distracted when the first call came. NAO was in turmoil after Stempel's ouster and Smith's elevation to CEO. VW could wait.

But VW was persistent. Beginning with that first call, someone from Wolfsburg phoned nearly every day. By the middle of November, Jens Neumann, a close aide to Piech, had taken over the recruiting job. He arranged a secret meeting between Lopez and Piech outside Frankfurt, just a few miles from Opel's operations in Russelsheim. Like a wisp of a cloud, the first rumor of VW's interest in Lopez wafted through European auto circles, denied immediately by GM. As the rumor persisted, Lopez himself issued a statement saying he had no intention of quitting GM. Yet, as 1993 began, the talks began to get serious. Smith, alerted to the speculation, asked Lopez if he was thinking of leaving. Lopez assured him he didn't plan to go, that his work at GM wasn't complete. But Smith, concerned that his longtime colleague might need some encouragement to stay, asked the GM board in January to name Lopez a vice president of the corporation, which it did. Though he was already a VP within NAO, the more powerful title gave Lopez greater weight within the corporation and was a stepping-stone to a bigger promotion.

A few weeks later, Smith, at GM's Chicago Auto Show lunch, was asked by reporters at his table whether he followed Lopez's Warrior Diet. "No, I threw it in the garbage," laughed Smith between bites of filet mignon. "But don't print that. We've got to keep Inaki happy."[12]

Even as Smith spoke, Volkswagen was making its move. It invited Lopez to come to Europe for what would turn out to be a high-level job interview with members of VW's top management. Lopez's schedule included constant travel and so a visit to Germany, ostensibly to visit Opel's operations, didn't raise any eyebrows. That week, GM Europe's top executives were attending a conference that included an annual review of future car programs. It was a routine event, with a slide presentation that included overhead transparencies with photos and some details about the upcoming products, including the next generation Corsa subcompact, Opel's most important product.

A few days later Lopez attended a meeting in Wolfsburg, where VW made its first firm offer of a job that would include Lopez's dream: a small car plant in his Spanish homeland. For years, while at Opel and later in Detroit, Lopez had wanted GM to build a super-efficient factory that would be the first example of a new concept called "agile manufacturing." Suppliers could come right into the factory to help autoworkers build cars. Factories didn't have to be set up with long assembly lines; work could take place in modules. Whole parts of the car, like the dashboard, could be brought to the factory preassembled. And the trucks that brought seats and engines and transmissions to the plants could be used to help carry finished cars away. Lopez estimated that such a plant could build a car in about ten hours, compared with eighteen hours at GM's most efficient factory, in Eisenach, Germany, or twenty-eight hours at its more traditional plant in Bochem. In the U.S., it took GM's factories between twenty-two and thirty hours to build a car, compared with about twenty hours at Toyota's plant in Georgetown, Kentucky.

Later, Smith would say that VW's willingness to build the plant was a key factor in winning him. It lead to the belief that GM thought the idea fruitless. Not so. In Europe, GM officials took Lopez's plant-of-the-future idea seriously; they thought it could come to pass someday. But Hughes, who assumed the mantle of GM's international operations from Smith on November 2, didn't think it should be built in Spain. GM already had a modern factory in Zaragoza. Hughes was eager to push deeper into the old East Bloc. GM beat VW into eastern Germany, home of the Eisenach plant. Hughes thought the next focus belonged in Hungary or Poland, emerging markets where the payoff would be big in sales, profits, and public relations for GM if it could act quickly. And over the long term, Hughes was itching to get into China, where agile manufacturing might be the method GM used from the first.

Lopez didn't make any promises to VW at the February meeting. But he made the first of the moves that would be called into question in coming months. Lopez asked for copies of the slides from the Opel future product planning meeting to be shipped to his office in Detroit. Because he was now a corporate VP, Lopez had the unquestioned authority to ask for and get the material. Five other GM officials made the same request. In the old days, the action would have been unusual because executives based in the U.S. rarely asked for product program information from Opel, since the cars wouldn't be sold in North America. But Lopez contended the information was useful because he was now in charge of worldwide purchasing. He needed to know what Opel planned to have for the future and the prices GM was paying in Europe for parts so that the company could compare them with those it paid for similar goods in the U.S.

Those weren't the only documents he took home from GM. A pair of the planners, who worked with Lopez on almost a daily basis that winter, noticed that every day Lopez's desk was piling higher with files. They started hearing from their colleagues that Lopez was requesting reports more frequently.

"We knew he was taking things and we wondered if we should tell somebody about it," one of the planners says. But with so much work to do, and knowing that Lopez had the complete backing of Smith and the board, the planners did not bring the subject up. It might not have done any good as far as keeping Lopez in the fold.

Many people at Opel and inside GM believe Lopez made up his mind to take the VW job during that February trip. Certainly, the rumor mill, which had quieted down somewhat when GM promoted Lopez, began to churn again. Lopez, through spokeswoman Simonetti, issued his second denial of any plans to leave GM. But late in February reporters cornered him at a luncheon meeting of the Economic Club of Detroit. And for the first time, he seemed to waffle. "Who can say? I will never say never. I do not plan to go now...but I cannot say what the future will hold." It was like throwing gasoline on already crackling firewood. And the flames were fueled by thousands of journalists from around the world descending on Geneva, Switzerland, for its annual Motor Show.

Normally, executives love the Geneva show. At an exhibition a third the size of the sprawling shows in Frankfurt and Tokyo, the bosses get a chance to see what their competitors are doing in a relaxed, carefree way. The food is good, the surroundings gorgeous, and the neutral site means little parochialism. But when Smith walked into the arena for the first of two press days, he was deluged with questions. No, he didn't think Lopez would leave. Yes, he hoped he would stay. He understood why VW was interested in Lopez because he was so bright. It was a tense, awkward couple of days for the problem-saddled CEO. He was hoping that Lopez would bring the weeks of rumors to an end quickly, but deep inside Smith knew the longer that they continued the greater the chances were that Lopez was going to leave. So in a move that was out of character for him, he placed a call to Piech, asking him, in essence, to "stay away from my guy." Piech's response was typically blunt: "I don't owe you anything," he told the GM chief executive.

Certainly, there was a tailor-made opportunity to stop the gossip once and for all. On March 6, in typical grand fashion,

Lopez had summoned GM executives and officials of GM's suppliers from around the world to Detroit for his first Supplier of the Year awards weekend. Later people called the extravagant festivities "Inaki's farewell dinner." Eighteen months afterward, Hans Weiser, head of GM's European parts operations, greeted his seatmate from the dinner by saying, "I'll always remember that fateful night." The sunny but cold day began with an eight-hour seminar at the GM Tech Center, where Lopez gave a long speech and handed plaques to each of the companies he had declared winners. In keeping with GM's increasingly global purchasing focus, the grand award winner was from France. That night Lopez presided over a celebration for 800 people intended to fête the hardworking group that had triumphed over GM's adversity. This wouldn't be just another dinner where men in business suits and wives in cocktail attire ate rubber chicken and listened to dull speeches. Lopez wanted a black-tie affair, a five-course dinner, good wine, entertainment and dancing—a festival. Members of his staff, charged up about the thousands of dollars he wanted to spend on the party, suggested hiring Detroit soul singer Aretha Franklin, who was available and happy to perform. But Lopez had seen the evangelistic youth troupe Up with People perform once in Europe and vetoed Franklin in favor of the politically correct, saccharinely sweet singers and dancers. A year later, dissecting the final days over beers in Traverse City, Michigan, Taylor still moaned over Lopez's choice.

The dinner in the Renaissance Ballroom of the Westin Hotel turned into a command performance for all of GM's highest-ranking officials, including Smith, who flew back from Geneva earlier than scheduled. Though chatting comfortably at a cocktail party before the dinner, he showed the effects of jet lag as he wandered over, unnoticed, to get a glass of white wine at the bar. (In the old GM, a dozen flunkies would have instantly offered him glasses, like swains lighting a chanteuse's cigarette.) Lydia Smith wasn't thrilled by the change in plans; the Geneva trip was her first back to Switzerland in the two years since her mother had died, and she had hoped to spend more time in her home country. She thought her husband could have skipped the event.

Lopez's charm was on high power; he kissed women on both cheeks, hugged men, and introduced his Margarita as well as his daughters, who'd later become embroiled in the controversy when investigators discovered one had carried some GM documents on a computer disc to Europe. The sprawling ballroom buzzed with conversations in English, French, German, and Spanish as people told their favorite Lopez stories. While the guests were finishing dinner, Lopez got up, a hand-held microphone in his hand. Striding across the floor to stand by Smith, who looked dubious as the spotlight shone on his dark hair, Lopez declared his allegiance to the GM CEO. "Jack Smith is my hero. He is my brother and I love him!" Lopez declared, pulling Smith to his feet so that he could embrace him—possibly the first time a GM CEO had been hugged in public by anybody other than his wife. Lopez presented Smith with a marble sculpture. It featured an arch that rose to form a small bust of a bald-headed man who distantly resembled Lopez. The Spanish executive gave similar trophies to other executives, then called on squirming reporters to rise. Once again, he repeated the story of the "yournaleests" of Spain as the scribes reached for deep gulps from their wine glasses. But, at Simonetti's request, he refrained from handing the reporters their trophies until after the dinner.

As Lopez rambled on, it seemed the entire room was straining for the magic words—"I will not leave GM"—that would end, once and for all, the swirling VW rumors. But they never came. Lopez made no reference to the German company, no pledge to remain at Smith's side. The suppliers, GM executives, and journalists sat through another ninety minutes of speeches and the boisterous singing of the youth troupe, realizing Lopez's omission was likely deliberate. As the evening ended, almost as if he knew what was to come in the week ahead, the visibly fatigued Smith, holding his wife's hand, trudged almost zombie-like out of the ballroom.

It was the last time that Lopez was ever seen publicly in the United States as a GM employee. The next day, he boarded a plane for Germany to attend a meeting of the International Strategy Board at Opel's Russelsheim headquarters. Once more he brought up the plant in Spain. Lopez had concocted a deal where Opel would have had to invest almost nothing to build the factory, which would have produced a car smaller than the Opel Corsa. Lopez had lined up Spanish investors and a commitment from the Spanish government to fund the factory, called Plant X. A few months before, at Hughes's request, Lopez had told the investors that the plant was on hold while GM attended to its financial crisis. Now Lopez wanted a promise that the plant could proceed. Hogan, who'd been named that January as head of GM's Brazilian operations, quietly backed Lopez because he could see ways that the factory's technology could be used in GM's booming Latin American operations.

But GM Europe's finance staff did not trust the free deal that Lopez said he had secured. They did not think GM could recover its investment, no matter how much it learned in the process. Finally, Hughes and other members of the strategy board told Lopez in no uncertain terms that the deal was dead. Any new factories would be built in Eastern Europe. That decision sent Lopez, in a rage, to Wolfsburg, where he signed a contract to become number two to Piech. His title would be director of worldwide manufacturing; the contract called for him to earn several million dollars if he could meet certain targets for modernizing VW operations and cutting costs. He was to implement a version of PICOS throughout VW's factories. And Lopez would get to build his plant in Spain.

Lopez got back to Detroit on Wednesday, March 10, went to his office, and phoned Smith. He was leaving, he told his friend. Smith had been expecting, dreading the call, but the reality of Lopez's words was like a bullet between the eyes. "What can I do to keep you?" Smith asked Lopez. He started to bring up possibilities: more money, more responsibilities, a bigger title. Lopez refused to discuss it. "No negotiations. I resign," he said. Even before the phone call, Detroit was abuzz with rumors that Lopez had quit.

On Thursday morning Lopez was in his office, his door closely guarded. In the afternoon, Lopez called his warriors into his office. He delivered the news and the room erupted. The young GM purchasing agents were in tears, pleading with

Lopez to change his mind. Despite the fervor that Lopez had instilled in them, it was a more emotional response than anybody had expected. Members of the purchasing team started calling other GM executives to ask them to do anything to keep Lopez from leaving. They in turn called Smith, who told them he didn't think there was anything he could do. GM issued a statement under Smith's name that afternoon, leaving a tearful Simonetti to take phone calls from mostly sympathetic reporters.

Within hours, VW announced it had hired Lopez. Now Smith was deluged with calls from angry GM board members. Chairman John Smale as well as directors Anne Armstrong, Dennis Weatherstone, and John Bryan all directed Smith to do what he had to do to keep Lopez. Smith had no choice but to negotiate. On Friday he launched into an unprecedented counterattack. He took a group of executives, including Wagoner and chief counsel Harry Pearce, to Lopez's house to talk him out of leaving. They offered him the job of president of NAO, taking over Smiths' duties in North America. It wasn't a job that Smith had been in any hurry to create. It was one that Hoglund, by all rights, should have expected to get, and it was the biggest trophy Smith had to offer. The day wore on as the executives by turn pleaded with and cajoled the Spanish executive. Later Lopez would contend he had been verbally tortured by the crew and threatened by Pearce with legal action, but the GM officials contend nothing of the sort took place. In the evening, seeing that the family patriarch was exhausted by the session, Lopez's wife and daughters ganged up on the GM officials and kicked them out. Smith left, wondering if the day had been a waste of time.

But it seemingly wasn't. The phone rang early at the Smiths' home the next morning, where neither Smith nor Lydia had gotten much sleep. Lopez was ready to change his mind, and he wanted to come over to talk about the NAO job. Smith was delighted, told him to come immediately, and phoned other GM executives to join them. But Lydia, increasingly angered by the stress that Lopez had put on her husband, said she had other things to do and set off in the family's Chevy Blazer. A few days earlier, when Lopez announced he was planning to take the VW job, she seemed to be the only one who knew he would be gone no matter what her husband and his colleagues tried to do. "Don't bother trying to talk him into staying," she said. But Smith wasn't ready to give up. That Saturday, Lopez, Wagoner, and Pearce arrived just after she left on her errand. The group settled into the Smith's white living room and began to discuss Lopez's future. The offer of the NAO president's job was made again by Smith, and this time Lopez accepted the job. In Florida during the weekend, Hoglund was inwardly steaming about the wooing Smith had done. "We don't crawl after people. It's not the GM way," he was later heard grumbling by some of the planners.

But he wasn't there to stop Smith. Lopez brought with him a copy of the contract he'd signed with VW. Could Pearce tell him if it bound him to VW? "It was in German, and I couldn't read it," Pearce said later. Smith, buoyant, said he thought any problems could be addressed. Lopez seemed confident enough to place a call to Germany to tell VW he wasn't going to come. At noontime, the group was still lounging about the living room, kicking around ideas for Lopez's new administration, when Lydia Smith came in the back door. She'd seen the cars still in her driveway and in the street outside, and drove past her house slowly, hoping the meeting would break up so she wouldn't have to confront Lopez. "Then I decided, 'This is my own house,'" she says.[13] Lopez came into the kitchen, ostensibly to kiss her on both cheeks, and Lydia mockingly shook her fist in his face. "You've given me two sleepless nights!" she told Lopez. He pulled back, protesting. "But I have had four sleepless nights!" he replied. Hearing this, one manager who worked with Lopez later scoffed, "He never lost a night's sleep over anything. Inaki could straighten things out in his mind so that they made sense to him."

That afternoon, Simonetti started work on the speech Lopez would give to reporters and employees on a television hookup on Monday. On Sunday morning GM public relations officials got on the phone to key reporters, confirming that Lopez was going to stay and hinting the company would name him to a top job at NAO. Smith made his own series of phone calls to members of the NAO strategy board, letting them know what had transpired. He ran into a buzzsaw of protests: Far from supporting the NAO leader in his attempts to keep Lopez, at least one third of the board felt Smith should have let him go. Meanwhile, Lopez, meeting at the Tech Center with a team of NAO planners and purchasing staff members, occasionally would disappear to do some telephoning of his own. It turned out he was trying to up the ante from Volkswagen by insisting GM was trying to tie him to a five-year contract. That wasn't true and Lopez knew it, and eventually Piech discovered Lopez was lying, too. He would get revenge on Lopez in a way the Spaniard didn't expect as he craftily negotiated.

Even as he was playing the double agent, Lopez and his team set to work with huge sheets of paper and Magic Markers. They were putting together a plan to dramatically remake NAO in the image of Opel's European operations. Down the side of one of the sheets, Lopez drew circles, each representing a core area of NAO operations: manufacturing, powertrains, chassis, safety, engineering. Across the top, he drew each of GM's car and truck platforms. Drawing lines down from the top, Lopez envisioned a system where each type of vehicle would draw on the expertise of each area of the company. There would be a cadence to the system; as one vehicle project was finished, the team that worked on it from each of the core areas would go on to the next vehicle, marching across the page. To make the system work, Lopez planned a full-scale housecleaning at NAO. He planned to toss out a whole flock of tradition-bound executives and install his own crop of baby boomers along with a handful of veteran executives he thought would be loyal to him.

The plan, if enacted, would have shaken GM even more than Stempel's plant-closing announcements or the boardroom coup. Lopez and his group literally were going to rebuild GM from scratch, with no respect for the past. If the UAW gave the company trouble, Lopez was even prepared to lock the union out. That would have shut down GM's operations and triggered plant closings at Ford and Chrysler, too, for their factories depended on parts from GM. It was a recipe for certain disaster, but one that did not seem to bother him.

Aspects of the plan were outlined on flip charts that would be shown to senior managers at the first meeting of Lopez's NAO strategy board the following week. "It was a new way of structuring an auto company that would have been enormously powerful," says one of the GM staffers who worked on the plan.

But VW, in Germany, had no intention of letting him try it. On Saturday, as the group was laughing in the Smiths' kitchen, the German carmaker issued an odd statement saying Lopez's departure from GM was going to be delayed for a year because he could not get out of his contract. That wasn't true; at the time, senior executives did not have binding contracts with the company, only employment agreements that discussed salary and job titles. But Piech, bent on winning Lopez, was not about to give up. German press reports, never confirmed by VW officials, hinted that the VW boss reminded Lopez of "our little secret"—a series of files that had been shipped by Lopez to Wolfsburg the previous week. Presumably in the files were the plans for the next-generation Corsa, material that VW wasn't supposed to have. Piech kept up the pressure, using the plant in Spain as a lure. Remember how much you've wanted that plant, he reminded Lopez. You know that you've made a lot of promises—to the Spanish government, to the people in the Basque region, to the investors, to the King of Spain. Lopez wavered, insisting that he would remain in Detroit for the kind of job that executives with far more tenure would kill to have.

On Monday morning word of Lopez's decision to stay made the front page of Detroit's two newspapers. Lopez came into his Tech Center office early in the day to alternately meet with purchasing staffers and go over the final draft of the speech with Simonetti, which included this sentence: "These last few days show that this company has soul and passion." She told him that requests had poured in for interviews, but he agreed to do only two, one with the author of this book and another with a reporter for the *New York Times*. At midmorning, Simonetti said good-bye to Lopez so she could head from Warren downtown to GM headquarters. "I'll see you later," Lopez told her. He was going to be driven downtown by one of his warriors. Simonetti remembers that Lopez seemed distracted, but she assumed it was because of the stress of the weekend and the big challenge he faced as head of NAO. She also was trembling with excitement because Lopez told her he planned to make her head of GM's public relations operations, an unprecedented leap five steps up the GM hierarchy and a move that would put her in a tiny group of prominent women at the car company.

But after Simonetti left, Lopez got on the phone to Margarita. "They were speaking in Basque, which was always a bad sign," says one of the people in the room. "He turned to [a warrior], and said, 'Let's go.' Everybody assumed that meant downtown to the [GM] building."

That morning, Smith was in Lansing, Michigan, at GM's mid-sized car factory, preparing to speak to a monthly session on quality. Gathered together were the heads of all of GM's car divisions and a number of its top executives. The morning had not gotten off to a good start: Michael Mutchler, head of GM's manufacturing operations and one of the men most unhappy with Lopez's strong-arm tactics, had approached Smith as he walked in the door and threatened to resign. Smith, shaken, urged Mutchler to hold on until he knew what Lopez was going to do. Though the strategy board had been informed of Lopez's appointment, other senior managers had as yet not been told anything officially about his pending promotion. So Ron Haas, vice president of quality, thought it would be a good time for the CEO to tell the group what he planned for Lopez. Smith, looking a bit uncertain, agreed. At the conclusion of his talk, he told the group that "this afternoon, we're going to announce a big promotion for Inaki at NAO." Haas noticed that Smith did not say Lopez was going to be named NAO president. "In retrospect, it's probably a good thing that he didn't," Haas said.[15]

Because as Smith was speaking, a friend of Lopez's arrived at the GM building with a letter from the Spanish executive. He told the guard he was to deliver it personally to Smith's secretary, Terry Miller, in Smith's fourteenth-floor office. She phoned Harry Pearce, who went to the lobby to fetch it. Though rambling and emotional, the words were clear: Lopez was jumping ship. Smith's secretary grabbed the phone to find her boss. He was just getting into a car to go to the Lansing airport, from where he would fly back to Detroit. It was around 12:30 P.M. and the press conference to announce Lopez's appointment was just two and a half hours away. Hearing the news, Bruce MacDonald, then GM's public relations VP, told Smith he would cancel the media session, shut down the satellite, and put out a statement. But Jim Crellin, GM's corporate news director, insisted that Smith should proceed with the press conference. Smith, stunned and practically in tears, agreed. He would meet with reporters and tell them the story of the past few days. First, he'd call Lydia. She wasn't home, having gone out for lunch. So he left a message and sat with MacDonald to put together a fairly frank chronology.

Around 2:30 P.M. reporters were starting to gather in the GM press conference room, chuckling over the events of the weekend. In GM's Washington office, the TV screen in its conference room ticked down the minutes and seconds until the satellite broadcast was to begin. Six-foot-six-inch Washington PR manager Bill Noack took the author aside, telling her to come into his office after the press conference to conduct a telephone interview with Lopez. The pair then joined the others in the conference room, chatting and watching the clock tick down. With four minutes and fourteen seconds to go, Noack's secretary came in to tap him on the shoulder with a message from Detroit. At almost that moment, in Bloomfield Hills, Lydia was rushing in the door, planning to sit in her airy white kitchen to listen to the news conference on the radio. She saw that the message light was blinking and touched the playback button. Her husband's voice, sounding as dejected as she had ever heard it in five years of marriage, came on the speaker. "Inaki bolted. I'll talk to you later," he said. She stared at the kitchen counter, the room seeming to spin around her.[15]

On her kitchen radio, station WWJ switched live to the GM building for the press conference. On the television screen in Washington one could see Smith, with MacDonald, walk up to the podium in the GM press room. His eyes red-rimmed and tired, he began by saying that GM planned to announce Lopez's promotion, "but he is gone and we don't know where he is. It is not clear to me what his intentions are or where he is at this time." He went into a version of what had happened the past few days, his fingers drumming the podium in quiet frustration. "I'm terribly disappointed in the way it has played out. We didn't want to lose Inaki. We thought we had brought him back into the fold," he said. Listening to her husband's voice, not being able to see him, Lydia feared he would break down and cry. Only seeing the press conference on videotape later did she realize that he had stayed in control.

The virtually all-male crowd, unused to such candor and raw emotion, at first hardly seemed to know what to ask him. It was like the awkward questions asked by reporters of family members of plane crash victims. Smith gamely answered everything thrown at him, disclosing for the first time the idea Lopez had for Plateau Six, his superefficient auto factory. It was a brave performance that raised hopes Smith would always be so forthcoming—something that was not to be. Later critics would say that the Lopez affair had badly damaged Smith's credibility. It proved he was no pro at negotiating, unlike Piech, who seemed to have no hesitation about reminding Lopez that he had him by the short hairs. Some inside GM argue that Lopez left because he was concerned, in the end, that he did not have Smith's full support. The plan he wanted to try was so radical that he was certain Smith would never let him do it. Lopez says that's not the case: "He would have supported me."[16] Says Smith: "We'll never know, will we?"[17] And the plant in Spain was so close to Lopez's heart that GM's refusal to build it for him simply showed he didn't have Smith's complete backing against Hughes. In the coming weeks, top GM executives, as well as former CEO Stempel, would say publicly that naming Lopez head of NAO would have been a disaster for the corporation. Mutchler, the most unhappy with Lopez, decided to withdraw his threat to resign and stay on.

The questions concluded, Smith walked out of the press conference and went back up to his office. That night, Taylor and some of the staffers who'd worked on Lopez's reorganization plan returned to the conference room where just a day before they'd been drafting the new look of GM. Through the door walked Bill Hoglund, back from Florida, his lean frame sagging and his face drawn. Spotting the flip charts on the easel, Hoglund picked them up, tucked them under his arm, promising to lock them away, and left. Sensing a chapter had ended, Taylor and the other Lopez warriors finally called it a night, adjourning to a dimly lit bar near the GM Tech Center. Joined by a dejected Simonetti, the group held their own wake for Lopez, getting royally drunk, laughing and crying at the departure of their leader.

Certainly Smith's sentiments were with them. That evening, he pulled his car into the drive and walked into the living room, dropping into one of the stuffed chairs by the fireplace. "Boy, could I use a drink," he said to Lydia.

That afternoon Smith had told the reporters that GM didn't know where Lopez was. In fact, as the press conference was under way, he was in a private plane with Margarita, headed for Chicago's O'Hare Airport. There the couple boarded a Delta flight for Frankfurt, where they were met the next morning by VW officials who whisked them off to Wolfsburg. Incredibly, Lopez was said to have had a panic attack. He phoned back to Detroit, saying he changed his mind again and wanted to come back to NAO. But Smith had had enough. The day before, when asked if he'd take Lopez back, he had answered, "I think this is over." Though secretly Smith would have welcomed Lopez on any terms, he knew the GM board would now never agree to let him return even though they'd begged him to keep Lopez at GM. So Lopez was stuck in Germany at VW, where an incredible corporate dogfight was about to begin.

CHAPTER • 8

Getting Back on Track

$\mathbf{F}$ar from paralyzing GM, Lopez's departure seemed to create an odd kind of euphoria among senior GM managers—like the high that a widow often feels during the crazed, shock-filled days just after her husband's death, when there are so many decisions to make in so little time. The ranks quickly closed behind Smith, who uttered not a word of public reproach against his friend. Even in response to the letters of sympathy that poured in from his colleagues and business associates, Smith was careful to mention Lopez's accomplishments. As the months passed, and GM's legal attack on Lopez and VW escalated, Smith took the high ground. But most of those those beneath him were not so charitable.

The most vehement in his criticism was Hughes. Almost overnight, the international chief went from becoming Lopez's biggest supporter to his most bitter enemy. At the Paris Auto Show in 1992, Hughes sprang to Lopez's defense in the wake of suppliers' gripes about his cost-cutting tactics. "The criticism is very unjustified. In five years, American suppliers will say, 'Thank you, Dr. Lopez,'" Hughes declared.[1] But when Lopez defected, Hughes, along with Opel chairman David Herman, led the public battle against him. Both men were widely suspected of leaking, or directing the leaks of, countless documents, information, and tips about the wrongs that Lopez had done as he laid the groundwork for his escape to VW. Hughes's attacks on Lopez escalated even as Smith became more and more philosophical. It became almost an obsession, and a topic that Hughes would voluntarily introduce into

197

conversations even when the discussion was on an entirely different subject. Other industry officials watched, almost in bemusement, as Hughes went after Lopez. "They had better not complain too much," Mercedes-Benz chairman Helmut Werner confided to the author during a dinner at the Geneva Motor Show in 1994. "Lopez was a product of the GM system."

As Hughes saw it, the Lopez battle was more than a case of one executive leaving his employer for another. That happened all the time in the industry, although less so at GM than anywhere else. The Lopez case was an intellectual-property dispute of the highest order. According to "the rules" by which people in the auto industry operated, an executive who left a company was allowed to take ideas, knowledge, brainpower. No company would try to stop another from using the experience of the executive that they'd hired away. There were some standout cases of times when that had been costly. In the late 1970s, Harold Sperlich, then an executive at Ford, pushed the number-two U.S. carmaker to build a small van meant for carrying people, not just cargo. Up until then the only such vehicle that had seen any market success was the Volkswagen Bus (later renamed the Eurovan). Sperlich argued that the baby boom generation, whose members had begun to marry and have their first children, would be the perfect market. His idea was never taken seriously at car-obsessed Ford. But when Sperlich jumped to Chrysler, the struggling number-three company was eager for anything that could set it apart from the competition. It latched onto Sperlich's idea, called it a "mini-van," and virtually created the market for people haulers in 1983 that it still dominates.

Some insiders at Ford grumbled, but no one ever accused Sperlich of taking documents dealing with the small van. The Lopez case was different. Hughes, and GM's chief counsel, Harry Pearce, saw grounds to go after the Spanish executive. They concocted a series of legal attacks. The first came just a few days after Lopez left Detroit. Seven of his purchasing agents, most of them Spanish as well, vanished from GM and Opel as soon as Lopez boarded the private jet that took him to Chicago. None gave notice to GM that they were leaving or told coworkers good-bye. "They were there one day, and then they were just gone," says a GM staffer. In court in Germany, Opel sought an injunction to stop VW from hiring or making job offers to any GM staffers or personnel.

Through the spring of 1993, rumors flew that Lopez had taken more than just a few colleagues and his know-how to VW. In May the German magazine *Der Spiegel* pulled it all together in one of the most famous cover stories in its history. Its title can be translated as "The Unscrupulous One." In it, a team of thirty *Spiegel* reporters laid out, in detail, the allegations of Lopez's actions, disclosing he had taken plans for the next-generation Opel Corsa, price lists for GM components, and the blueprints for the Plateau Six plant that he had tried to convince GM to build. The cover caused an uproar, and made Lopez, already a business-world celebrity, a hunted man. Things came to a head in Oklahoma City. It was an unlikely spot for a stop on the Lopez tour, but it was the site of the General Motors annual meeting that year. Hughes joined Smith and Smale at a news conference afterward. The session was drifting to a close when a local reporter, asking a question that sounded scripted by GM's public relations department, shouted from the back for an update in the Lopez case. Hughes replied that GM had filed a lawsuit seeking criminal charges against him. It was like dropping a bomb, and the questioning resumed furiously. Obviously unhappy to be asked at length about the man he had once considered a friend, Smith quietly said, "It's a tragedy."

Smith didn't just mean Lopez's defection or the alleged theft of the documents. A few weeks later, on a steamy June night, the Big Three carmakers put their gleaming wares on display on The Mall in Washington. Dozens of cars were parked outside the Smithsonian Institutions as GM, Ford, and Chrysler celebrated the auto industry's newfound sales comeback in a massive PR campaign to woo Congress. Along with a herd of executives from the carmakers, Smith spent the evening shaking hands and schmoozing with members of Congress, who filled the red-white-and-blue tents across from the Smithsonian Castle. Lopez was on his mind as he picked up a buffet plate, took a couple of slices of ham, and invited the author to join him. "What are you going to do about Inaki?" Smith was asked before he'd even had a chance to take a bite. The mournful look, so familiar that spring, came into his eyes. "You have to understand what he did. He has stolen our future," the CEO replied. Smith explained that Lopez was one of the few people at GM who understood the new manufacturing concept called agile manufacturing. It was just beginning to be discussed in automotive circles as the successor to lean manufacturing, a phrase coined by professors at the Massachusetts Institute of Technology to describe the efficient methods Japanese automakers had developed to produce cars and trucks.

Agile manufacturing was more than just an exercise in efficiency. It was a whole new mindset that would allow carmakers to change the types of cars and trucks, and their volumes, according to what customers demanded. It put the emphasis on speed, not on sales numbers. In an agile atmosphere, carmakers would be able to make profits similar to those they earned in the old days when they maximized economies of scale. Agile manufacturing required a company to remake itself from the inside out so that it could be able to act quickly. It required new relationships with suppliers, who would have to be able to respond to the car market as rapidly as the automakers did. The idea was at the heart of Lopez's plans for the Plateau Six plant, Smith explained, which made it even more important that GM pursue the case. It also made it even clearer why Lopez was so valuable to GM—and why VW courted him so ardently. At a time when GM hadn't yet embraced lean manufacturing, Lopez was one of the few people at GM who understood what came next and could help others embrace it.

Throughout the year after Lopez left GM, as the all-out battle between the carmakers escalated, German prosecutors conducted their investigation. During the summer of 1993, it appeared that GM would win. Investigators discovered boxes of GM documents in a vacant apartment in Wiesbaden, about fifteen miles from Opel headquarters in Russelsheim, that had been rented by a pair of the warriors. VW and Lopez claimed the documents had been planted at the apartment to make them look bad. But the disclosure fueled intense speculation that VW's board would dump Lopez. "Is he dead meat or what?" PaineWebber analyst Steve Girsky cracked. His goose, however, was not quite cooked. Forced by the furor to defend himself, Lopez contended GM was pursuing him because it was embarrassed to have lost him to VW. At one particularly painful court hearing, a number of Lopez's closest GM aides, including Taylor and Simonetti, were called to testify about the events in the days before his departure. Simonetti, making her first-ever trip to Europe, was on the stand for several hours. She told of meeting with Lopez the weekend he was offered the job of NAO president to draft the speech he would give on Monday. (Lopez, in one press report, denied having met with her and said the speech was written by someone else on the PR staff.) She maintained her dignity and her utter loyalty to GM during her testimony. But afterward Simonetti sat by herself for hours in the Kurpark, across from the elegant Nassauer Hof hotel in Wiesbaden, staring at a fountain and trying to make sense of the events that brought her to testify against her former mentor.

Despite what seemed like irrefutable evidence against Lopez, here was not enough to bring charges against him. In Germany prosecutors must go further to build a case than in the United States. Reasonable suspicion of wrongdoing is enough to file charges in the U.S., which must then be proved in court. In Germany, prosecutors must present an actual chronology with evidence that a crime has been committed before the case begins. The prosecutors, in effect, conduct a mini-trial of their own as they build a case. That is why the Lopez case dragged so long without criminal charges actually being filed against him. It is why GM and Opel kept going to court, seeking temporary injunctions against Lopez and the "seven warriors" who absconded to VW with him. And it is a reason GM appealed to the Justice Department to launch an investigation of the Lopez battle on the grounds of intellectual-property theft.

As the controversy swirled around them, Lopez and his boss, Piech, became larger-than-life personalities. German magazines showed Lopez walking the streets of Amorebieta, where there was talk of building a statue in his honor. Piech posed for *Spiegel* floating in his pool, wearing a skimpy thong bathing suit and a glint in his eye. And the pair actually found time to tackle the massive financial problems that faced VW. Lopez renamed his PICOS program KVP and began the same attacks on VW's tangled supply base as he had conducted at GM. He suffered one setback: VW, in deep financial trouble, told him it did not have the money to build his cherished plant in Spain. It almost seemed like punishment for the consternation he had caused the company. The distractions of the court challenges may have made his job more difficult to pull off, for VW's balance sheet did not improve quickly. Finally, two years after he got to VW, the German carmaker began to show progress, though far slower than Lopez had seen at GM. "In ten months at GM, we had things fixed," Lopez reflected during the 1995 Geneva Motor Show. "I have never seen a company turn around so fast. Here [at VW], we are twenty percent there. We have eighty percent to go but we know what we have to do to get there."[2]

Lopez, by that time, had emerged as something of a victor. Thus far he had escaped criminal charges. He still had a job despite constant rumors that VW's board wanted to dump him—or send him off to Spain, where he would be immune from prosecution by German authorities. Rumors circulated in the summer of 1995 that he and Piech were no longer on speaking terms. It did not matter that GM and VW continued to hold high-powered legal negotiations to settle the case (GM was represented by Ira Millstein, counsel to the outside directors, while VW hired the former U.S. ambassador to the Soviet Union Robert Strauss's Washington law firm.) Looking robust and confident as he talked about the time he had spent at GM, Lopez contended in 1995 that he was a target only because GM knew how valuable he could be. "These people who are saying these things about me—they were not saying them when I was there," said Lopez. His machismo seemed to soften as he reflected on how his departure had hurt Smith, the man who had put his faith in him and had taken such a risk on his behalf. "Jack Smith is a good man," he said, as his wife Margarita, standing nearby, nodded in agreement. "Jack Smith will save General Motors. You must tell the people at General Motors to follow Jack Smith."

After Lopez left, Smith showed his faith in Wagoner by giving him the worldwide purchasing job in addition to his duties as CFO. It was a surprise move, since most in the company expected that a purchasing executive like Taylor or Perriton would move up. And Wagoner did not seem to have much purchasing expertise. However, he'd taken a keen interest in what Lopez was doing in Europe, where Wagoner served as CFO in the late 1980s. GM Brazil was implementing a European-style purchasing organization when Wagoner arrived, causing a smaller yet vocal uproar among Brazilian parts companies. Lopez paid a visit and was pleased to see his ideas being put into practice. When the Spaniard left GM, Smith decided Wagoner should have his job. "Jack just one day asked me, 'Would you be willing to take this thing on?' and I thought about it and said, 'Hey, if you think that's the right thing to do,'" Wagoner says.[3] "It wasn't as far-fetched as it seemed from the outset because I had some understanding." Having two high-profile executives in the purchasing job gave the once-maligned speciality a much higher strategic position within GM. "It's a huge piece of our business, and we've consistently [underestimated] it," Wagoner says. "Look, our main responsibilities are engineering and manufacturing, but if we don't purchase well, we blow all that."

In the months after Wagoner took charge, GM executives were publicly conciliatory toward the suppliers whose feathers had been ruffled by Lopez's aggressive approach. Wagoner met with many, patiently listening as they railed about Lopez, and assuring them GM would reform. That gave rise to the thought that Wagoner, with his easygoing personality, would be softer in demanding savings, which did not prove to be the case. Under Wagoner, the purchasing managers were just as demanding of efficiency as they had been before. While the grumbling among suppliers died down, it did not completely cease.

Unhappiness among the parts producers helped exacerbate GM's biggest problem: product development. In 1994, more than a year after intense rehabilitation work began, Smith told GM's top 100 managers, "Product development is our biggest competitive disadvantage." GM took far too long, and spent far too much money, to conceive, design, develop, and manufacture its cars, and it could not figure out how to target them to customers once they reached showrooms. According to a Harbour Associates study, it cost GM $2,000 more per vehicle to bring an automobile to market than Ford spent, $800 more than Chrysler. GM's "everyone for himself and his car project" culture that permeated the company until the early 1990s was partly to blame. So was its emphasis on profitable large cars to the detriment of wider-selling medium and small cars.

In the late 1980s, GM's management committee was faced with funding a pair of $30,000-plus luxury cars whose combined sales probably would not top 100,000. At the same time, development work had begun on the next-generation compact Chevrolet Cavalier and Pontiac Sunfire, of which the two divisions could sell upward of 300,000 a year. Cash was running short and the managers had to decide which car to support and which to delay. The choice, almost without debate, was the luxury program, which eventually gave birth to Oldsmobile Aurora and Buick Riviera. They were prestigious cars but hardly addressed GM's basic need to attract large numbers of younger consumers. "Why in the world would you fund Aurora and not the Cavalier?" a former GM executive grumbles. The answer was easy: Aurora and Riviera potentially earned GM higher returns. And they were the kinds of cars that GM executives liked to drive.

Such decisions led to a stop-and-stop mentality that was destructive to North American net income and devastated the morale of the product development teams. A Japanese auto industry study showed that for every day a company delayed an active car program, $1 million was lost in potential revenue and in the cost of starting up the program once it had stalled. Every six months a company fell behind, the cost was $180 million on top of what had already been funded. And the longer a program took to become a car or truck, the less likely it was that the vehicle would meet buyers' tastes, needs, and desires because the market research that had been done at the beginning of the program might be outdated. With all its capabilities, it took GM a minimum of four years simply to follow the steps of product development. Counting delays that set in, it usually took the company five to six years to complete a project. Japanese automakers could follow the steps in three years, and in some experiments were able to complete a car in as little as twelve months.

Fixing product development would be tougher than any of the planners, strategy board members, or Smith imagined. There was no one place to start, and plenty of history to battle. Though engineers, manufacturing experts, and marketing staffers had begun by the early 1990s to work more closely in teams, traces of the old walls between the disciplines existed. GM's designers, once called stylists, still seemed a breed apart. They isolated themselves from the rest of the GM Tech Center in their streamlined Saarinen building. GM was also rife with duplication. There was no single way to develop a car, just as there was no standard steering wheel, lug nut, or single key that would open the door and turn on the ignition. (The latter was one of the most irritating things customers reported about driving GM cars. Women, concerned for their safety, complained of having to fumble with one key to open the door and another to start the car. Men grumbled that they weren't able to switch off the ignition, jump out and open the trunk with the same key. GM for years had gotten its ignitions and locks from different suppliers. It finally went to a single key in 1994.) Duplication, as Lopez had discovered in his eight months in worldwide purchasing, was a major financial drain that could turn into big savings if it were addressed.

Late in 1992, the planners had come up with a starting point. The previous June the planners had told the board NAO would cut platforms from twelve to seven, but at the time they had not figured out how or what would happen once there were fewer platforms. Now they had some firmer ideas about how to coordinate the streamlined operations. Using Smith's emphasis on "common processes, common systems" as a focus, they devised a concept for a single starting point to bring all of GM's tangled product development operations together. They called it the Vehicle Launch Center. At first the name was confusing, because in automotive terms a car is "launched" when a factory first begins to build it. By contrast, the launch center was meant to be an incubator for each new car and truck program. Under the concept, teams of engineers, designers, manufacturing experts, and marketing staffers would begin their work at the VLC, which GM set up in early 1993 in the basement of a building at the Tech Center, under the direction of executive Gerald Collins.

In theory, each vehicle would spend its first year at the VLC, going through a checklist of the early steps it needed to take before funding could be approved and the team could break off on its own. There would be three different checklists: bill of materials (BOM), which would list the components needed to build the vehicle; bill of process (BOP), which would state the manufacturing methods GM would use to build the vehicle; and bill of design (BOD) which would denote the features it would have. There had to be a complete BOM, BOP, and BOD before a car could leave the launch center. Each GM car or truck would begin life in the same fashion, meeting the same criteria and specifying how it would proceed. And the vehicle teams would be able to draw from ideas that other teams had used. For example, if a mid-sized car team came up with an easier way to manufacture a door panel, the idea could then be shared with the next project that went through the launch center. Once the early work was completed, the vehicle was supposed to be released from the launch center back to the platform that would be in charge of completing its development and marshaling it to a manufacturing plant. The VLC seemed the answer to GM's long search for a way to coordinate car and truck programs that had always gone their separate ways, sharing little information among themselves. "This requires a real element of teamwork," Collins said.[4]

Before any car or truck development could begin, however, GM's market research staff was to play an important role. In the mid-1980s, Robert O'Connell, the former chief financial officer banished to GMAC in the board's management coup, had hired Vince Barabba to head GM's market research activities. Barabba was a former director of the U.S. Census Bureau and had worked for IBM and Eastman Kodak. Tall, outspoken, bearing a slight resemblance to actor Irwin Corey's mad scientist, Barabba was a true outside voice within GM.

He'd first visited the GM building in 1982, while he was still at Kodak, to talk to GM's senior management about innovation. Trying to get across how Kodak scientists translated their ideas into consumer products, he picked up a Kodak disc camera, whose negative was a round, notched piece of film, and began flashing pictures of the men in the dark suits seated at the long conference table. At the rear of the room was Smith, then head of GM's worldwide planning.

For a market researcher, GM seemed to be an untapped font of opportunities. With its five million vehicle sales a year, it certainly had access to more customer input than any other company. Barabba, like Purcell a student of GM history, discovered that GM's marketing efforts were sophisticated even in the 1930s, when it routinely canvassed its millions of owners for their views on GM cars. Barabba found almost unlimited resources in his work, but he did not always find executives receptive to what he had discovered. He had developed a research model he called "voice of the customer." In a 1990 book, Barabba discussed his theory that market research could be refined so that companies could more precisely determine exactly what customers wanted. Instead of just asking customers, "Do you want round headlights?" voice of the customer research involved giving customers a series of choices— "Would you rather have round headlights or square ones?"— and then finding out how much they were willing to pay for the options they chose. "Would you pay ten dollars more for the round headlights? Would you pay thirty dollars more?" Small groups of potential customers would attend clinics, held in shopping mall parking lots, where the market researchers would show them fake versions of GM cars to test their reactions to ideas under consideration.

Such research was being conducted in the 1980s, Barabba says, but top management did not always place as much of a priority on his researchers' conclusions. That changed when Smale became GM's chairman in 1992. Deeply concerned about GM's fuzzy, unfocused marketing efforts that set cars competing against each other for buyers, he asked to talk with Barabba. The two marketing experts formed an almost instant bond. And with Smale's powerful backing, the work of Barabba and his feisty young crew of voice of the customer researchers became of paramount importance within GM. The teams of designers, engineers, manufacturing experts, and marketing officials working on GM vehicles could not proceed until the work by Barabba's teams had been concluded. From a company that had virtually ignored market research in the 1980s, GM swung almost completely in the other direction. This caused some grumbling among members of GM's product development organization, who felt they knew at least as much about the car business as the shoppers in Schenectady whose opinions suddenly carried so much weight.

But Barabba's market research would not just stop with a set of detailed questions. It potentially would change the way GM cars were conceived. He argued that GM needed to more closely fulfill the needs of the customers who ignored its autos. Barabba's research showed buyers in the 1990s were far less wedded to a particular size of vehicle, like a compact car, than they were to what that car could do for them. They might need to haul two children, or lug home antique furniture, or be comfortable at freeway speeds. It was one reason why minivans were so hugely popular. Even grandparents who could have been counted on in the past to buy Buicks were purchasing Chrysler people-haulers because they better fit the needs of their active life-styles. Barabba argued that the most successful auto companies would drop vehicles into slots in the market that meet the needs of the customers, not just crank out replacements for existing models.

All these ideas were critical to the first step of the product development process that Smith hoped to institute in NAO in 1993—the four-phase process, which was intended to bring discipline and consistency to the way GM brought its cars and trucks to life. The model came from Opel's operations in Europe. It was close to the heart of Peter Hanenberger, the courtly international development czar who can explain technical concepts better than anyone except perhaps Microsoft founder Bill Gates. The four-phase process was Opel's attempt to mirror the Toyota development process, widely believed to be the best in the industry and the focus of a 1990 book, *The Machine That Changed the World*. The Toyota process was developed over the past twenty years and generally results in cars that are easy for workers to build, easy for owners to operate, high-quality, and customer-pleasing. It is a series of steps that begin when the first idea is sketched by a Toyota engineer and ends when the car rolls out of the factory.

Opel first embraced the four-phase process in the mid-1980s, when its engineers were working on the replacement for the small Corsa. The ambitious goal was a car that could be transformed into different versions, such as a two-door, four-door, hatchback, or small van, and could even be used as the basis for other car models. Ideally, Corsa could become GM's world car, easy to build in other countries like Brazil and Mexico, and easy to adapt to different markets' needs. (It was smaller than most vehicles sold in the United States, and thus it was not intended for the NAO lineup.) But for Opel to maximize Corsa, it had to keep such concepts in mind from the beginning.

Thus came the four-phase development system, which actually has five phases. The first phase is called "bubble up" because ideas for the car bubble up among the developers like spring water. This is where brainstorming goes on, where customer research is performed, and the early sketches of the car take place. Key suppliers might sit down to offer some ideas for parts and processes that could be used. By the end of bubble up, the developers have a detailed idea of the customer who will buy the vehicle, a comprehensive list of features it will have, an understanding of how it can be built, and what it will look like. If two parts of GM will share the car, like NAO and Europe, developers from both organizations take part in these intitial sessions. Bubble up lasts about a year. In Phase zero, the car has received "concept initiation" status and the team that will do the development work is put in palce. Experts from throughout GM lend their guidance. Up until the end of phase zero, which lasts another year, changes can be made in the car's design and the methods used to build it without much expense and delay. Designers have built clay scale models of the car so the team can see how it will look. If the car is going to be aimed at other world markets, it is here that plans are made for the versions that will be sold. The first two phases are the most information-intensive. By the end of phase zero, GM executives must decide whether to spend the money needed to bring the vehicle to reality or whether more development work needs to be done.

Phase one marks "concept approval," when the project is funded. Now engineering work begins and the expense mounts. The automaker places orders with its suppliers for the tooling it will need in its assembly plants to build the new vehicle. It begins laying out the changes it needs in the factory, often with the use of tiny plastic machines and robots like Lego toys that can be reassembled to test work flow. The plant manager, and sometimes auto workers, takes part. Though it seems simple, projects at GM often bog down here due to fights between GM and suppliers and shortages of key engineers. By the end of phase one a full-sized model exists. In phase two, that model is translated on computer from model to driveable prototype, built by hand from the components that have been ordered based on the engineering specifications. It is here that problems in tooling should be caught and corrected in order to avoid delays later on. Safety experts, who participated in earlier development phases, perform crash tests while environmental engineers test the engine's emissions and noise levels.

By phase three, the vehicle is finished. Pilot versions are being built, one at a time, first on a special assembly line that is used for training, then on the factory's assembly line. Marketing staffers firm up their plans and set the car's price. Early production moves at a snail's pace while adjustments are made and workers learn changes in their routines that the new vehicle requires. Sometimes workers build a handful of the new unit on the same assembly line as its predecessor. This is called a "running model change" and allows the factory to remain in operation even as the production of the new vehicle begins. It is a common practice at Honda, which can retool overnight for a new model year without any interruption in production. More often, however, the factory shuts down for several weeks so it can be overhauled. In GM's case, shutdowns of several months were the norm. When it reopens, production of the new model cranks up slowly, and then more quickly to

Robert Stempel in a characteristically pensive pose. The ousted CEO saw the problems facing GM but seemed too hampered by tradition to act quickly. (*GM*)

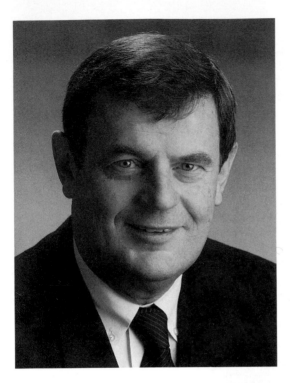

Jack Smith as he looked in his happiest days as president of GM Europe and head of GM's international operations. (*GM*)

Lloyd Reuss, the optimistic GM president whom Stempel picked over Jack Smith as GM's number-two executive. His belief that "the market will come back and save us" nearly sank GM in the early 1990s. (GM)

Jack Smith as he appeared during his senior year at St. John's. He and his classmates did not sell enough ads to publish a bound yearbook and had to settle for a printed brochure. (*Courtesy Joseph Lane*)

Thirty-seven years after graduation, Jack Smith joins some of his classmates from St. John's Preparatory School in Worcester, Massachusetts. *From left:* Don Moran, Jack Conley, Jack Smith, George Sullivan, and Joe Lane. (*Photo by Tasse, Worcester, Massachusetts*)

Seventeen-year-old Jack Smith (*center*) rests his head on his hand during class at St. John's. (*Courtesy Joseph Lane*)

Harry Pearce points to the crumpled GM pickup truck used in the faulty *Dateline NBC* report. After his dramatic press conference, Pearce is surrounded by members of Detroit's automotive press corps. (*GM*)

The first Saturn car and its proud parents. *From left:* Robert Stempel, UAW president Owen Bieber, Roger Smith, and Saturn president Richard "Skip" LeFauve. (*GM*)

Roger Smith passes the torch to a new management team in 1990. *From left:* Robert Schultz, Robert Stempel, Roger Smith, Lloyd Reuss, and Jack Smith. Two years later, only Jack Smith would remain. (*GM*)

Three variations on the Opel Corsa, GM's true world car, built everywhere but North America. Its success frustrated NAO engineers, who called it "that stupid little car." (*GM*)

Ignacio Lopez de Arriortua and his father confessor, Father Joseph Coyle of Three Rivers, Michigan, at the infamous Supplier of the Year awards dinner in Detroit in March 1993. (*GM*)

Lopez poses with members of Detroit's automotive press corps, to whom he gave "hero" awards along with GM's top management. *From left:* GM spokesman Bill O'Neill, James V. Higgins of the *Detroit News*, Marjorie Sorge of *Ward's Auto World*, Edward Lapham of *Automotive Industries*, Joe Szczesny of the *Oakland Press*, the author, and Toni Simonetti, Lopez's spokeswoman. The dinner marked the last time Lopez was seen in public as a GM executive. (*GM*)

"Job One," the official start of production.

The final three phases of the four-phase process take about two years. That is not the end of the product development cycle, however. For about a year after the new vehicle goes into production, the development team spents a lot of time in the factory, diagnosing what went wrong and making notes on what went right. Then work begins anew on the vehicle that will replace the one that has just been introduced. At Opel, the system operates on a cadence. Vehicles follow each other through the steps of the production process—Corsa might be followed by Omega, which is followed by Vectra and Astra. Each specialty—engineering, finance, labor relations, manufacturing—has kept track of the advancements that are made with each new product so that the methods used can be shared with the program that comes next. And each size of vehicle reports to a vehicle line executive, who will stay with the car through at least two complete overhauls, about ten to twelve years. There is no question who is in charge.

It is a system that results in a company clearly focused on the vehicles it produces. Opel, despite the changes Smith made in the late 1980s, could not have prospered without a stream-lined, focused product lineup. "Product is everything," says Opel president David Herman. "Without product, you are dead. Dead."[5] But that was never the case in the U.S., where product was secondary to finance and car guys never made it to the top. That was why the vehicle launch center was so important, Smith felt. Europe did not have one, but Europe had only one center of product development. Before they were abolished, BOC and CPC each had their own processes, but in actuality every car and truck project proceeded at a different pace. The launch center was to be the starting point so that the four-phase process could be implemented in NAO. Smith did not want to see it attempted in bits and pieces, as had happened inside GM in the past. The developers for the Aurora and Riviera, due out in 1994, had seized upon the four-phase process. Smith was glad they had done so, and now he wanted the rest of NAO to follow suit, making it clear that this was not a "flavor of the month" directive. "Jack has said, 'This is not an option,'" said the University of Michigan's David

Cole, who closely advised Smith on technical matters.

The VLC was part of Smith's greater plan to turn the Tech Center in Warren into an active resource for product development. The sprawling campus was supposed to operate as a support staff for the divisions, but like the rest of GM, it was filled with small empires with little coordination and no direct link to GM's operations. The Tech Center played a minor role in production work, even though there were many opportunities for it to do so. Safety operations fell under GM's corporate side. GM's research and development center spent as much time on "pie in the sky" projects with no connection to the automobile as they did on practical applications. Manufacturing was off by itself. So was design. The people within the company who had embraced the gospel of the quality movement had little success winning converts. Now that was going to change.

Smith put Arvin Mueller, a veteran GM executive, in charge of the refocused Tech Center, which Mueller said would flow from the the rest of GM. "NAO is an outfit that has fifty-eight products, seven marketing divisions, and ten thousand some-odd divisions. [The Tech Center] is not adding on to that—it is an extension of it," he said. But there were particular challenges: GM's technical development operations were spread across the bottom half of Michigan. Some engineering work was done in Lansing, 100 miles to the northwest; truck development work took place in Pontiac; and GM had two test tracks—in Milford, Michigan, and Mesa, Arizona. It would not be able to group all of its technical support operations in one place, as Chrysler and BMW were able to do with their gleaming technical development centers.

On the organizational chart, the regrouping of the technical disciplines seemed simple. In reality there were conflicts, beginning with the rivalries and distrust that had grown up among the various organizations, particularly in GM's engineering community, the heart of its product development process. Jay Wetzel, who'd been in charge of engineering at Saturn, was named GM's first North American chief engineer by Smith. Eventually, in a later series of management moves, Wetzel would take GM's design operations under his wing as well. Steeped in the teamwork of Saturn, Wetzel, who'd been given the responsibility for the "bill of materials" in the early steps of product development, wanted the NAO engineering operation to be the equivalent of an automotive "home room." Wetzel likened it to the high school classroom where students spent part of each day hearing announcements, eating lunch, and studying. He wanted the engineers from around GM to pool their knowledge in NAO engineering so that each part of GM could benefit from others' ideas. Yet Wetzel realized that each engineer would have trouble visualizing how his work fit into the big picture, not just of a car project, but of the GM community. One wall of Wetzel's office was covered with sheets of paper, each headed by a different engineering task. Each task was broken down into easy-to-visualize steps, like those used in manufacturing to trace the path of a car or a component through a factory. The exercise allowed Wetzel to see ways engineering tasks could be improved, where backlogs occurred, and possible ways problems could be resolved. It was, he said, the "engineering factory."

Wetzel was anxious to see NAO's engineers, so demoralized by years of product delays, mobilize themselves. With the new platform organization, it was a perfect time for the engineers to have real influence in GM's product development process. He had worked with Hanenberger years before at Pontiac, and knew how focused and motivated the European engineers could be. Wetzel wanted NAO's engineers to be the equivalent of their international counterparts by the end of 1994. "We have to operate like we're on a mission here, with a passion. We need to be engineering commandos, to have that passion, that urgency," he said. Secretly, he wanted to combine the teamwork and customer-centeredness he'd seen at Saturn with the fire that he'd seen among Lopez's purchasing managers.

The combination of Saturn principles and Lopez's practices raised eyebrows at GM, but Wetzel, who'd taken part in so much change in his GM career, did not want to hear the excuses of the past. He wanted to hear about problems so the organization could fix them. On laminated file cards, like those printed with the Saturn mission statement that founders had carried in their breast pockets, Wetzel prepared a list of ten priorities he wanted to see the engineering organization accomplish. Most were technical in nature, but nearly all made sure the engineers concentrated on serving the NAO organization and GM's customers. He wanted all his engineers to understand what was expected of them. "The responsibility of leadership is to set the direction, mobilize the teams, and constantly prune away the ambiguity and the roadblocks," Wetzel said.

Among Wetzel's ten priorities was an emphasis on quality. This was music to the ears of Ron Haas, vice president for quality at GM, who'd been pushing for years for the automaker to pay more attention to the details on its cars and trucks. In quality studies by marketing firm J. D. Power and Associates and in *Consumer Reports'* car-buying issues, GM routinely did poorly. Buick had put on its own quality push in the late 1980s with good results, and Cadillac crowed when its product development organization won the Malcolm Baldrige National Quality Award. But the idea hadn't spread further. That had begun to change in 1990, when Saturn's small cars hit the market. They stunned the industry by capturing the number-three spot on J. D. Power's customer satisfaction index behind Lexus and Infiniti. Winning the CSI was a clear sign that what Saturn had done was on target. Smale, for one, was impressed, and began to urge other parts of GM to step up their quality drive. In the new NAO organization, GM would not introduce any vehicles before their quality met tough standards. It might mean some slow production startups, but GM could not afford to put cars out on the streets and risk damaging recalls later on. Only with the best-quality cars could GM begin to spark the kind of customer enthusisasm that Smith and Smale wanted to see. A payoff came in 1995, when GM cars beat their U.S. competition on J. D. Power's measure of initial quality. Japanese carmakers still took the top spots.

Mueller, Wetzel, Haas, and the others in charge of product development at GM had even greater goals in mind as the NAO organization moved beyond its initial stop-the-bleeding phase and into its restructuring. One of the top priorities was lean manufacturing. For decades consultants had concluded

GM's manufacturing operations were the least efficient in the U.S. auto industry. One of the biggest problems was GM's excess capacity. As Stempel realized, GM could build almost twice as many cars and trucks as it could expect to sell in a year. The costs of maintaining that kind of excess capacity were enormous. Under the restrictions of the UAW contract, GM was barred from simply letting workers go. It had to pay them virtually all their wages and benefits for the life of the contract. During each contract, GM set aside upward of $4 billion to cover such costs.

But the excess capacity was not the only problem. GM used too many parts, compared with its competitors, in each vehicle it built. And because there were too many parts, there were too many steps involved to assemble each vehicle. In a one-story building deep within the Tech Center lay the GM Knowledge Center, where engineers routinely dismantled other companies' cars, then took apart each major piece—doors, trunks, instrument panels—to see what went into making them. Some of the comparisons were startling: GM put twenty-six pieces into a small car door, while a competitor built its door from five pieces. That meant twenty-six separate connections that had to be made, either by a robot or a worker, compared with five steps for the competitor. Piece by piece, GM's factories were simply more labor-intensive. By the mid-1980s, Ford, hit by a financial crunch earlier in the decade, had closed all the factories it planned to shut. Chrysler had trimmed the bulk it gained when it bought AMC in 1987. GM, by contrast, was just getting started.

In 1992 and 1993, copies of *The Machine That Changed the World* lay conspicuously on executive desks or sat on their bookshelves, and the topic of lean manufacturing arose frequently in meetings and interviews. Unlike in the Roger Smith era, where lean manufacturing might have been just another watchword for cutting jobs, Jack Smith's strategy board seemed to understand that the transformation had to come from within. It didn't do GM any good to slash jobs only to still be inefficient once the cutbacks were complete. And GM was twenty years behind Toyota in embracing the concept of lean manufacturing, meaning the progress it made would pale in comparison with its Japanese partner. Yet Gary Cowger, head of GM's advanced manufacturing operations, knew that GM had to do more than become lean. It had to become flexible—a concept at which his predecessors had scoffed.

Until the 1980s GM and its competitors based their operations on mass production. The more cars they built and sold to dealers, the bigger their profits. Factories were classic "flow shops" that had to keep moving, churning out cars, to keep the company in the black. Back aisles were stocked with boxes and crates of parts used to build the cars, sometimes a week's worth. Japanese automakers, by contrast, had found they could not sell the large numbers of cars that their U.S. competitors could force onto consumers. They had to make money by selling a mix of vehicles, and had to be able to build each one at a profit. Their factories became "job shops" that built cars almost to buyers' orders. They kept costs low with "just-in-time" inventory systems, in which parts were delivered to factories only a few hours or even minutes before they were needed.

At Mazda's Hofu plant in Hiroshima, Japan, production schedules for the week were made up the previous Friday, based on customer orders. In Detroit, those schedules had to be set three weeks ahead of time, based on forecasts. Further, Hofu could build nine different vehicles on two assembly lines, everything from Mazda's tiny Carol (whose round design was a forerunner of the Dodge Neon) to the plump MPV minivans. Mazda called it "mixed production," but it was the same as the flexible production system that Cowger wanted to see at GM. Yet the factory was only a start. The vehicles built in Mazda's plants were designed so they could be assembled in its flexible system, a concept called "Design for Manufacturability" or DFM. They were created to be easy to build, much as the Corsa had been in Europe. DFM was a foreign concept at GM, where the philosophical walls between design, engineering, and manufacturing were as thick as concrete. Under the NAO structure those walls were starting to come down, and Cowger could see the opportunities were finally there to make GM a lean organization and someday a flexible one. Certainly, the savings from the idea would be enormous.

Cole, at the University of Michigan, concluded that if Smith were able to pull off all the changes that he had planned in GM's product development process, GM could cut as much as $4,000 to $5,000 per car—for total savings of nearly $25 billion through the middle of the 1990s, as much as Roger Smith had earned (not counting Hughes and EDS) during his decade as CEO. According to Cole's calculations, GM would save the most in five key areas:

- *Plant closings* already announced by Stempel would save $1,000 per car, or $5 billion by the time all the factories closed.
- *Cuts inside ACG*, the components division, would save another $1,000 a car, or $5 billion
- *Design for manufacturability* and streamlined assembly operations would save $500 to $1,000 a car, or $2.5 billion to $5 billion, once all the cars and trucks in GM's lineup had been redesigned. That would take longest, since many would not be overhauled until the end of the 1990s.
- *Streamlined engineering* under Wetzel's engineering factory would save $200 a car, or $1 billion.
- *Quality improvements* throughout GM's operations would save $1,000 a car, or $5 billion.

A year after he came up with his list, Cole quietly shook his head over the opportunities he thought NAO had missed and what the company could have accomplished had it been on target with its myriad ideas and goals. "Obviously I'm disappointed," he said. "I guess they've done what they could do with what they have to work with." For in 1994, it was clear the momentum that seemed to sweep the NAO organization in the first heady months was gone and the company seemed to have stopped in its tracks, trying to figure out what to do next.

CHAPTER ▪ 9

Lost Momentum

On a Friday morning in mid-October 1994, Smith looked at Rick Wagoner and shook his head. "I knew at the start of this week that it was going to be a tough one. But I never expected it to be this bad," he told the forty-year-old NAO president. "Let's hope we don't have too many more like this," Wagoner replied.[1]

His wish would not come true. The next few weeks would be the most dismal of Smith's reign as CEO since Lopez's public betrayal. He would watch as Wall Street's crystalline support of GM's comeback shattered into jagged pieces. GM stock went into a nightmarish downward spiral. And the carmaker, almost paralyzed by its inability to communicate in a time of crisis, could do little to stop the plunge. It was a painful reminder to the giant car company that it could not let up on its turnaround efforts, or risk being abandoned by investors who continued to be wary about GM's chances for longterm success.

The crisis was triggered by two events that came just days apart. On October 21, GM reported its first quarterly North American loss in a year's time in the third quarter. Just two days earlier, U.S. Transportation Secretary Federico Pena unexpectedly trashed the safety of GM's 1973–87 pickup trucks and threatened to order GM to recall them. Taken individually GM might have been able to absorb either and keep moving forward. But both Chrysler and Ford reported earnings of $1 billion for the third quarter, making GM's loss look dreadful by comparison. And Pena's denouncement stunned an auto industry that thought it had a friend in the Clinton administration. The first Smith knew that Pena planned to take action came in a morning phone call in which Pena did all the talking.

In the following four weeks GM shares fell to nearly their lowest point under Smith's leadership. Analyst after analyst on Wall Street slashed earnings estimates, downgraded GM stock, and declared GM's recovery had stopped in its tracks. But the chorus of discovery came well after the fact, for GM had lost its sense of urgency the previous autumn, a year after Smith became CEO. Only a booming industry recovery kept GM's flagging momentum from being more widely discerned. The one-two punch of Pena's attack and the disappointing third quarter earnings report finally brought to the surface months of difficulties that Wagoner and Smith faced in trying to get NAO back on track.

Never underestimate the importance of momentum in the auto industry. It can make a hot car even hotter, a healing company robust, a promising young executive a star. In the car business, success breeds success. And it takes more than spin doctors to get momentum rolling. There has to be a spark to fire it, and it can be a single standout car. After a terrible start to the 1980s, Ford built speed with a series of new designs capped off by the groundbreaking, aerodynamic Taurus. A few years later, Chrysler was wandering close to bankruptcy for the second time in a decade when its leaders woke up and reorganized the company. Lee Iacocca, in his last years as CEO, slashed spending by $4 billion and focused Chrysler on building vehicles, not buying other companies as it had done with mixed success in the mid-1980s. What really saved Chrysler, though, was Jeep Grand Cherokee, followed by the Dodge Viper and the LH mid-sized sedans. By the time the Dodge Ram truck, Neon subcompacts, and Stratus and Cirrus compacts came along in the mid-1990s, Chrysler's sales had moved into high gear.

In the early 1990s GM couldn't boast any cars or trucks as hot as Taurus or the Chrysler fleet. But it did have the excitement of financial success—enough, some thought, to overcome the inevitable letdown that occurred when Lopez left in March 1993. As spring approached, it was clear the car company was starting to climb out of the red ink canyon in which it had been mired for so many years. GM's finances the first half of that year were visibly stronger, as it abandoned unprofitable fleet sales and put the emphasis back on individual customers. Although still weak, GM's lineup, was actually selling. In April, the Chevrolet Cavalier—an eleven-year-old, barebones compact, virtually ignored the past few years as Saturn got all the accolades—became the best-selling car in the United States. Cavalier's success was due in large part to a new concept that was emerging in the industry, value pricing. The idea was part of Fundamental Change and was fleshed out by Vincent Barabba, GM's effervescent director of consumer research. As Saturn had learned, customers hated to haggle over car prices. And young, cash-strapped buyers were most likely to despise it. They felt demeaned enough having to buy small cars without having to dicker for them.

Barabba knew that GM could earn more money on building cars if it had to make few changes on each model. For years automakers had loved option packages that offered customers a series of features like air conditioning and power steering for a lower price than they'd pay by picking out each item individually. Carmakers still earned a profit. Why not package cars this way? Barabba suggested. It would simplify orders for cars, orders for parts that went into them, make a dealer's job easier, and make customers happy. Cavalier was a leading success of the strategy, and there were dozens more; Oldsmobile eventually switched its entire lineup to value-priced cars and GM launched a whole campaign in California built around the concept of streamlined prices.

Over the summer and into the early fall of 1993, GM sales strengthened, cost-cutters kept discovering new ways to save money, and it became clear that Smith was going to make good on GM's promise to break even, before interest and taxes, for 1993. The single hitch seemed to be the slow start to the 1994 model year. GM had trouble launching production of some of its new vehicles. A study showed GM hadn't been able to kick off a new model year without hiccups for the past five years in a row. In the old GM, the news would have been kicked under the rug; in the new GM, the NAO strategy board vowed to find ways to avoid the slow startup problems the following year so the trouble wouldn't be repeated. None of the vehicles coming out that fall was particularly crucial. The big launches would come in 1994, when the new Chevrolet Lumina and Cavalier were introduced.

A year into Smith's tenure as CEO, it was time to stand back and take a look at what had been accomplished. In mid-November GM held its first meeting with auto industry analysts in the year since the tension-filled November 12 session a week after Smith had been named GM's CEO. The gathering in Rye, New York, about thirty miles north of Manhattan, was tantamount to a celebration. Outside, the air was crisp and the sky was blue as the investment advisers arrived in chauffered Lincoln Town Cars, taxis, and their own cars for the daylong session at the Rye Hilton. The burned-out people from GM's finance team, who had worked such long, exhausting hours for so many months, thought they were beginning to see results. GM was going to make it, and the first vision of the power that GM could become someday was beginning to emerge.

Speaker after speaker emphasized to the analysts that the carmaker wasn't going to get fixed overnight, and that the common practices and common processes that Smith was insisting upon were going to take more discipline for a much longer time than anybody had thought. And GM faced a potentially huge financial headache. Late in 1992, amid the financial crises, GM recalculated its unfunded pension liability to reflect ultralow interest rates then in effect. To the pension staff's horror, GM's unfunded liability had mushroomed to $24 billion, the greatest of any U.S. company. Pension liabilities reflect the amount companies have to pay each of their workers and retirees over their remaining lifetimes. The numbers are based on complicated forecasts that reflect assumptions on how long workers will live and the yield from investments that companies make with employees' pension contributions. Each year companies contribute cash to their pension funds, but they also gamble that investments made with that money will grow to cover the rest of their pension liability. The federal government allows a company to have less in its pension fund than it would cost to pay pensions to every worker, but it requires the company to demonstrate that it will be able to fully fund the pension. Unfunded pension liabilities were key issues in the bankruptcies of Eastern Airlines and Pan American World Airways, and the specter of Chrysler employees on the street without pensions spurred Congress to approve federal loan guarantees in 1979.

GM's unfunded pension liability had been growing steadily during the early 1990s. Chrysler also had an unfunded pension burden of about $4 billion, a major obstacle for a company one third the size of GM. Only Ford, whose pension was actually overfunded, escaped the problem. GM's liability swelled in the wake of the lowest interest rates since the 1960s. Low interest rates meant GM earned less on its investments. Coupled with its huge base of potential retirees, the problem loomed large and critical. It shocked GM's ratings agencies, whom the company needed to convince of its health in order to see its long-term and short-term debt upgraded. But GM's treasury staff found what it hoped would be a solution. Treasurer Heidi Kunz and a team of pension experts decided to ask the government for permission to transfer 185 million Class E shares into the pension fund. The shares were not publicly traded, but GM had the right to issue them as a cash-raising tool at any time. So, in effect, GM was issuing EDS to itself in order to pay its unfunded pension liability. Kunz maintained it was a bookkeeping matter that would not hurt the value of EDS but would greatly reduce GM's liability. At the same time, GM would contribute cash to help pay down the pension liability. The plan was announced on the eve of the analysts' conference and seemed to meet with their approval. At the very least it showed ingenuity, and at the most it took care of a thorny problem.

Even though the pension problem was far from being solved at that point (the government ultimately approved the idea in early 1995) and more work needed to be done to implement Fundamental Change, Smith told reporters at an early-afternoon press conference that GM would be profitable in North America in 1994. Even if the economy wasn't quite as strong as GM's economists expected? a reporter asked. Smith paused, and uttered a line he would repeat many times in the next twelve months. "No excuses," he said. Later he joked that if he'd known the next year would be so hard, he would have asked for an excuse. With that declaration, it seemed to GM employees that the long years of worry were coming to an end, and that finally the payoff would start—both for GM and for themselves. Word was spreading inside the company that Smith was happy with the progress that had been made, and was ready to ease back on the pace. According to word of mouth, the CEO wanted the NAO organization to settle in like the foundation for a new house that had just been poured.

When GM signed a new contract with the UAW in October, maintaining the wages and benefits that had been in place the previous three years, it seemed like the strongest sign yet that things were returning to normal. A number of Wall Street analysts worried that GM had missed a golden opportunity to attack its labor costs and increase its flexibility within its assembly plants. Inside GM, however, the status quo looked good. Certainly, GM wouldn't have signed the contract if it couldn't afford it. The truth was that GM could not afford to take on the union when it was implementing Fundamental Change. But since the union seemed mollified, GM staffers began to expect that they'd begin getting raises and be paid bonuses for 1993. Money has always been the big status symbol in the auto industry, especially at GM. Until the bonus-dry 1990s, up to 60 percent of a top executive's annual compensation came through bonuses. A typical middle manager could receive a bonus half the size of his annual salary. Now that GM was back on its feet, many people within the carmaker figured that it was time to be paid back for getting through the crisis.

Thus it was a painful blow when that expectation was bitterly dashed by the man who had raised GM's collective morale the previous February. In an early January 1994 interview with the *Wall Street Journal*, chief counsel Harry Pearce said GM hadn't done well enough in North America for UAW members to get their profit-sharing checks. So that meant that staffers wouldn't get their bonuses or raises. Pearce's remarks made perfect sense to Wall Street and to those outside the industry. After all, without profits how could GM pay profit-sharing? And who could expect a bonus in a year when GM still wasn't making money in North America? Some thought the GM employees were lucky to have their jobs. But GM's president's council hadn't made up its mind about salary increases when Pearce made the comment, nor had GM's board discussed executive compensation. It could not do so until GM's fourth-quarter results had been reported. Pearce spoke on his own—and, inadvertently, his words helped to slow the momentum that had been driving GM.

Over the next few months a series of miscues began to collect. Each on its own wasn't dangerous, but combined they began to stagnate GM. The stallout was almost imperceptible. Indeed, as GM executives got ready for the North American International Auto Show in the first week of 1994, a positive feeling was in the air. The show, held each year in sprawling Cobo Conference Center on the banks of the Detroit River, is the U.S. industry's annual celebration of itself, almost Detroit's version of the Academy Awards. Some years, as in the movie business, there isn't much to get excited about. During the early 1990s slump, when Japanese companies seemed invincible, Detroit companies could seem downright desperate. At one end of the hall would be sparkling imports—the earliest Lexus luxury cars, Infinitis, and peppy Mazdas in their crayon colors. By contrast, offerings from GM, Ford, and Chrysler seemed mired in the past, boxy, cheap-looking, their interiors stuck in some early 1980s time-warp.

Not in 1994. Chrysler, which always went full out to impress the 2,500 international journalists who flock to Detroit, uncovered the Cirrus and Stratus compacts and a flock of intriguing concept cars. Ford put the U.S.versions of its European Mondeo compact on display along with its hot new Mustang. And GM, for once, seemed to have plenty, too. Oldsmobile was showing off the Aurora and Buick had its new Riviera, both of which would go on sale in the next few months. And Cadillac was going to unveil the LSE, an American version of the Opel Omega that would be introduced at the Geneva Motor Show two months hence. In two years' time, if all went well, LSE would join the Cadillac lineup in yet another bid to attract car buyers under fifty.

As reporters jammed ten-deep around the turntable where the car was under wraps, consumer research boss Barabba and Tech Center chief Arvin Mueller seemed on edge. The LSE was supposed to bear the fruit of Barabba's voice of the customer research, which involved taking suggestions from customers, defining what they really wanted in cars and putting it into production. For Mueller, LSE represented the early days of a marriage between engineers and product experts from NAO and their counterparts at the Technical Development Center in Russelsheim. Up on the turntable, Cadillac general manager John Grettenberger was about to unveil the small Lexus-fighter he'd been seeking for years. True, the cobbled-together concept car wasn't the all-new luxury auto he'd wanted to develop in the United States, but it would fill a big gap in his product lineup. Smith, about to see the first example of his global product strategy come to life, jumped up to help Grettenberger pull a cover off the car.

The first cherry-red lines of the converted Omega car came into view—and gradually it dawned on those who took a close look that it was a dog. Mounted on the front end was a sculpted grille with the unmistakable wreathed Cadillac symbol, which had been banished from the Eldorado and Seville luxury cars just a few years before. The car looked lumpy and its rear end was confusion. Unlike Seville, whose striking exterior lines still seemed smooth and clear three years after its debut, the LSE seemed ungainly, not elegant; a Buick or an Oldsmobile, not a Cadillac. When the rounded, classic-looking Omega went on sale in Europe a few weeks later, the contrast to the LSE was sharp. Why hadn't GM just left the car alone? people wondered. Why not put faith in the Opel engineers and leave Omega intact, except for an Americanized interior?

Almost immediately after the show, the Opel designers went back to work on a new rear end for the car. Showing the pieces of clay to a visitor at the Technical Development Center in Russelsheim, they explained how they'd smoothed out the bulbous behind that had plagued the Cadillac. But they were stuck when it came to the front end: Cadillac insisted that the car have a carved-in grille so its buyers would know they were getting a Cadillac. Resignedly they complied, though the new front end was much less garish, at least in white clay, than the Polaroid snapshots of the old front end tacked up to a bulletin board. When Barabba's crew began testing the LSE over the next few months, they learned that the tepid reaction at the Detroit show was just the beginning. LSE flunked not one but two buyer clinics. The market researchers brought together Lexus, Infiniti, Nissan Maxima, and Acura Legend owners and asked them about LSE, not telling them it was a Cadillac. A key point would be their answer to the question, "Would you consider buying this car the next time you are in the market?" Of several hundred people who took part in the clinics, just a handful said they'd consider buying the LSE. The research team didn't give up. In the coming months they'd keep trying to come up with a model that was appealing to tough-to-please import owners. That impressed some GM veterans who say that in the old days LSE would have been quietly scrapped, or worse, introduced in its original form and shoved down dealers' throats. A year later, LSE was renamed Catera—a made-up name rhyming with Sahara—and developers hoped it would be ready for introduction in the United States in 1996.

LSE's stumble was a cautionary note at a time when others were celebrating. February brought Rick Wagoner's announcement that GM had met its target of breakeven earnings before interest and taxes. Late in 1993, Smith had moved his watch from his right wrist to his left, and reporter Alan Adler, then with the Associated Press, noticed it at the auto show and asked him about it. "I've moved it, and that's significant," Smith responded. News that Smith's watch was back on his left wrist—something Lopez had said would be done only when GM returned to record profits—became the story of the holiday season. If Smith was declaring victory, it was time to relax. Maybe the worst days were over after all. On a net income basis GM had lost $1 billion in North America, a sharp contrast to $15 billion in losses over the previous three years. The bleeding had slowed from a gush to a trickle. At the press conference and later in an internal telecast, Wagoner tried to stress the point that GM had significant work to do to get its operations in shape to compete with Ford, Chrysler, and the Japanese.

It was a message nobody seemed to be hearing. With the bleeding under control, the big job was over. What was left? The leadership hadn't explained that part, and certainly the typical employee at GM couldn't say what the second phase of the turnaround plan was to be. In fact, the biggest job was yet to come, and GM was in no way prepared to move forward. The planners knew it and they had informally prepared a pair of documents that, had they been adopted, could have served as GM's badly need Plan B. They could have kept momentum going and headed off the crisis that struck GM in the fall of 1994.

Before he left his planning job to run GM's Brazilian operations in early 1993, Mark Hogan, along with Bob Purcell and the rest of the planning team, sketched out proposals to transform GM's wide-ranging marketing organization and its equally broad product planning system. Fundamental Change II, as the planners called it, was a clean-sheet approach to make GM dealers more responsive to customers and position its cars and trucks so that customers weren't overwhelmed by the different brands and divisions. The planners tackled the problem by asking themselves what would happen if GM was able to take a clean sheet of paper and remake the way it sold its cars and trucks. Why did GM need 10,000 dealers in the United States? they asked. GM's dealership body had mushroomed after World War II, when Americans moved from cities into new suburbs, and again in the 1970s, as they moved from the older suburbs into even newer ones. The rationale had always been that the more outlets for GM vehicles, the better shot GM had at capturing buyers. Put enough GM dealers on main roads, and consumers would undoubtedly go visit at least one when the time came to buy a new car.

In the days when GM had 60 percent of the car market, when cars wore out quickly, and appearances changed significantly every model year, that massive organization had its benefits. But in the reality of the 1990s, with strong competition from Ford, Chrysler, and Japanese and European brands, the proliferation of dealers was a nightmare. Nothing pointed it out more clearly than the success of Saturn, which had just 300 dealers to sell about 300,000 cars a year. Each Saturn dealer sold an average of 1,000 vehicles a year, compared with 300 cars a year or less at the traditional GM dealers, who found themselves competing with one another for the same customers. On New York's Long Island there were sixteen Oldsmobile dealers aiming at 2 million people in one of Oldsmobile's least successful markets. Saturn allowed just two dealers for Long Island, and they often ran out of cars. The planners knew a quick and logical solution would be to yank the right to sell GM cars from superfluous dealers who hadn't met their quotas for years, had poor quality service, and did little to keep customers coming back. But dealers in the United States, in general, enjoy strong protection under state franchise laws that generally bar a car company from pulling a franchise if the showroom is not bankrupt. Dealers take plenty of steps to make sure those laws stay in place; in most state capitals, the lobbyist for the state auto dealers' association is one of the most powerful men, or women, in town.

Knowing they couldn't simply slice the number of GM dealers without lengthy and expensive lawsuits, the planners took a different approach. Why couldn't those dealers stop competing and instead strengthen their ties to one another and to GM? Why not make the dealers ambassadors for GM products, able to service and repair all makes of GM cars, not just the ones they sold? This would truly be listening to the voice of the customer, who couldn't understand why he or she had to travel across town to a Chevrolet dealership for an oil change on a Cavalier when the Pontiac showroom was a block away. The planners suggested that instead of each division tending to its buyers' needs individually, GM should come up with one customer service approach, one toll-free hotline that any company customer could call for help.

Further, the planners thought it was time, during the transformation that was taking place throughout GM, to strengthen each GM division's identity. Smith had often reiterated his belief that there was room for each GM division, despite frequent calls for GM to streamline its ranks by dumping one of its brand names. If that was going to be the case—and not all the planners thought it was necessary to keep all of the divisions—then make their identities crystal-clear and supply them with products that would reinforce those identities. Make Saturn the clear foreign car competitor. Make Chevrolet the clear mass-market leader. Transform Cadillac into a clear luxury marque. And, at the same time, streamline the divisional organizations. There were far too many regional offices, zone offices, district managers. A Chevrolet manager once counted eight levels between the customer and Chevy general manager Jim Perkins. That meant any message that customers were sending had to fight its way through layers of bureaucracy before it could get to the top. The more people involved in selling cars, the less profit GM could take in on every vehicle. Ford and Chrysler didn't carry such overhead, and the GM planners could see the difference it made in net income per vehicle. They thought the plan could be a logical handoff from the original Fundamental Change program, and figured it would run from 1993 through 1994.

But the planners knew that to carry out Fundamental Change II, GM would have to go back to basics on the way it conceived, developed, and manufactured its cars and trucks. There was no point in having clear identities in the showroom if vehicles weren't created to meet those identities. So the planners sketched together what they called Fundamental Change III, a scheme for making it easier and clearer to bring vehicles to market. A key portion of the plan would have given most of the power in making decisions about vehicles to the platform organizations—the teams of engineers, designers, manufacturing experts, and market researchers—that worked on each size of vehicle. Each platform would have a clear leader who would have the right to block anybody who tried to meddle with the car or truck under development. The idea of a platform honcho was rooted in Toyota's organization, which had superpowerful chief engineers called *sushas* who could stand up to executives who got in the way. In Europe, Opel had similar platform chiefs in its program managers. In the past, GM's car and truck divisions could lobby for or demand different kinds of models to fill out their lineups, even if they threatened to cannibalize the sales of another division. Under

Fundamental Change III, that could no longer happen. Nor could executives stick their fingers into car and truck programs as they had so many times in the past.

The planners wanted Fundamental Change III to begin concurrently with Fundamental Change II, which they hoped to kick off in 1993. But they figured it would take longer to fix product development because of its complexity. So they saw Fundamental Change III as the company's focus from 1993 through the end of 1995. Some in the group argued there should be another plan to take GM forward after the three Fundamental Change plans were finished. They even came up with a name for it: Operation Gladiator, the blueprint for a lean organization. Hogan, figuring he couldn't pitch too much at once, decided to save the fourth plan for later.

Emboldened by the board's reception of the original Fundamental Change plan and the widespread acceptance of its ideas, Hogan and Purcell went to see Mike Losh in late 1992 to talk about ideas for Fundamental Change II. It would be up to Losh, whom Smith had named vice president for sales, service, and marketing, to implement the changes that the planners suggested as part of Fundamental Change II. But Losh did not agree with the planners. In an eerie echo of Lloyd Reuss's refusal to consider the original Fundamental Change proposal, Losh told Hogan he did not see any need to change GM's marketing organization so dramatically. The meeting turned acrimonious. Members of the planning team say that Losh, irritated by the sweeping suggestions and the potential job cuts the planners proposed, all but threw the visitors out of his office. Fundamental Change II was tucked away in planners' files in a folder next to Fundamental Change III. Without the reforms of II, the planners knew that it was hopeless to even talk about fixing product development. Hogan says diplomatically that the plan "died in its embryonic state."

Inside the company, the episode coincided with the breakup of the group of strategists whose work had been so crucial to GM's turnaround. In January 1993 Hogan was given the GM Brazil job that Wagoner had held before Smith named him GM's chief financial officer the previous November. He hadn't been on a list of possible candidates that had circulated a few months before inside GM's international operations. When his appointment was announced, it was as much as surprise in Latin America as it was to Hogan himself. Just a few months later, Purcell was gone, too. GM's chairman, John Smale, thought GM should conduct a worldwide study that pulled together the products GM planned to build in North America and elsewhere for the rest of the decade. Smale wanted to see whether there could someday be one big product development plan with a few core vehicles that could be sold in nearly all GM's major world markets. Purcell was detached from the planners to work on the study in concert with John Smith (no relation to Jack) who ran GM's European planning organization. Their report projected the company over fifty years— something no one else at GM had ever dared try to do. When the plan was complete, Purcell went to GM's electric car program and Smith headed for GM's Allison Transmission operations in Indianapolis.

Though other planners took their places, the successors lacked the spark, chemistry, and influence of the group whose ideas helped to save the company. And as 1994 wore on, it soon became clear that without a team of visionaries keeping the strategy board intent on implementing change, NAO's sense of urgency was in danger of disappearing.

In one of the early drafts of Fundamental Change the planners wanted GM to anoint the 1994 Chevrolet Lumina a landmark product and put major resources behind making the car a success. As things turned out, it was just as well that GM didn't do so. Lumina was originally set to be introduced in late 1993, the long-awaited replacement to the disastrous mid-sized car that was first introduced in 1988. A member of the GM-10 family, Lumina was supposed to be GM's best crack at winning back mid-sized car buyers who'd defected to Taurus, Toyota Camry, and Honda Accord. From the start it was a piece of junk. Quality was lousy, the car was simply ugly, and its interior was cheap. To top it off, it hit the market first as a two-door—ludicrous considering its main competition was the four-door Accord. Buyers fled Lumina, and the only market GM could find for it was rental car fleets. Frequent travelers joked that the only thing worse than getting stuck in a holding pattern at O'Hare Airport was finding they'd been assigned a Lumina on the ground.

By 1993 more than 70 percent of Lumina sales were to fleets, often at a loss of $2,000 a car or more. Even though Chrysler had made air bags standard on all its U.S.-built cars in 1989, GM decided not to spend the money to put bags on Lumina until the car was overhauled. That cost it sales even among fleet buyers, whose corporate customers were refusing to lease or purchase cars that didn't have the safety features. Insurance companies were giving discounts to firms that bought cars equipped with air bags, and GM simply could not compete with Ford Taurus, which by then had a driver's and passenger's airbag at a price similar to Lumina. Chevrolet officials were praying for the day when Lumina was finally overhauled, and hoped 1994 would finally bring them relief from six years of painful sales. It didn't turn out that way.

Instead, 1994 was a year in which GM's problems became magnified, possibly unfairly, in comparison with success at Ford and Chrysler. It became clear that year that the GM system was more of a threat to the company's turnaround than anyone had expected in the heady days of 1992. It was one thing for a group of baby boom planners to huddle long hours in a conference room, fixing GM on paper. It was far yet another thing for Smith and his team of managers to actually implement the suggestions. GM's culture, they learned painfully, was a force of its own, one that had to be respected and taken into account at every step they took.

It is always difficult for a carmaker to get a new vehicle off the ground, but until the 1980s Detroit automakers always focused on selling the sizzle, not the steak, of a new vehicle. They put their efforts into creating enough hype and desirability for a car that buyers would lust for it, thirsting to be the first on their block to own one. Since people traded cars in much more frequently, or seemed to in the pre-1980s, buyers were much more tolerant of glitches and problems that might arise in the first run of a new model. Anybody who was truly concerned about quality knew enough not to buy a car the first year it was on the market. All that changed in the 1980s, when

Japan's share of the car market climbed toward 30 percent. It was safe to buy one of their cars in the first year because many had already been introduced in Japan before they went on sale in the U.S. Detroit executives sniffed that Japanese companies got a chance to get the bugs out before the cars were shipped to America, a luxury Detroit didn't have. But that was only partly true, and it became close to an obsolete concept when Japanese carmakers began introducing all-new cars in the United States. By the 1990s, Japanese companies, particularly Toyota and Honda, were aces at launching virtually clean new cars. The reason was that their vehicles were designed to be built simply. The Japanese companies made maximum use of common parts and components across their vehicle lineups, so that the pieces used to assemble new cars and trucks were already familiar to the people on the assembly line and to the suppliers producing those parts.

By contrast, U.S. carmakers still run into problems getting their new vehicles onto the market, mainly because they make such dramatic changes in appearance, technology, and factory tooling between old and new models. Chrysler and Ford weren't immune from such troubles; early versions of Chrysler's key LH sedans and Neon subcompacts had to be recalled for glitches. Ford Contour and Mercury Mystique compacts had to be repackaged with fewer luxury options because their high prices drove buyers away. But for GM, the launches of the new Chevrolet Lumina and Cavalier were crucial. And in each case the carmaker couldn't pull them off cleanly.

GM planned to spend the fall of 1993 tearing up its big car plant in Oshawa, Ontario, so that it could install the equipment it needed to build Luminas and generations of cars that came after it. In the past, at model change time GM installed only the tooling and machinery needed to build the revised version of a car. It never worried about what it wanted to build in the plant three or four years down the road. Because it had so many plants, GM never worried about having flexible factories that could build multiple kinds of cars. But the 1990s were different. GM had seen how much cheaper it could be if a factory could produce three or more vehicles without needing different kinds of machinery. At Toyota's Georgetown, Kentucky, plant, workers built two-door, four-door, and coupe-style Camrys, the Avalon full-sized car, and were expected to add a minivan or a sport utility by the end of the 1990s. Quality was even higher than at Toyota's plants in Japan. One reason for such flexibility was that the vehicles were designed in Japan to have interchangeable parts; only the exterior sheet metal was different.

That was what GM hoped to do at Oshawa and at all its factories as the 1990s progressed. But the job turned out to be bigger than GM had ever expected. Oshawa, where Smith had his office when he ran GM Canada, was plagued by a mixture of outmoded, inflexible machinery and failed attempts at high technology. GM officials literally had to rip out acres of equipment and reroute the assembly plant, a construction job that lasted nearly five months instead of the expected three. Then, when production finally began, GM was stuck building two-door Monte Carlos for weeks while engineers and auto-workers figured out how to mesh four-door Luminas alongside. The Monte Carlos looked fine and buyers liked them, but the two-door models weren't going to be Chevrolet's savior; the Luminas were. The slow Lumina launch brought back nasty memories of the bungled startups of the five previous model years. Because the four-doors were so slow to hit the market, GM couldn't introduce the cars with the bang it had hoped for. As winter turned into spring, and spring into summer, there simply weren't enough Luminas to supply all 5,000 Chevy dealers.

Not only did GM miss the chance to launch the cars in the spring; in the fall of 1994 it was forced to reintroduce a car that it had begun touting a full year earlier. Inside the company, executives praised Chevrolet for pulling off such a big improvement. Outside GM, at least at first, there were shrugs. Lumina looked pleasant, it was roomy inside, the $15,000 price tag was a bargain, and the quality was fine, but it was hardly the pacesetter that Chrysler's LH cars had been two years before or Taurus eight years before. It had two air bags, it was reasonably priced, it seemed solid; had GM introduced the car in 1991 or 1992, Lumina likely would have been a real help to

Chevrolet. But coming late as it did, Lumina couldn't give GM much of a boost in the strongest car market of the 1990s. In spring 1994, demand for new cars suddenly exploded and automakers found themselves with more buyers than they had vehicles to sell. It was an odd situation for an industry that often overhyped its products.

And GM was in no way ready to meet the demands of the surging car market. Its forecasters had completely underestimated how much of that demand would be for trucks, sport utilities, and minivans. In 1980, such vehicles, grouped in the category of light trucks, comprised 25 percent of vehicle sales. By 1994 they comprised nearly 40 percent and would have climbed higher had GM had competitive minivans and a full supply of sport utilities. Nearly 60 percent of Chrysler sales were light trucks, as were just over 50 percent of Ford's sales. GM's forecasters doubted the rising trend toward light trucks would last, and predicted sales would top out at 40 percent of the market. GM set up its production schedules according to the forecast—and was caught short of supplies for its most popular and profitable vehicles when the market took off. One of the reasons it could not build more trucks was that it did not have enough automatic transmissions to install in them. Engineers came up with a way to convert automatic transmissions used in GM cars for use in trucks—at the breathtaking cost of $300 per engine. Management cringed but ordered the conversions as a short-term solution while they tackled the truck capacity question. And the strategy board took a more controversial step. They delayed a few of GM's plant closings until later in the decade. The vast majority of the shutdowns would be complete by the end of 1995, but some plants won a delay until as late as 1998. In one case, at Tarrytown, New York, home to the "dust-buster" minivans, GM began transferring veteran workers to other plants in 1994 as job openings occurred, and hired temporary workers to fill in until the factory closed in 1996. Normally it couldn't do this. Temporary workers became permanent and joined the UAW after six months. However, the union agreed the company could collect union dues from the workers without making them permanent. It potentially saved GM the expenses it would incur in special plant closing benefits for its veterans who would not have jobs when the plant ultimately closed. But the plant closing slowtdowns dismayed analysts and Stempel, who felt GM was dragging its heels on the plan that cost him so much agony. "We took the blows, we took all the gaffe for announcing closures. Let's follow through, fellows," he said.[2]

Just when GM didn't need it, questions about Saturn arose. Sales had accelerated in each year the small cars were on the market. But as Saturn passed from babyhood into its toddler years, the enthusiasm of its buyers masked problems at the Spring Hill factory and controversy within GM over what the company's future should be. When GM's board cut the size of the plant in half, the move put double the pressure on Saturn to become profitable. It would not be able to count on revenue from half a million cars to cover expenses, even though the budget for product development had not been cut. According to the business plan, GM expected Saturn to break even by the end of 1993. And it did so, but not without some difficulty and some financial maneuvering. In 1993, Saturn dealers accepted a cut in profits so the company could keep more money. Saturn pulled its advertising. And GM credited Saturn's books for technology in use at Spring Hill even though it hadn't used the ideas anywhere else.

Meanwhile, Spring Hill did not pan out to be the state-of-the-art factory that GM had hoped it would be. It was configured in the years just before automakers caught on to the benefits of flexible manufacturing, which allowed easy changes of the tools and dies used to make cars so that more than one kind of vehicle could be built on the same assembly line. Saturn could build only one kind of car. And it took longer than industry officials thought was necessary: The average Saturn took thirty-two hours to build, about the same as a mid-sized Buick or Oldsmobile built in a much older factory. Further, the Saturn platform couldn't be used as the basis for another car, meaning GM couldn't spread the expense of the car to another division. GM already had two other small car platforms, one to build Chevrolet Cavaliers in the U.S. and one for Opel Astras in Europe.

It took longer than GM hoped to find out Saturn's true

efficiency levels because the Saturn factory didn't hit full production until a third shift of workers was added in 1994, four years after the factory opened. Auto plants are supposed to be at their maximum efficiency when they're operating full-out. Saturn took far too long to get to that point, and its policy that allowed workers to stop or slow the assembly line meant speeds could be erratic. Perhaps because of the stop-and-start quality of Saturn's production methods, there were signs of fracture within its workforce. Begun with a core group of dedicated zealots, its makeup changed in 1993 when GM began placing laid-off workers from closed plants at Saturn. Many of the newcomers mistrusted the whole concept of the small car plant, weren't used to a team approach, and began complaining about injuries to their hands and backs caused by the inconsistent rate of the assembly line. Dissidents began to gather support for challenging long-time union president Mike Bennett, whose rank gave him the power to fill a number of positions within the plant. The Saturn contract also gave him power to make far more decisions than a typical local union leader, and the more recent arrivals felt he favored the original crew. Bennett held on to his job in the face of several attempts to defeat him, but the voice of Saturn, which started out in unison, began to lose its harmony. When GM offered workers a chance to transfer back to their original plants in 1994, more than 1,000 applied, surprising Saturn union officials and company managers who had no idea of the depth of discontent. Eventually, 185 took jobs back home in places like Janesville, Wisconsin, and Flint, Michigan, helping to relieve tired colleagues burned out from months of steady overtime.

It may have been just as well that Saturn never attained its original size; because in 1993 and 1994 a debate raged within the NAO strategy board over what to do with it. In the fall of 1993 Saturn officials made a proposal to double the size of the Spring Hill factory, or to add what they called a "second module." They argued vehemently that the car company needed to grow to fulfill its mission of attracting young buyers to GM and to assure that the Saturn customer service gospel did not dwindle in the face of increasing competition. They wanted Saturn's lineup to expand, possibly to include a larger car and maybe even a sport utility vehicle. But the proposal as it was made that fall was doomed. Chrysler was on the verge of introducing its small, peppy Neon cars. Chevrolet and Pontiac were only a year away from launching their J-car subcompacts. Would the world want more Saturns despite their sales success thus far? Many people within GM didn't think so. And Smith, at the time, was opposed to making bigger Saturn cars. That would run counter to the creation of Saturn as GM's premier small car division. Plenty of other GM divisions had bigger cars, Smith said. If anything, Saturn should consider going smaller, and picking up a car like Geo Metro from Chevrolet or taking on a version of the Opel Corsa. Later, he changed his mind and Saturn started work on a bigger car that GM hoped would be shared with Opel, and possibly Oldsmobile.

Smith also wasn't happy to see that the expanded factory wouldn't make money until late in the 1990s. After four years of expenses and slim profits in the early 1990s, GM couldn't afford another five years of Saturn losing money. The coup de grace came from Yokich. A longtime opponent of the special Saturn contract, one of Yokich's goals was to bring Saturn back into the fold under the conventional union agreement, whose terms he had a tremendous say in dictating. Yokich did not want GM to add more workers at Spring Hill. He told the company he would not go along with a second plant there; if GM wanted to increase Saturn's size, it must consider adding on at an existing plant, like nearby Bowling Green, Kentucky, or at Willow Run, Michigan, or Wilmington, Delaware, which Stempel had ordered shut. And those workers had to come under the traditional contract. That pretty much killed any chance of expanding the small car company. Meanwhile, Saturn's independence as a separate car company was all but lost in October 1994, when GM reorganized its North American Operations and folded Saturn in with its small car platform. Named to head the platform was Saturn president Skip LeFauve It became clear, however, that Saturn would soon share parts and processes with the rest of GM. (LeFauve was soon overwhelmed by the workload, leaving Saturn without an active champion. After Bennett complained to *USA Today* in

July 1995 that Saturn was being ignored, GM named Saturn marketing chief Donald Hudler to succeed him.)

Worries about Saturn's future weren't GM's only small car problems in 1994. Almost as if on cue, as soon as problems with the Lumina were resolved, the launch of Cavalier and its sister Pontiac Sunfire blew up. Cavalier hadn't had a complete overhaul since it was introduced in 1982, but, incredibly, it was GM's best-selling car in 1993, thanks to aggressive marketing targeted at young buyers. GM had tremendous hopes for Cavalier in its first year. It boasted about the productivity improvements it expected from the car. It had cut the number of parts to 2,329 from 3,259 and the number of hours needed to build one car from thirty-two to twenty-three hours. But these improvements didn't translate from computer screen to assembly line. One problem lay within GM's own system. Large metal parts for the cars, called stampings, were made at one of GM's parts factories and shipped to Lordstown to be installed on the cars. These stampings were made on big presses that basically cut out the pieces from sheets of steel, then embossed them several times with dies so they'd be the proper shape. Each time the metal is stamped is called a "hit." When the stamping process was completed, a piece of sheet metal was shaped to clearly resembled a car hood or a truck lid. GM planned to reduce the number of hits from about six to about three on each large Cavalier and Sunfire stamping. But the dies that its engineers had crafted to do the stampings were not cutting each piece accurately in so few hits. The machines had to be stopped and started again; ultimately the dies had to be remade so they'd be more accurate. As a result, GM could not get enough correctly made stampings to ship to the Lordstown plant. There were also supplier problems. Midway through the product development process, when Lopez was fielding his first PICOS teams, GM switched suppliers on several components. When the project arrived at Lordstown for initial production, the suppliers GM had chosen could not supply components at the rate GM needed.

The delays were frustrating because GM was trying to make up for a long history of poor labor relations with the

Lordstown plant. It was keeping one-third fewer workers at Lordstown to build just as many cars as it had before. They were introduced to a new team system like the kind used at Japanese auto plants. Workers are supposed to eyeball each other's work and call down to colleagues if a faulty car slips through their hands. GM had installed a system like the one at Saturn, involving cords that workers pull to shut down the line when they see poor quality. Not used to the opportunity to speak up, some Lordstown workers didn't report problems; others yanked on the cords far too often.

Under GM's production launch plan, the company had expected to build only about 1,400 cars the first month, then accelerate to about 30,000 four months later. Instead, GM was able to build only 155 Cavaliers and Sunfires in the first month, and production had climbed to only 2,559 three months later. By the end of five months, GM had built only a total of 40,000 cars, fewer than it wanted to build in a single month. And in February 1995, it had to recall the first 38,000 because the welds that connected the steering column to the car were missing. Without the connections, the steering column could break during parallel parking, as happened to seven customers. It was the kind of problem that experienced workers at a plant like Toyota's factory in Georgetown, Kentucky, might have spotted before a single car left the assembly line.

GM officials refused to discuss Lordstown's problems in detail and did not let visitors into the factory while it solved the problems. But Stempel says GM failed to address each problem as it occurred. Instead, it let the issues build up until all needed to be fixed at once. "I'm appalled at the Lordstown situation," Stempel says. "That should be running at clock-work, spitting them out like bullets. You can't make that investment, and take this long to come up [to full production speed] with something you are supposed to know how to do."

At the same time that GM was dealing with the Lumina and Cavalier problems, its relationship with the UAW seemed to be deteriorating. In 1994 the union used strategic local strikes at key GM plants to send the company a warning. It still nursed the resentment of not being able to play a role in the massive job cutting program that Stempel had announced nearly three years before. Union leaders fumed as GM closed factories and trimmed jobs at plants that remained open. As those plants had been cranked up to full capacity, the fewer number of workers at those factories were being crushed by the workload. Five times in 1994 the union staged brief shutdowns, demanding that GM hire workers to supplement those who were becoming burned out by constant overtime. Had the relationship between the union and the carmaker been better, GM might have been able to place some of the workers who were on indefinite layoff and yet earning virtually full pay and benefits. But the UAW-GM contract said workers didn't have to move if the new job was more than fifty miles from their old plant. GM could hire temporary workers, but they became union members after six months and went on the GM payroll. Despite his efforts to smooth the relationship with Yokich, Smith found he was still being ambushed by the UAW's wily tactics. But it was nothing compared with the body blow he received from the Clinton administration in the GM pickup truck case, which he thought had gone away.

Everything exploded during the third week of October. Smith was in his office on Monday morning when a call came from Pena. He'd called a press conference for the afternoon, and word had leaked in Washington that the government was finally going to say what it planned to do about GM's 1973–87 pickups equipped with side-saddle gas tanks. The conversation was pretty much one-sided; Pena explained he considered the trucks unsafe and felt GM should fix them. That was the only warning GM got; Pena had not notified GM's Washington office, its legal staff, or the White House of his plans to discuss the truck case. And Pena did not merely ask for a recall as he told Smith he would do; he denounced the trucks, warning that hundreds of people would die if they were allowed to remain on the road. He said he would hold a public hearing on December 9 to address the matter, which was bound to be a public relations nightmare for GM. Nobody knew at the time that Pena's own staff had recommended against a recall, concluding that the death rate in GM truck accidents was no greater than in accidents involving competitors' trucks. Certainly, the White House was as surprised as GM's legal staff, which watched the session in stunned silence on a television set in Pearce's office.

The next day, Smith had been scheduled to fly to Washington to participate in the one-year anniversary of the industry-government Clean Car program. The government had pledged to throw open its research labs to the automakers, who in return pledged to come up with a car that could get triple the typical 27 mpg that a car of the 1990s obtained. Smith immediately canceled the trip and sent Hoglund in his place. The lanky executive, fuming during the White House ceremony, caught sight of Vice President Al Gore leaning on his crutches behind a tree, still recovering from damage to his Achilles' heel during a basketball game a few weeks before. Striding over, Hoglund gave the vice president hell for Pena's remarks. Gore, chastened, insisted he knew nothing of what Pena would say until the Monday press conference. (In early December 1994, after intense negotiations between GM and the Justice Department, the two sides reached a settlement that called for GM to contribute $51 million to auto safety programs. The deal came just days before Pena's planned public hearing. It was a victory for GM that Pena argued was far better for truck owners and future buyers than risking a court battle with GM.)

Pena's initial verdict was only a warmup for the walloping GM would get from Wall Street in the next few days. It fell to Losh, newly named chief financial officer, to deliver to reporters and analysts the news that GM had stumbled on its path to profitability. GM lost $328 million in the third quarter. That was hardly a bloodbath; the previous two years, third quarter losses were over $1 billion. But the analysts, who hate surprises, felt GM hadn't warned them sufficiently of bad news to come. Losh, apologetic, couldn't give them the answers they wanted. Soon after, GM ended the quarterly press conferences that reporters had seen as a sign of its new openness. Everything came home to roost—the bad blood with the UAW, GM's poor relationship with its suppliers, GM's inability to get its retooled plants started up on time. By the beginning of the following week, GM stock had fallen 20 percent. And Wall

Street was asking some tough questions about GM's progress—or lack of it.

Steve Girsky, the blunt analyst with PaineWebber in New York who began his career on GM's finance staff, wondered just how much GM was losing because it couldn't get cars out on time. He decided to start tracking vehicles as they were introduced by various carmakers to see how closely the companies were able to stick to their preintroduction production schedules. Girsky, who has since joined Morgan Stanley, wasn't so much concerned with the pace at which the cars were introduced as he was with whether the vehicles were coming out on time. In November, after the surprise of the third quarter earnings, Girsky calculated that GM had lost as many as 240,000 vehicles—a full assembly plant—due to the slow launches. It cost GM an estimated $800 million to $1 billion, or about one fifth of its net income for 1994.

Girsky figured Lumina alone cost GM between $200 and $250 million in 1994—and the company lost half a point of market share because it simply didn't have enough cars to sell. In the fall of 1994 GM launched an advertising sweep touting Lumina as a well-built bargain—it sold for around $16,000 versus $20,000 for a competing Toyota Camry—yet dealers didn't have cars to show to buyers. It was a paradox that the company that couldn't give the old Lumina away may have miscalculated the appeal of the new model, which seemed particularly affordable in light of six recent interest rate hikes that sent car-loan payments close to $400 a month. Officially, GM blamed both slow start-ups on the fact that each factory was being retooled so that it would be easier in the future to start up new vehicles. But analyst Girsky, voicing a fear that was becoming clearer by the minute, warned that GM was going to miss any benefits of the strongest U.S. car market of the decade because it was too screwed up inside to take advantage of it. Although it was the largest auto company in the world, GM was unable to capitalize on its size, he said. In a booming car market, with buyers lining up for hot vehicles, GM should have been able to step up production at its plants and fill up dealers' lots with new cars and trucks. Instead, fights with its suppliers, its workers, shortages of engineers, and too few resources stretched too thin were causing the company to stumble.

GM's lateness in realizing a crisis was at hand in the early 1990s and the carmaker's inability to keep momentum going once a turnaround had begun were hurting the company financially. Girsky figured out that if GM were as streamlined as Ford, which had attacked its operations in the 1980s, it would have earned $3 more per share of common stock in 1994—more than $2 billion on top of its net income of $5 billion. If GM could have trimmed its operations to the levels at Chrysler (admittedly an impossible thing to do, given GM's level of vertical integration), GM could have earned $7 to $8 a share more in 1994—or more than double its actual 1994 earnings.

Girsky was quick to praise GM for the progress it has made. Yet, he warns, "GM needs time to fix itself. The company...is in the worst position of the Big Three when it comes to weathering a downturn." Girsky put his finger on Smith's biggest fear: that GM hadn't done enough during the period of Fundamental Change to avoid losing money once the auto boom turned south, which it showed signs of doing in early 1995, almost as suddenly as the upswing had occurred the year before. GM has always been a company that boomed in strong economic cycles, only to crash in soft sales periods. That was never a concern in prior GM administrations, but this time it was the top priority to fix NAO before industry sales fell apart. And now Smith and Wagoner had to figure out what to do to take GM into the twenty-first century.

CHAPTER ▪ 10

What's the Persona?

The biggest single question Jack Smith and his management team must answer is deceptively simple: What do they want General Motors to be?

Will they be satisfied if GM merely remains the world's biggest auto company, as it has been since the 1920s, or should they try to make GM the world's premier auto company, unchallenged in performance, unquestioningly the industry's leader? Naturally, the correct answer would seem to be the second one. And, publicly, that is GM's stated goal. In GM's annual report for 1994, the corporation proclaims that it wants to become the world leader in transportation. It is a vow that GM's executives repeat like a mantra at nearly every opportunity. But rarely do they follow it with a clear definition of just what it means. Such a fuzzy goal could be proclaimed verbatim by British Airways, Airbus Industries, or Canadian Pacific Railway. There are too few clues that will help GM employees, dealers, customers, and investors understand what will comprise the soul of the great machine that Smith has had an unprecedented opportunity to craft. Without specifics, GM falls right back into the old trap of big dreams and failed execution.

Yet for many people in the company the financial comeback is validation enough that GM's turnaround has been a success. Certainly, Smith and his team made the right moves to stem the financial crisis that nearly brought GM to its knees. In that context, GM's recovery has been swift and impressive. The Smith years have been a textbook case of the kind of bold steps a company must take to bring its balance sheet in line with reality. Making the turnaround even more sweet is that the solutions came from people within the company who had a stake in its survival, not from the recommendations of multi-million-dollar consultants hired simply to fix a problem. Because of those efforts, GM will not go out of business, as some of the most perceptive members of the finance staff and senior management feared was possible in 1992. Executives received their bonuses again in 1995, the first in five years—the most concrete sign that the turnaround worked and the good old days had returned.

Yet the actions that GM took, such as closing plants, cutting fleet sales, slashing purchasing costs, and refocusing its core product lineup, are big-ticket items whose bottom-line impact is felt for a relatively short period of time. With its immediate crises solved, GM is faced with the far more time-consuming, much more frustrating job of renovating its operations and creating a truly world-class company—if that is indeed what it decides it wants to be. Here is where the break with the past must come once and for all. GM cannot write its own definition of leadership: It must bow to what the business world is recognizing as the best, whether in North America or across the globe.

As most see it, a world-class company is one that is consistently profitable throughout a business cycle, something GM has never been in its nearly ninety years. To become the best in its class, GM must be more than a corporate squirrel that stores away enough money in strong car markets to make up for its losses in weak sales periods. It must examine every corner of its operations and retool them, much as it reorders its factories at the start of every model year, so that it defeats the inherent cyclicity of the car business.

A world-class company also is one that provides leadership to the rest of its industry—significance, not just size. Perhaps the man who best understands this is GM's secretive chairman, John Smale, who has been even more invisible than Smith. In the three years since he directed the boardroom coup that elevated Smith to the CEO's job, Smale's biggest contribution may have come in prompting GM to examine just why it lost its grip on industry leadership, and the kinds of things it can do to become a force in global business yet again.

In the fall of 1993 Smale put some of his philosophy into words. In a widely quoted speech entitled "Why Great Companies Lose Their Leadership," which was written by planner Purcell, Smale said failure did not occur overnight. A company's downfall might not even appear in its financial results before a final crisis, such as the one at GM. But a careful look will show that the roots of failure developed years before. Rarely are the failures due to unexpected disasters, said Smale, turning to Shakespeare. "The fault is not in the stars, but in ourselves." Smale defined three areas of industry leadership. The first is intellectual leadership, in which a company breaks new ground with inventions and ideas unique to its industry. As examples Smale pointed to Bill Gates at Microsoft, George Eastman at Kodak, and Alfred Sloan at GM. Second on his list was capability leadership, which Smale said was a matter of ability rather than vision. It was one thing to create a new product, another to make it the industry standard that all competitors rush to copy. "It's the company you look at when you're benchmarking your own company's capabilities," said Smale. Finally, a company could reach for results leadership. This, said Smale, was the art of putting all the elements together to produce a superior bottom line: market share, profitability, cash flow, and return on investment. It was the most visible aspect and probably the most rewarding.

During the early days of Smith's tenure as CEO, members of the NAO strategy board took a cold, hard look at how GM was doing in each area. And the executives sadly concluded that the company had failed in each regard. That was understandable. Even GM's great chief executive, Sloan, had warned that it was probably harder for a major company to keep producing great results than it was to become major in the first place. When a company sits atop its industry for many years, the human factors of pride, arrogance, and complacency overtake the best intentions of those in charge. Bureaucracy replaces a spirit of entrepreneurialism. Momentum is mistaken for leadership. Individual efforts are directed inwardly, not externally. There is more emphasis on studies and reports, less on getting out and visiting customers and eyeballing the competition. "Very few, if any, great companies develop all of these faults, but even fewer avoid developing at least some of them," said Smale.

Under Smith, GM began to battle its way back to achieving some semblance of each type of leadership. But it has not yet made the commitment to grasping hold of all three kinds. If that is what it decides it wants, GM must shatter the fast-creeping practice of comparing its performance with "the way things used to be around here," or judging itself only against Ford and Chrysler. GM's mere size will always tip the scales in its favor in the minds of many people inside the company whose universe is still solely GM. Instead, executives must look across industries, at General Electric, Motorola, Rubbermaid, and Allied Signal, and benchmark themselves against the culture of creativity that is vibrant at each of these companies, whose leaders are visible and visionary.

NAO president Wagoner, who will have to direct some of the toughest changes, agrees GM must broaden its outlook. "You've got to be hungry to benchmark yourself and learn from it, not argue against it," he says.

Yet Wagoner has had to battle a stifling atmosphere that began to develop at the company about the time he became president of NAO in 1994. Throughout GM, there was a feeling that no one will be able to tell if Smith's turnaround has worked until after GM gets through the next cyclical downturn, which many in the auto industry fear is under way. Late in 1994, sales began to soften because of interest rate hikes and affordability concerns. The average price of a new car topped $20,000, sending the average monthly payment to $374 on an 11 percent car loan (the interest on which is no longer tax-deductible). The affordability crisis brought forth the first worries about what would happen to GM once the downturn hit with full force. In the best-case scenario, GM slides through softer sales without having to cancel or delay product programs, lay off workers, or close factories, and its balance sheet does not fall into the red. In the worst-case picture, everything goes to hell and GM's board orders another turnaround attempt.

Because of the looming downturn, an attitude quietly

started to burble up—one of "we'll fix it later." For many people, particularly GM's leaders, the thought of procrastination was chilling, considering that for decades GM operated exactly this way. It was the kind of inertia that threatens to make the first three years of Smith's turnaround just another halfhearted attempt to tame the monster. In the vast scope of GM history, the Smith years are still just a blip on the radar. Only the toughest, most determined, most self-directed leaders can fight this feeling. It is a reason why in 1995 Wagoner has insisted that GM must maintain a sense of urgency despite its quarters of record net income. "Rick has turned the heat way up," purchasing executive Taylor said in the spring of 1995. "He's running out of patience. He isn't listening to the same old excuses anymore."

But Wagoner had a difficult time in keeping NAO focused. With record profits and executive bonuses making a comeback, it became increasingly apparent that such determination was difficult to find beneath the top five tiers of management. People were ready for a break. In the old days at GM, and in many American companies, weary managers confused working long hours with working well-directed hours. At GM, the feeling often still is, "We're exhausted. Look at how little time we've spent with our families the last few years. It means this must be working." To the contrary, the customary GM workload does not translate into success—only to half-lived lives whose reward is a big check at year's end, not the satisfaction of contributing to a vibrant enterprise whose achievement is self-generating. Spending fourteen hours a day at a desk in Warren without gauging how the competition is doing, let alone keeping track of other industries, is a sure ticket back to the tunnel vision that plagued GM for so long.

What is desperately needed within GM now is a clearly articulated set of goals and priorities for the rest of the 1990s. To join the slim ranks of world-class companies, it must address its biggest problems, not leave them to be solved by future generations. Looming like icebergs are the major areas that GM cannot ignore if it is to sail toward the shore of leadership. Some are hard and quantifiable; others will require change as deep as that which has already occurred.

Aggressive financial performance. This is the measurement by which GM has been judged repeatedly in the past and always will be in the future. If the expected mid-decade downturn does not hit with swift and sudden severity, many industry analysts believe GM is headed for outstanding corporate earnings. GM earned a record net income of $5 billion in 1994, and industry analysts believe it will set new records in coming years, perhaps earning as much as $8 billion in 1996. Meanwhile, NAO, which earned about $750 million in 1994, could earn upward of $2.5 billion in 1996. Without the burden of major new car and truck introductions looming until late in 1996, there is an expectation of a rush of black ink. Yet those record earnings could well be short-lived. By 1997, most economists believe auto industry sales and indeed the U.S. economy will soften significantly, and so, say the analysts, will GM's earnings. Depending on whether the U. S. economy has an easy-to-handle "soft landing" or a meaner crash, GM could fall back into the red as the decade comes to a close. And NAO, which has only just climbed into the black after five years of losses, is likely to bleed again later in the 1990s.

Internally, GM's forecasters believe NAO's losses will be between $1 billion and $2 billion at the bottom of the coming downturn. Outsiders are not as optimistic. Concerned by GM's inability to wring savings and efficiencies out of its product development, analyst Girsky of Morgan Stanley anticipates NAO could lose as much as $4 billion—double what the GM analysts expect. With so much uncertainty about when the recession will hit, GM must closely monitor its financial situation, using tough measurements that managers of the past disdained. It cannot take its eye off the ball when it has a good quarter, like the record-setting performance turned in during the winter of 1995. Smith and Wagoner have vowed to remain vigilant. Unlike his predecessors, Smith is not obsessed with net income or market share. His most important measurement is GMs net margin. This figure reflects a company's net income divided into its sales and revenue. The emphasis on margins has become far greater in the auto industry and the larger corporate world during the 1990s because Wall Street, investment banks, ratings agencies, and shareholders have realized that net income can be inflated with one-time gains to make a company's performance look good.

Net margins, on the other hand, are a cleaner measurement because they use the ultimate performance measure—revenue—as a basis around which to compare income. Smith's goal is to have all sectors of GM earn an average 5 percent net margin over a business cycle, which lasts about seven to eight years in the car business. That is about $5 for every $100 in revenue. He acknowledges that because of the cyclicity of the car business, some years will be better than others. In essence, GM will need to overperform at the top of a business cycle to make up for underperforming at the bottom. However, Smith emphasizes he wants GM to get through soft sales years without losing money.

Consistently achieving a 5 percent net margin across GM will be difficult, and may seem impossible. The challenge will be toughest in NAO, whose net margin in 1994 was just 0.7 percent, or 70 cents on $100, compared with a net margin at Ford of about 4 percent and Chrysler's net margin of 7 percent. Smith's goal of 5 percent translates earnings into $5.2 billion a year, based on NAO's 1994 revenue of $110 billion. That figure is just the average. In peak cycle years, NAO should be earning $7 billion to $8 billion to make up for years in which it breaks even or loses money. According to Girsky's projection, NAO will not be able to reach Smith's 5 percent figure in a single year during this decade. When it can do so depends on whether NAO is able to follow through on its drive to improve its manufacturing efficiency, cut its product development cost, and in general change its ways. "We have to be willing to learn from others and ourselves and make the changes necessary, not be afraid to change," Wagoner says.

If GM were operating in a vacuum, this would be much more simple. But GM has a seemingly immovable object to tackle in its union.

Repair the relationship with the UAW. What makes this goal second only to financial success? Simple. GM's lack of labor peace is a distinct competitive disadvantage. It cannot achieve its greatest hopes financially, competitively, or culturally until it has a sustainable relationship with the UAW that does not fracture every time an issue arises. This barrier often seems insurmountable. There is a fundamental atmosphere of mistrust between GM and its union that goes back nearly sixty years, to that first sitdown strike in Flint, Michigan. Over the years, GM executives have displayed little more than thinly disguised disdain for the union, and UAW leaders, sometimes justifiably, sometimes not, view GM executives as liars. In the company's glory years, GM officials always dealt with the UAW by throwing money at its members. It was easier to toss out an extra $1 an hour or more money in cost-of-living allowances than to address the central issues in every set of contract talks. When conflicts arose, the UAW challenged GM, at least publicly, by playing its single trump card. Unfortunately for GM, there has been no end to those conflicts. And the UAW has shown time and again during the past ten years that it has no reluctance to play that card. It has learned, says former UAW president Douglas Fraser, that "You have your greatest amount of influence five minutes before a strike deadline."

The always rocky relationship was exacerbated in the 1980s when Roger Smith sent the union conflicting signals. On one hand, he seemed eager to try new concepts in labor-management relations, like NUMMI and Saturn, especially when they resulted in more efficient ways to build cars. On the other hand, he seemed to be bent on eliminating jobs among GM's regular workforce. That wasn't the case at all, because Smith, as Stempel calculated, actually added UAW jobs during the 1980s. But he did so gracelessly, not hesitating to use threats to try to intimidate the union. Smith's strongarm tactics contrasted with Ford's decision to give the UAW a voice in running its plants. As early as 1984, Ford was willing to guarantee nearly all the jobs in its factories in return for getting workers' cooperation in some of the innovations it wanted to try, like training people to perform more tasks than their ordinarily narrow work rules would allow. Smith refused to do the same at GM. He would guarantee paychecks but not jobs, figuring that all GM had to do to get workers' cooperation was guarantee that they would be paid.

In 1990, just a few weeks after Stempel became CEO, GM and the UAW signed a pact that virtually assured workers would be paid whether or not they were on the job. Under the 1990 agreement, workers could be placed on temporary layoff for only thirty-six weeks. During that time they would receive state unemployment benefits along with company subsidies that added up to about 90 percent of their regular pay. But after the thirty-six weeks were up, workers went back on GM's payroll and remained there until GM could find some work for them to do. Further, workers could be ordered to accept jobs only within 50 miles of their home plants. They did not have to accept transfers farther away. Implicit in the GM-UAW deal was the prospect that GM would eventually shut some factories. The contract basically gave GM permission to cut its production to match its market share. It gave the union members guaranteed income and unprecedented protection that few others in the labor market enjoyed.

Even though he kept his plant-closing list close at hand, Stempel never suspected that the economy would collapse as quickly as it did. And he could not have suspected that GM's board would shake management by the shoulders and order it to shrink its manufacturing capacity so quickly and drastically. The huge plant closings meant guaranteeing workers' pay, which cost GM about $4 billion—as much as it spent to develop and launch Saturn—during the first three years of the contract. That financial hit was just another arrow in Smale's quiver that ultimately forced Stempel to step aside. Under Smith, GM passed on its first chance to dismantle the thorny provisions. Despite the expense, in the fall of 1993 GM accepted the contract for a second three years rather than risk a confrontation it would surely lose, and in so doing, it sent an unintended signal that things were better inside the company than they really were. Many analysts groused that GM should have taken the risk of a strike rather than be saddled with such an competitiveness-stifling agreement.

But Jack Smith knew that a walkout would mean a serious setback to his goal of shoring up the relationship with the union. When he became GM's president in 1992, he met almost immediately with Steve Yokich, heir apparent to UAW president Owen Bieber and head of the union's GM department. Over Smith's first months as president, and early in his tenure as CEO, Yokich and Smith forged an open relationship that seemed to bode well for the future. Each clad in a casual sweater, they shared a telecast together in January 1993 that outlined GM's goals for the future. Smith spoke to a gathering of the UAW's top 300 local presidents later that month on "White Shirt Day," the anniversary of the day when the company recognized the UAW in 1937, making the blue-collar workers feel their workshirts were as good as the bosses' dress shirts. At a farewell party in 1994 for GM's longtime Washington lobbyist, Jim Johnston, Yokich spoke warmly of Smith's efforts to improve communication with the union. It seemed like the animosity was finally dissipating. Unfortunately, that friendship did not extend to the factory floor.

In 1994 and early 1995 GM was hit by eight local strikes at key plants, an average of two each quarter. The cause was simple: Car and truck sales had heated up much faster than GM's slimmed-down factories could handle. Stempel's massive cutbacks, based on economic, assumptions made two years before, were taking effect just when GM and other carmakers faced their best auto market in five years. For once, its long-range thinking resulted in short-term pain.

The hot market made GM run its plants on nearly continuous overtime, but the cutbacks meant those plants had smaller employment levels than the last time auto sales boomed in the late 1980s. Thanks to the job cuts, the workforce was comprised of veterans whose average age was nearly fifty and who were beginning to buckle under the strain. (GM officials often boasted that their payrolls had not added a new blue-collar social security number since 1986, as if a lack of younger workers was something to brag about. Most of the people at Honda, Nissan, Toyota, and Mazda plants were under thirty.) Under orders from their bosses to improve productivity levels, GM's plant managers did not let up on the workers despite their complaints. So UAW leaders authorized a series of local strikes at key parts and vehicle plants, from Dayton, Ohio, to Anderson, Indiana, to Flint and Pontiac, Michigan. The walkouts had a domino effect on GM assembly plants, which were unable to operate without frequent supplies of components. In almost every case GM yielded, agreeing to transfer workers who would take jobs, extend the life cycle of products built in the plant, and make investments to ensure the plants' futures. The moves were frustrating to those who wanted to see GM get tougher with the UAW—a strategy that could prove even more disastrous than the tentative course it was following. "It's clearly a problem. The solution of it is not trivial, and the implementation of it does need to recognize that a solution that is one-hundred-percent acceptable to us is not acceptable to them, and vice versa," says Wagoner. "It's an issue of communication and trust, constancy of purpose. You do not just go to the UAW and say, 'We'd like to solve this issue.'"

But GM needs to make a greater effort, contends Yokich, elected president of the UAW in June 1995. The past year, the union conducted an in-depth study of GM's operations, including suppliers, parts plants, and car and truck factories. It understands, perhaps even better than GM, the automaker's parts flow and which factories are key to supplying which vehicle plants. "They don't understand that we track them," Yokich says.

Despite his clear affection for Smith, Yokich does not apologize for the series of strikes that made the CEO's life miserable the first three years of his tenure. Says the union leader, "Every one of those strikes is because they don't know how to react to pressure, or they don't know where we're getting our information, or they can't understand anything about running their business."

Besides showing some sensitivity, there is not much that GM can do quickly—or even accomplish in the next round of labor negotiations in 1996. Having just about completed trimming 55,000 blue-collar jobs from its payrolls through the wave of plant closings, GM cannot afford to turn around and add significant numbers of new workers. GM's average hourly labor cost in 1994 was $44, up $10 an hour in just five years. The problem is toughest in its ACG components plants (renamed Delphi in 1995), which must compete against companies paying nonunion wage rates a quarter of those GM pays. Saddled with UAW wage rates, ACG must cut more deeply in other areas, like materials costs, or vastly improve its factories' efficiency.

Almost as difficult as improving efficiency is changing attitudes on both sides. Some GM employees harbor an almost bitter hatred of the union, as deep as any distrust between workers and management. The emotion stems in part from GM employees' envy that the blue-collar workers, long mired at the bottom of GM's status barrel, receive better benefits than do GM salaried employees. Some of those white-collar employees are the sons and daughters of blue-collar workers, and they took their staff jobs as a way up the ladder, to see their efforts at self-improvement pale against the well-protected labor force. Despite repeated attempts by management to eliminate the perk, GM workers still receive fully paid medical and dental benefits. They receive thousands of dollars for tuition allowances, legal aid, and child care as well as four weeks' vacation time. But there are some shared burdens. Like their salaried counterparts, they receive no profit-sharing payments in the years that GM did not pay bonuses, although the payments were reinstated in 1994. And like their white-collar colleagues, many blue-collar employees are just as eager for signs from GM management about the path the company hopes to take. Says Yokich: "GM has to learn in every segment of management that the UAW isn't here to put them out of business. The UAW is here to save jobs for themselves and for several generations to follow.... They have to expand their horizons and look at their workers as the answer, not the problem."

Like it or not, the destinies of GM and the UAW are enmeshed. GM cannot prosper unless the cars and trucks that its UAW members build are the best possible quality. Union members can't build top-notch vehicles unless the people inside GM develop them cleanly and efficiently. GM is failing to take advantage of one of its greatest assets. And the UAW is failing to see eye-to-eye with the people who can help assure that it does not become a has-been champion of workers' rights. NUMMI and Saturn have shown that management and labor can work together successfully. The time may have come for drastic changes in the labor agreement that governs GM's plants. Historically, the UAW has prided itself on pattern agreements that give equal pay and benefits to workers across the auto industry. But each company is vastly different in the 1990s, and GM needs as much flexibility as it can muster to face its competitive challenges.

How visionary Yokich and his leadership team will look if they take the risk to say, "Our contract is working against GMs best interest and against our best interest. Let's try something better." They are smart and savvy and will be able to protect the improvements they fought so hard for while ensuring the UAW's future prosperity. And think how imaginative Smith and Wagoner will be if they are the first GM leaders to truly welcome the UAW into the very fabric of GM. Ultimately, says Yokich, the issue is one of trust. "And how do you get trust? You make an agreement and you live by it," he said.

Certainly, the union leader understands the challenges that he will face the last years of the century as he strives to make the UAW's voice heard and its views respected. As he took control of the UAW at its convention in Anaheim, California, in June 1995, Yokich told two thousand delegates, "We will soon be entering the twenty-first century. You and I have to take a hard look at ourselves to make sure we have the continuous vision to build a great society. Simply by going to work, and working hard, doesn't make a vision come true." Said Yokich, "We will have to try new things. If they don't work, we'll discard [them]. If they work, we'll build on them." Without the union playing a key role, every dream that GM designers, engineers, and product development experts have for their cars and trucks will be dashed.

Fix product development using the best ideas from GM's international operations. Among the people who know the company well, there is a quiet fear developing that GM is turning into two auto companies. One, GM's international automotive operations, or IAO, will fulfill Smith's quest to be a leader in global automotive transportation. Its operations will be lean and flexible, its balance sheet a solid source of cash even in times of softening sales. Its savvy engineers, filled with energy by the opportunity to compete in challenging world markets, will be able to come up with half a dozen cars from each platform that can be built in plants in Europe, Asia, Latin America, and even Africa. The other company, NAO, will be the problem child, always needing attention, a drain on cash, saddled with a culture that looks inward, and unable to bring out cars and trucks according to schedule.

It is not something that anyone wants to admit will happen, but it is close to being a snapshot of reality. The problems with GM's product development process in North America threaten to hold NAO back from being a contributor to, and a beneficiary of, GM's global prosperity. And it also is keeping GM from competing in the U.S. market with good-looking, well-built, profitable new cars and trucks. No one will be able to judge the success of the GM turnaround until the vehicles conceived, designed, developed, and produced under Smith go on sale. Until that happens, GM is stuck with a product lineup with roots that are half in the 1990s and half in the 1980s. It cannot achieve the kinds of savings it wants in purchasing, materials, manufacturing, and engineering until each vehicle in its lineup is revamped. That is why fixing product development is a main focus for Wagoner and the NAO strategy board. "It's not bigger than life. We can do it. We've got to stick with it," Wagoner says.

GM is sadly behind its rivals in the time it takes to develop a new vehicle. It averages fifty months from Phase Zero—not counting on average thirteen months in Bubble up. Chrysler needs only thirty-seven months to do what takes GM one-third longer.

When Smith and his team took over in 1992, GM was already making decisions on the cars and trucks it would introduce in 1997. Thus the ideas and concepts that have evolved the past few years won't show up until late this decade, probably in 1998 and beyond. Those vehicles will be the first that spent time in GM's Vehicle Launch Center, where development teams were supposed to share theories, develop common processes, and come up with the BOM, BOP, and BOD for each car. In reality, the VLC has taken longer to kick into high gear than anyone at GM anticipated. It took about a year to sort out issues like whom the developers worked for—the VLC or the platform organization where they had come from. Then it was difficult to get the product development teams to break down their suspicion of sharing information with each other for fear it would benefit another project before its creator had a chance to use it.

Two years after they were conceived, the BOM, BOP, and BOD checklists are still not completely finished. Meanwhile, members of the strategy board had different views about the role the VLC should play in vehicle development and the kinds of changes that could take place in a program after it leaves the center. Smith, who emphasized consensus, wanted the discussion to play out without interference. All this was frustrating to GM's product planners, who were trying to set up a schedule of new product introductions through the decade. Group executive Robert Hendry, who is in charge of NAO's business support group and a member of Smith's personal inner circle, says GM leaders did not expect the process of setting up the VLC to be an easy one. "I think just because you set direction, lay out an implementation plan, and involve people doesn't mean things are going to go smoothly. There are 300,000 people [in NAO]. You're not going to get buy-ins and get everybody involved," he says. Despite the start-up problems, Hendry says he believes GM still would have set up the NAO launch center because it was a symbol of the single direction mandated by Fundamental Change. Says the executive: "Had we not done it, those words 'getting common' would have been just that. Words."

But the launch center could not address the problems that occurred when vehicles that already had been in development left Tech Center studios for assembly plants. First, the introductions of Lumina and Cavalier fell behind schedule. Then the rest of the vehicles GM planned for the 1990s seemed in danger of missing their targets. Deeply concerned by what was happening, in 1994 the strategy board hired consultants A. T. Kearney to study the product development process from beginning to end, trying to see where the bottlenecks occurred. The $8 million study infuriated the planners who had worked on Fundamental Change III, which had a series of suggestions on how to improve the product development process. Privately, Hogan fumed that spending the money would have been unnecessary had the strategy board simply paid attention to what its own staffers had pointed out. But Smith contended that A. T. Kearney was an independent voice to whom everyone in GM would listen.

The study recommended that GM create a new class of automotive super-chiefs whose job would be solely to oversee car and truck projects for at least two development cycles. The officials would be called Vehicle Line Executives, or VLEs—the same executives that the planners had pushed for in Fundamental Change III. These executives took charge of vehicle development projects for ten to twelve years, and had the authority to make decisions that once would have been made by higher ranking executives. Becoming a VLE is a long-term prospect that would take a manager out of the running for higher-level jobs. But it also makes sure somebody was accountable for the programs, and that car guys who loved their jobs wouldn't be yanked upstairs when they'd be happier working on vehicle projects. With such authority comes the responsibility to keep a program on schedule, and to lobby for its needs. GM said in August 1995 that it would pick sixteen to eighteen VLEs by the end of the year. Hendry says it was important for GM to know how it was going to implement the new positions before it made the appointments. "There is the issue of direction, and there is the issue of decision," he says. "We're going to have strong program management. That's clear. The next question is, What is that? What are the skill sets required, and what are the processes that need to be in place to support that person? Those are not trivial questions—those are major questions. The bigger the company, the more important those are," he says. Hendry calls such investigations "implementation planning." And before the research is complete, he contends that neither Smith nor any GM leader should order a change. "You're going to have false starts, and you could fail. You could be in worse shape than if you let the current system run," Hendry says.

That's exactly what a number of engineers and manufacturing experts think happened in GM's product development process. They seemed to have ammunition to prove their case. A warning flag went up in March 1995 when GM executives quietly acknowledged to auto industry analysts that they were pushing back the introductions of some of GM's next wave of cars and trucks by up to six months. Reviewing its product development programs, GM discovered that it had little in the pipeline for 1995 but a big wave of products from 1996 through 1998. Although GM hired 2,000 engineers in 1994, causing its white-collar ranks to grow for the first time since the cutbacks were announced in 1992, its "engineering factory" was in danger of being overtaxed by the upcoming flood of new product introductions because it was short of skilled engineers in crucial areas, like designing the dies used in stamping metal. The delays were simply part of a long-term attempt to keep the factory running more smoothly, GM executives claimed. Wagoner argued eloquently that five years from now analysts would praise GM for keeping its focus on its long-range success and not worrying about missing a model year.

Regardless, the delays—followed by a second pushback in summer 1995—seemed a sign of trouble for a company whose future depended on the success of its new cars and trucks. And they seemed to reflect a real grasp of the fact that Smith's team could not be considered a success until the market could judge those vehicles. Thus far in Smith's tenure, each of GM's new vehicles has turned out well despite the glitches in start-ups. Once they reached the market, Lumina, Cavalier, Aurora, and the restyled Chevrolet Blazer all were strong sellers without costly rebate programs. All were begun under Smith's predecessors, and, except for minor tinkering, reflected improvements made by the executives who were in charge before Fundamental Change.

Sadly, the contrast between the all-new GM vehicles and the rest of the aging lineup was unmistakable. Oldsmobile's stand at the 1995 Detroit Auto Show, for example, placed Aurora up front along with a concept car dubbed Antares that was a sneak peek at the future Cutlass. At the rear of the display, separated from the front by a waist-high curtain, were the old-style boxy Olds cars. Cadillac did not even hold its annual press conference because it did not expect to have a new car for at least another year. Meanwhile, new vehicles were pouring onto the car market at a rapid pace. Starting in 1994, Ford's new entries included the Windstar minivan, the Contour and Mystique compacts, a restyled Explorer sport utility, and the Lincoln Mark VIII and Lincoln Continental. Chrysler had rolled out the Neon subcompact, the Cirrus and Stratus compacts, and the Dodge Ram truck, and planned new versions of its market-leading minivans for fall 1995. Toyota was set to introduce a new version of its Camry sedan, a small sport utility, and a U.S.-built minivan to replace the Previa.

GM partisans could find ways to pick all their competitors apart. They argued that Ford had lost touch with reality in pricing some vehicles much higher than market would pay. Chrysler was dogged by quality problems and worries from a spring 1995 takeover threat by Kirk Kerkorian and Lee Iacocca. Toyota was forced to replace an ailing president in summer 1995 and saw massive cost increases due to the strong yen. But GM's three major competitors could boast something in common. A glance over their lineups showed mostly new cars. A glance at GM's still showed mostly older ones. "There is nobody stepping up and saying, 'We're running out of time,'" fumes a GM manager. "It's a real simple issue: Is the customer going to care? We essentially go through the motions without saying, 'We're going to have to roll up our sleeves, get into this, and get it accomplished.'"

If GM sticks to the schedule in place in 1995, analyst Christopher Cedergren of AutoPacific Group estimates that the bulk of GMs new car introductions will happen between fall 1996 and fall 1998. The 1996 model year brings a new Saturn sedan, the first complete overhaul since the small cars were introduced in 1990. A year later, GM is scheduled to introduce three important vehicles: Cadillac Catera, Oldsmobile Achieva/Pontiac Grand Prix, and its first all-new minivans since the APV "dustbusters" were introduced in 1989. Sometime in 1997 the Chevrolet Malibu debuts along with the Oldsmobile Cutlass (which may be called Intrigue). And the following year GM will revamp its top-selling vehicle, the Chevrolet CK pickup. The big wave hits the market just when industry sales may slide—a bleak prospect for an auto company that needs to keep its hitting streak intact. And the later GM introduces its new vehicles, the longer it will take to correct any major design flaws should something go wrong. By missing a feature on the next Cutlass Supreme (scheduled for 1997), GM would have to live with the problem until 2004.

Wagoner says GM's problems in its product development process should be smoothed out by 1997. "The good news is, we don't need a tear-up. We simply have to improve what we've got," he says. In the meantime, NAO is exploring ways it can develop cars in conjunction with IAO—steps toward the global strategy that is a pet project of GM's CEO. In fall 1996 GM plans a new line of minivans in the U.S. that also will go on sale in Europe. And Cadillac will launch Catera, a version of the Opel Omega that went on sale in Europe in 1994. Both projects sprang into existence shortly after GM's management shakeup in 1992. The carmakers put together a team of U.S. and European engineers to explore ways to develop vehicles that could be sold in GM's two biggest markets. This was going to be the beginnings of the global auto company that Smith had envisioned.

The different cultures of each organization made for tough going, at least initially. The NAO engineers were defensive at the idea that the Europeans were there to teach them to build vehicles. Opel is not GM's low-cost producer. It is able to charge about 25 percent more for its products than GM can charge for comparable vehicles in the United States, and thus the competitive pressures have not been as great to keep costs to a minimum. Various laws in Europe prevent dealers from selling more than one company's cars in each showroom, making intra-company comparisons much harder than in the U.S. Opel also lagged behind NAO in development of safety equipment such as air bags and anti-lock brakes, since Europe has been late to embrace these features. Luxury features have come later, too. Air conditioning, which is ordered on nearly every car sold in GM's U.S. divisions, is still not widely installed on European cars. And while 85 percent of the cars sold in the United States have automatic transmissions, only 20 percent of those sold in Europe have them. It is a sore point among some engineers that Opel touts the flexibility of the

Corsa platform. Grumbles one, "They keep talking about everything they've done with that stupid little car, and we can't even do core products."

Meanwhile, the engineers from Opel saw that their NAO colleagues, burned out from years of delays and cancellations, did not have the respect for deadlines that they were used to in Europe. They learned that their U.S. counterparts still waited for approval before proceeding on minor issues upon which the Opel engineers could proceed without delay. A rivalry of sorts developed on the minivan project, the first in which the Opel and NAO engineers worked together from the start. The European engineers wanted to build a slimmer vehicle that could fit more easily in Europe's narrow streets. But the NAO engineers argued it should be bigger because most of the minivans would still be sold in the U.S. and Canada. In 1994 only 200,000 minivans were sold in Europe, less than the sales of GMs minivans in the U.S. alone. The NAO engineers won that argument. But the Europeans quietly spread the word that they'd been able to find ways to reduce the minivan's weight by 1,500 pounds, improving its fuel efficiency.

Jurgen Stockmar, recently named head of GM's Technical Development Center in Russelsheim, Germany, smiles when he hears of some of the conflicts. Says Stockmar, "You have to give your people some time at first to get completely and perfectly comfortable with what they are doing. Then they must have some time to develop their own ideas, to implement their own ideas. And, at least, that will take you three or four or five years. "

And the anti-Opel grumbling among some in NAO seemed justified in the summer of 1995, when a scandal ripped through the German company. Prosecutors in Darmstadt, the same jurisdiction that handled the Lopez investigation, announced they were probing allegations of kickbacks from Opel suppliers to high-ranking executives. The probe centered on Opel's extensive plant expansion and renovation programs during the early 1990s, and it threatened to become the biggest bribery investigation in German corporate history. Opel had been tipped off about irregularities by a supplier in 1994. It had contacted German officials but did not expect the program to turn out to be as serious as it did.

Prosecutors alleged that 200 people, including 65 at Opel, were involved in a ring of deceit. The suppliers, mostly construction companies, offered cash, vacation homes, and home renovation projects to the Opel officials in return for work on its plant. The factories ranged from Opel's home plant in Russelsheim to the treasured Eisenach complex in eastern Germany that had been Lou Hughes's pet project. According to the allegations, Opel officials took the bribes and, in return, billed the company for the amounts involved. Thus, an official might get a swimming pool installed, and the supplier would get Opel's business and was paid unwittingly by the company for the pool installation. The deception alone was enough to anger the carmaker, but real tragedy ensued.

Hans-Juergen Perizonius, an Opel official, and had been sent to NAO in 1994 to run its worldwide painting technology organization. It was a key position because paint technology is among the most difficult and expensive in the automotive world. Prosecutors in Germany contacted Perizonius to tell him he was under investigation. They had searched his home there. They told him to come back for questioning. Instead, Perizonius went to the garage of his rented house in West Bloomfield Township, Michigan. He closed the door, connected a hose to the exhaust pipe of his Oldsmobile, and turned on the engine. He was found dead several days later when worried colleagues at NAO reported he had not come to work. The police found a rambling suicide note to his family in which he asked to be remembered as a good provider.

GM issued a brief statement disclosing his death, but only the suburban *Oakland Press* wrote a story. In July 1995, German news magazines, which had pursued the Lopez story, discovered the link between the suicide and the bribery investigation. The tensions mounted until reports surfaced that Ferdinand Beickler, who'd preceded Jack Smith as president of GM Europe, and Fritz Lohr, the Opel engineering chief who had accompanied Smith to visit Lopez in Spain, were involved. Both were retired but served as members of Opel's supervisory board. The two executives, revered by many in Europe and at NAO, vehemently denied any link. But the prosecutors found evidence that they were involved. At an emotional special meeting of the supervisory board, the pair resigned, as did Opel manufacturing chief Peter Enderle, who'd been suspended a few weeks before. Enderle's resignation was as deep a blow inside GM's international operations as the departure of Beickler and Lohr. From Mexico to South America to Asia, Enderle had been involved in Opel's quest to build its car worldwide. "That's a real loss," says Hogan, who had worked with Enderle in brazil.

The Opel board's action, along with a strong statement from Smith vowing to find any perpetrators, seemed to quell what threatened to become the successor scandal to the Lopez uproar two years before. And Opel officials, in meetings with employees and strongly worded statements to the press, emphasized the organization needed to return to business as usual to stay competitive. That included its joint projects with NAO.

The two technical organizations are constantly looking for ways they can share automotive components so that engineers on each side of the Atlantic do not waste their time developing the same part twice. This is an area where GM can have a huge advantage over its competitors. The potential savings, as Lopez discovered, are enormous. It may be in this area rather than actual vehicles that GM is able to leverage its ability to become a global manufacturer. "You will certainly see that we will have common componentry," says Stockmar. Meanwhile, there is an active team looking at whether Chevrolet, Opel, and Saturn can share one platform for their small sedans in the early twenty-first century. If so it's likely that Opel would develop the platform that Chevy and Saturn would use at plants in the U.S. But the idea of a common platform shared among the U.S., Europe, and the rest of the world, the way Europe and the world share the Corsa, is still as much as six or seven years off, says Hanenberger. The success of such an idea rests on NAO's embrace of the product development process that GM uses in the rest of the world. Says Stockmar, "With 1,000 people working on both sides of the ocean, you have to be led with discipline. It can be five-phase or four-phase, it doesn't matter."

Find, encourage, promote, and keep talented employees, particularly women and minorities. The best process in the world will not matter if GM does not have the kind of people who can carry it out. At times it seems the only people who gain authority at GM are simply those who stick around the longest. Lopez's decision to leave may have caused tremendous uproar, but in a way he was merely joining a prestigious alumni organization. Look through the ranks of other corporations, and you will find dozens of GM alumni. Chrysler CEO Robert Eaton and president Robert Lutz both worked for GM. Dennis Pawley, Chrysler's manufacturing chief, worked at GM before joining Mazda and subsequently going to Chrysler. Mike DaPrile, manager of Toyota's standout manufacturing plants in Georgetown, Kentucky, spent nearly thirty years at GM, running a series of plants including GM's Wentzville, Missouri, factory, one of Roger Smith's group of new plants. His wife, tired of hearing him complain about the difficulties on the factory floor, sent his resume to Toyota without his knowledge. George Borst, head of strategic planning at Toyota's North American operations, worked his way up the Chevrolet system before joining Toyota in the 1980s.

There might as well be revolving doors at the entrance to GM's finance operations in New York. Even in Jack Smith's early years, GM's treasury office was a hunting ground for Wall Street brokerage firms and investment banks. Since there can be only one CFO—and there are dozens of MBAs in GM's New York ranks—it is understandable that people look elsewhere. But the number of CFOS, treasurers, and other finance officials with GM backgrounds in corporate America is truly staggering. "There's a real brain drain going on at GM," says analyst Girksy. Smith seems unconcerned about the loss of the finance staffers. When asked about it he said, "We've always been a great training ground. We can't keep people." And, certainly, in the days when Wall Street salaries soared and GM could pay no bonuses, GM couldn't compete on pay. Its only weapon was frequent promotions, which it used to hold on to some of its most sought-after young executives, such as Losh and Wagoner. Now, with NAO back in the black and the corporation earning record profits, GM can pay more competitively and fend off some of the headhunters. Still, a number of the people who have left GM in recent years say no amount of money would have convinced them to stay, given their lack of voice and opportunities for real authority. Ironically, as people within GM's ranks have left, its top management has grown in size. When Stempel was CEO, GM had thirty-seven vice presidents in addition to fifteen members of senior management. Under Smith, the vice presidents number forty-seven, and there are fifteen senior officers. Many of the additional vice presidents hold jobs in GM's international operations.

If such disillusionment affects the corporation's talented white males, GM can be an even tougher place for the handful of women and minorities who try to rise through the ranks. There are no women or minorities among GM's top four levels of management. When Smith picked an all-new management team in 1992, it was exclusively white males. He did not hesitate to let Wagoner skip two tiers of GM's management ranks (there are five tiers of management jobs). But no woman or black manager has yet made such a jump. There has never been a woman general manager of one of GM's U.S. car and truck divisions; until GM named attorney Maureen Kempson Darkes head of GM of Canada in 1994, no woman had ever held a significant operations job. She is one of just four women vice presidents (GM has two black vice presidents). Because GM has always been a place where close-knit groups of people advance together, none of the top managers seemed to think Smith's choices of his longtime colleagues were unusual. Bill Hoglund, trying to defend the choices Smith made for his team, said, "When Rome is burning . . . " only to be interrupted by a female reporter. "You don't look for Caesar's wife to put out the fire?" she asked.

GM's track record is actually better than its Big Three rivals. Still, women buy half the cars and trucks sold in the United States. And non-whites—Asians, blacks, Native Americans, and Hispanics—buy a quarter of all vehicles. When

Smith looks at the members of his president's council, he sees no one who can give him another perspective by gender or race. But among his vice presidents, Roy Roberts, head of the GMC truck division, is a loud voice calling for change. Roberts, who is black, is in his second tour of duty at GM. He rose through engineering, manufacturing, and components jobs, was manufacturing boss at Cadillac, and worked in GM's personnel operations in the mid-1980s. But he left GM in 1987 for a senior position at Navistar, the heavy truck company. He did not see much hope of advancing at GM, and he wanted the hands-on experience he thought Navistar would give him. "I left for opportunity. I wasn't mad at anybody. But I didn't feel what I said or did was central to the business," he says. "I'm glad that I did it. I got the chance to run an entire business," from product development to design to marketing and manufacturing. Roberts was mentioned as a candidate for Navistar's top job. But in 1989 Roberts surprised Navistar, his GM colleagues, and possibly himself by going back to GM at the invitation of Roger Smith. "I said to myself, 'Roy, did you run away from some problems? Or should you be right in those problems trying to fix them?'"

His voice rising with a preacher's fervor, Roberts recalled that his father, a factory worker in a foundry in Muskegon, Michigan, taught his children to face prejudice and predicaments head-on. "I didn't believe for one minute that everybody was going to love the thought that I was there. But you can't worry about it," he says. "I don't come to work for you to love me. I come to work so that you will respect me and help me get the job done."

There are more than a few people at GM who don't love Roberts, who has a flair for fashion, an enthusiastic speaking style, and does not hesitate to debate issues in strategy board meetings with Smith. In 1994, GM executives were red-faced when Roberts's application for membership in the Bloomfield Hills Country Club was rejected. The club, whose members have included every recent GM CEO and president, is almost a second home for the corporation's older managers. It had just one other black member when Roberts's name was put forth. It only takes one "no" vote for an applicant to be turned down, and no one needs to state a reason for opposing a candidate. Roberts's rejection immediately brought forth charges of bigotry, though members say Roberts likely didn't make it as much because of his flamboyant personality as his race. They simply did not feel comfortable with him and voted "no," not realizing how the world outside would view Roberts's rejection. Smith, who had to be talked into joining the club when he was named GM president, quit in protest, as did Losh. Roberts shrugged off the incident, turning his attention back to GM.

Since his appointment as head of GMC, Roberts has put together a diverse staff. He's culled people from GM's international operations and given important jobs to women and minorities. Despite his heritage, Roberts has deliberately shied away from having an all-black staff. "We are aggressively, positively working with females and minorities. I seek out diversity. If I hire nine black males to sit on my staff, you get a black male answer. If you get nine white males, you get a white male answer. I've got people on my staff that no damn way would let me go to the market with an advertisement that doesn't think about women." At every GMC press conference, Roberts emphasizes his trucks' appeal to "the females" who buy at least 25 percent of all trucks sold in the United States. That may cause some titters in the audience, but Roberts insists diversity is a question that must continue to be raised. "Nobody has the corner on the market on brains. We've got to have Hispanics and Asians and females and African-Americans. We've got to have all of them playing, because guess what? They comprise our customer base," Roberts says.

He knows he is a lightning rod for criticism. But that's nothing new. "For thirty-five years, every job I've had, I was the first black to have it. That's a lot of pressure. That can be good and that can be bad. If you're doing good, it's amplified. If you're doing bad, it's *amplified*. You don't want that. You'd like to be as natural as anybody else in the corporation. It's not a comfortable feeling." Still, Roberts, rumored to be a candidate for a higher-ranking GM job, says GM is making substantial progress. He believes the next five years will yield a more diverse company, where many voices and views can be heard and not all the faces in the room will look the same. "There really are a lot of things happening here. This new management has a higher degree of sensitivity and understanding. They're all international. They all have more understanding of the diversity issue than any other management of the corporation. I think every division is going through its learning curve. We think you've got to work it. You've got to work it from the top of the organization to the bottom. Not many companies have done it very well." But Roberts adds, "I'm impatient."

So are people who would like to see GM open up more to the world at large. When John Smale and the outside directors led the boardroom coup in 1992, there was intense speculation that Smale would really be running the company and would recruit other newcomers to fill key positions. Smale has had significant influence on parts of GM, but only in the past year has GM begun to look beyond its walls to fill important jobs. The most visible example is the hiring of Ronald Zarrella, former president of Bausch & Lomb, as group vice president for NAO sales, service, and marketing. The job became vacant in June 1994, when Smith made a series of management changes including naming Rick Wagoner as president of NAO. Because Smale reportedly wanted Losh out of the marketing job, Smith gave his protégé Wagoner's old job as CFO. The sales job, which is one of the most influential marketing positions in American business, remained open nearly four months longer while a battle waged over who Losh's replacement should be.

Certainly, there was no lack of candidates inside GM. Skip LeFauve, the president of Saturn, seemed to have the best shot at getting it. The small car company was universally admired for its quirky and entertaining ads, created by San Francisco advertising firm Hal Riney, that featured Saturn customers, cars, sometimes its autoworkers. Saturn was widely hailed as an even bigger marketing success than its cars' sales success. And there were people within GM who thought LeFauve could bring that to the corporation. But LeFauve had always said he'd prefer to retire from Saturn, plus he also was under consideration for an equally important job in charge of GM's small car platforms, which he eventually got in October 1994. Among the other candidate's who were mentioned—or put themselves into the running for the job—were John Middlebrook, the respected head of Pontiac, and Ed Mertz, the veteran general manager of Buick. Mertz admitted he hadn't been interviewed but said, "I think it would be fun."

But Smale didn't want GM to look only at its ranks. He wanted whoever got the job to be someone respected in the business world for his marketing skills. Except for LeFauve, that couldn't be said about any of the other internal candidates. So in the spring of 1994 GM hired headhunting firm Russell Reynolds to come up with a field of possible candidates. To give Russell Reynolds more time, Bill Hoglund agreed to run the marketing operations for a few months. He'd already told Smith that spring that he wanted to take an early retirement. Hoglund was only sixty, but he'd been bothered by bad health, and was ready to trade the twelve- to fourteen-hour days that the recent years had brought for more time at his home in Naples, Florida. (A lifelong smoker, he'd always had trouble quitting and would occasionally alarm visitors with his cough and his froggy voice.)

Zarrella was first approached by the headhunters in June. He was caught off guard by the call, since he had not applied for the GM job and really did not want to give up his comfortable life in Rochester. But he was a car fan—his garage included a top-of-the-line BMW 835i and he was about to put a down payment on a Chevrolet Blazer. (Zarrella held off the purchase for a few months. Once he'd been offered the GM job, he said, "I got a much better deal.") Tall, solidly built, with a pleasant face and a quick wit, Zarrella demonstrated a sharp understanding of the need to focus GM's brands. He seemed like a good fit to the GM executives who interviewed him, especially Wagoner, who invited him on a skiing trip within weeks of his arrival at GM. Zarrella did not seem to be flustered by the wave of attention he received when he got to town. He noted that a number of people had asked him why he took the GM job "and they give me the kind of look that tells me they think I was crazy to do so." But the GM job could be a dream opportunity for him—and he could be a godsend for GM's marketing efforts if given the authority to act without interference from the division general managers. Already in summer 1995, GM was buzzing with word of Zarrella' ideas to transform GM's brands—some of which came straight from Fundamental Change II.

The argument GM insiders use against hiring outsiders is that the company is too complex to be grasped quickly. Anyone who comes in from the outside must spend months first learning GM, time that can be put to better use by giving the job to somebody inside the company. That's rubbish. GM is a complex company, but so are most others in American business. In General Electric's 1994 annual report, CEO Jack Welch cautions his wide-ranging company against getting too tangled up in itself. "We are going to de-complicate everything we do and make at GE. Our communications with each other will be increasingly straightforward, our presentations to each other and our customers will be simpler. Their richness will come from the dialogue, not from the complexity of the charts," Welch said. In the past, GM was incredibly difficult to understand because of the interlocking relationships, the many different ways of doing the same task, and the lack of reason that seemed to go into much of its decision-making. With the common processes and common practices that Smith espouses, GM is on its way to being a much more streamlined organization. When that happens, it will be an easier place for outsiders to understand—and it will be easier for insiders to see the direction that GM is meant to take. GM no longer has the market clout that allows it to be a world unto itself. To grow and prosper it needs to be a greater part of the world at large. And welcoming people whose training has taken place elsewhere is one of the simplest and most rewarding ways for that to happen. They should not have to come to GM to have an influence on the company. It is incumbent upon the people who are running GM to get away from the Tech Center, get out of Detroit as much as possible so they can see, firsthand, what is going on in the auto industry and in the business world. "The best thing for all these guys to do is get out of their offices," says Ron Pinelli, an analyst with AutoData.

Clarify GM's brand images to meet its customers' needs. On his first day as CEO, Jack Smith ruled out ditching any of GM's seven car and truck divisions. It may be time to reconsider. With its product development process overloaded and the U.S. auto market becoming ever more competitive, GM simply cannot leave things the way they are. Maintaining each division costs too much money and is splintering GM's market impact. With 60 percent of the market, Sloan's approach made sense. With GM's market share falling ever closer to 30 percent, it does not. In 1980, GM and Ford were nearly twenty market share points apart. In 1995, GM and Ford are only six market share points apart. GM's 32 percent of the market is spread across seven brand names, and Chevrolet has about half those sales. Ford's 26 percent of the market is divided up among just three—Ford, Lincoln, and Mercury. The identities of Ford's three brands are well defined. GM's seven are not. Analyst Christopher Cedergren says GM could prosper with three—Chevrolet, Oldsmobile, and Cadillac.

Before any of that can happen, GM needs to decide how it will approach the car market. In his first months as marketing chief, Zarrella worked his away around each of the car and truck divisions. He set executives to work justifying, to him and to themselves, every single nameplate and every version of every car in their lineups. Zarrella was discouraged by private talk that GM could always battle its competitors by cutting prices on its cars and trucks. He worried that GM was acquiring an image as the bargain car company, not as the one with the best-quality cars. He did not want GM to always have the lowest-cost cars in every segment. And, like Roberts, he was concerned GM was not trying hard enough to reach different kinds of customers, not just white males.

Luckily for Zarrella, some of the groundwork has already been laid by Barabba's needs-based marketing research. The concept could truly revolutionize the car business if GM has the guts to actually implement it. Think for a moment what would happen if GM took a clean-sheet approach to selling cars, much as the planners did when they wrote the doomed Fundamental Change II. Under Barabba's theory, GM first would quiz consumers on what they really needed. If they had no use for two-door coupes, GM wouldn't build them. If they wanted a small car with a lot of interior room, GM would begin work on one. Instead of simply restyling the same cars over and over again, GM could go where its customers wanted and, in the process, perhaps even be the industry leader in finding new segments of the market instead of being late to enter them. That idea, of course, requires the full faith and confidence of GM's board, the NAO strategy board, and GM's divisions, who would have to sell the cars. And that is a lot of bureaucracy to have to fight—unless someone like Zarrella is simply empowered to make the change. And it seems he has been: In late 1995, Zarrella plans to name thirty brand managers who will create images for GM vehicles. They were supposed to report to the VLEs, but they report to division general managers, who report to him.

Once GM decided what kinds of vehicles would fit its customers' needs, it could begin the task of refocusing its approach. There seem to be two choices here. One is to let GM's sales and marketing staff dictate identities. They could haul in the consultants, decide which brands and nameplates are valuable and which can be discarded, and dishearten a lot of people wondering what the future will hold. That's probably what will happen: In 1995 Zarrella was searching outside GM for some of the brand managers. The other choice is to give the brands the option of creating images that they can most happily embrace. Two of GM's brands—Chevrolet and Oldsmobile—have already begun the work of rejuvenating themselves. The tasks began out of necessity, but the efforts have already paid off in stronger sales. Both divisions began their separate struggles in 1992, as GM's board was dumping Reuss and the rest of Stempel's management team.

Chevrolet may have called itself the "Heartbeat of America," but in 1992 it was hard to find a pulse. Its best-selling car was the Cavalier, introduced ten years before as one of GM's small J-cars. Oldsmobile, Buick, and Cadillac versions had long been discontinued, but Cavalier and sister Pontiac Sunfire remained. Lumina, the GM-10 that was supposed to be a Honda-fighter, was instead an embarrassment, with no air bags and a rattling, tinny body. Chevrolet had a slew of loyal pickup truck buyers, but Chevrolet Blazer was losing ground to Ford Explorer and faced another threat from Jeep Grand Cherokee. Yet in their research, Chevrolet strategists discovered that the Chevy name was dear to the hearts of many people. Older customers remembered the days of the Chevy Bel Air, when Dinah Shore would send a giant "mwah!" from her lips to her audience at the close of her Chevrolet-sponsored television show. Baby boomers had memories of their fathers' Impalas or their mom's Chevy station wagons, and many still lusted after Camaros and Corvettes. Young buyers who couldn't afford new cars their first time out often owned used Chevys. The researchers found Chevy's brand name was every bit as strong as Harley-Davidson, which became a cult motorcycle in the 1990s, playing on its muscle heritage.

There was no question that GM had a valuable asset. But what could it do to repair it? The answer came by deciding what Chevrolet ultimately wanted to be: GM's middle-of-the-market entry in cars and its strongest player in trucks and sport utilities. It needed the best possible products at the most reasonable prices in order to compete with Ford, which was breathing down Chevy's neck with five of the top-ten-selling cars and trucks in the industry, and with Chrysler, whose minivans owned the segment and whose new cars were stealing Chevy's traditional customers.

Jim Perkins, Texas-born Chevrolet general manager, had timing on his side. Between 1992 and 1996, Chevrolet was set to overhaul its two most important cars, the Cavalier and the Lumina, as well as restyle its top-selling sport utility, the Chevrolet Blazer. Along with the renewed product lineup, Perkins got some public relations help from Bill O'Neill, who'd masterminded GM's attack on *Dateline NBC* and who'd served on the original NAO strategy board in his job as director of NAO public relations. O'Neill's move to Chevrolet was seen by some as a step down, but it was a smart move for Chevy because O'Neill quickly set out to make Chevy's public relations more customer-friendly and its product message simple to understand.

With a stronger lineup and motivated messengers, Chevrolet needed something to tie it together. The answer was Genuine Chevrolet (as opposed to "Fake Chevrolet?" some cynics sniped). The slogan, which replaced Heartbeat of America, was more than just a tagline. Chevrolet wanted it to be a symbol of its renewed emphasis on its customers and something for its employees to keep in mind as they did their jobs. Foulups in production of Cavalier and Lumina didn't help Genuine Chevrolet get off to a good start. Because dealers simply had little to sell, Chevrolet's car sales almost fell below a million vehicles in 1994 for the first time since the end of World War II—half as many cars as the company had sold at the beginning of the 1980s. A last-second sales campaign pushed the number above one million. But on the truck side, Chevrolet was booming.

The restyled Blazer got off to a splendid start. By early 1995 dealers had six-week waiting lists and customers were trying to buy Blazers off delivery trucks when the vehicles arrived at showrooms. Blazer became the vehicle of choice among GM executives, who once disappeared behind the smoky windows of big Cadillac sedans. All over NAO, they were now scrambling up behind the seats of their sport utilities. Even the big, bulky Suburban, a gas-guzzler at 14 mpg, became a cult car among Hollywood celebrities and trend followers. Chevrolet discovered that it had the most complete lineup of sport utilities in the industry—from Geo Tracker at the small end to Suburban up top—and pushed the people-haulers to the hilt. With minivans set to arrive in 1996, and Chevrolet Malibu coming the following year, Chevrolet's future seemed brighter, if only it could get enough vehicles to dealers in time to capture customers before the recession hit.

As for Oldsmobile, new products will be the only thing that ultimately will revive it. Between 1984 and 1992, its sales, once a million a year, fell 60 percent. Once the step up from Chevrolet, Oldsmobile didn't seem to have a reason to exist. It sold fewer cars than more expensive Buick, and its buyers' average age was over sixty. It tried to attract younger buyers by saying, "This is not your father's Oldsmobile," but increasingly, it wasn't their Oldsmobile, either. Thousands of middle-aged buyers who'd been loyal to Olds over the decades were deserting the division for Ford, Chrysler, and Japanese carmakers. Oldsmobile Cutlass was the best-selling car in the 1970s, but in the 1980s it was beaten out by Honda Accord, and in the early 1990s Ford Taurus grabbed the crown. Although it

had 1,800 dealers, Oldsmobile sold only 400,000 cars a year—
222 apiece. The typical Saturn dealer sold more than 1,000
each. Oldsmobile dealers were piled on top of one another in
bigger car markets while Saturn dealers were carefully targeted at key markets. Sufficiently alarmed, the planners had
discussed combining Oldsmobile with Saturn, since Saturn
buyers had no place to go after they had outgrown their small
cars. There was even talk of ditching Oldsmobile altogether.
But nobody reckoned with John Rock, Oldsmobile's sometimes
profane but determined general manager.

Rumors of Olds's demise were just the tool Rock needed to
blast his sleeping division back into business. "The medicine
was something like chemo. Tough, tough. I wouldn't want to
go through it again. But it probably saved Oldsmobile," Rock
says.[1]

One of Rock's first moves was to comb through
Oldsmobile's lineup and ditch the slowest-selling versions of
its cars. First to go was the front-wheel-drive Toronado. Then
the rehab work began. In 1994, Oldsmobile was scheduled to
get Aurora, a $30,000 luxury sedan with a Northstar V-8
engine. There had been big fights over which division would
be chosen to sell Aurora. For years Cadillac had been demanding an entry-level luxury sedan so it could compete with
European and Japanese luxury cars. Buick wanted it, too (and
got one, the Buick Riviera). Tests by GM's market researchers
showed that buyers who liked the car when they only knew it
by its name turned up their noses as soon as they heard the
Aurora was an Oldsmobile. There were even attempts, in 1992,
to kill Aurora because its product development costs had
soared. Rock saved the car but he knew he could not let dealers
simply plunk it down on showroom floors and sell it with the
old high-pressure tactics they'd used for years. So he took two
steps.

Dealers chosen to sell Aurora received special training in
customer satisfaction, designed to take the tackiness out of the
sales process and assure the buyers they should be proud of
spending their money on an Oldsmobile. Then Rock tried to
make Oldsmobile in general a much more customer-friendly
place. He borrowed from Barabba's value pricing strategy to

create a series of one-price Cutlasses and Oldsmobile 88s. Each was sold at a set price—$14,999 for the Cutlass, $18,999 for the 88—equipped with popular options like antilock brakes and air conditioning. The prices were lower than buyers would have paid had they chosen the options individually, but Oldsmobile still made a profit because it could order the cars in bulk instead of budding them individually. Dealers grumbled but buyers liked the idea, which Rock called "simplified selling." Eventually, he instituted one-price selling across Oldsmobile's entire model lineup.

Aurora, meanwhile, was a smash from the day it was introduced. Nowhere on the car did the Olds logo appear; instead, it bore a stylized "A" that Oldsmobile eventually stole as inspiration for a new corporate logo. To give the car an identifiable theme, Oldsmobile borrowed from American composer Aaron Copeland's familiar symphony, *Appalachian Spring*. Soon the strains of "Simple Gifts" became known, to some people, as "the Oldsmobile song." Aurora brought Oldsmobile a slightly younger buyer—not as young as the division had hoped, but with an income level well above $100,000, exceeding the highest levels of any GM car sold, including Cadillac. There was a cautionary note: Instead of stealing buyers from BMW, Mercedes, or the Japanese, Aurora seemed to be attracting mainly Cadillac and Buick owners, a trend that the industry calls "cannibalizing." Oldsmobile seemed to be facing a challenge in broadening Aurora's appeal. And it faced another problem: If customers decided they didn't want Auroras, Oldsmobile had nothing else to offer them. Olds's next wave of products, including replacements for Achieva, Cutlass Supreme, and Cutlass Ciera, is not due until later in the 1990s. Rock hoped to transform Oldsmobile by its 100th birthday in 1997, but the real evidence may not be in until sometime after that. In the meantime, Olds will struggle.

Still, Rock, who sips from a mug emblazoned, "Coffee from Hell," has become something of a folk hero inside GM for taking the risks needed to save Oldsmobile. And he isn't finished yet. Rock says he wants the once-stodgy division to be the first automaker to let buyers place orders through on-line computer services. In 1996 Oldsmobile is expected to have completed linking its dealers to its computer network via satellite, and customers potentially would be able to link up as well. Rock talks of letting shoppers place an order to the company, using a credit card for a deposit, and showing up at the dealership only when their car arrives. They'd be assigned to a salesperson who would deliver the car they wanted—or, if they wanted another model, to sell them that one. Like his simplified selling, the idea is bound to cause consternation among Oldsmobile dealers because it threatens to change the way dealers have earned their livelihoods.

But Rock doesn't care. If Olds does not change, it will not survive. And, he says, that applies to GM as well. "I think General Motors wasted a lot of time getting together. Time is our worst enemy," Rock says. "But nevertheless, I don't know if God himself could handle GM any faster."

Jack Smith would never have the audacity to compare himself to Our Lord. But as far as many people at GM are concerned, he has been most responsible for GM's resurrection. Now, as the 1990s proceed, one of the biggest tests at GM will be his leadership. Aside from some expected retirements among GM's division general managers and vice presidents, GM's top management should remain intact for the rest of the decade. Smith, who turned fifty-seven in 1995, conceivably could stay through 2003, while Wagoner and Hughes each have twenty years left in their GM careers. That is not the case with members of the GM board who led the management shakeup, starting with GM chairman John Smale, who is now sixty-seven. The next major management move at GM will occur sometime within the next few years, when Smale decides to retire from the board. No one is encouraging Smale to do so— nor, says Smith, should GM be in a hurry to see Smale leave.

One thing that will not change when Smale leaves is the function of the GM board. In 1993 the board adopted formal guidelines to preserve its newfound activism. Writing in the *Harvard Business Review* in 1995, Smale said the guidelines' existence formally recognized that the GM board is separate from the management of the company and had separate responsibilities and obligations. "The board's basic responsibility is to see that the company is managed in a way that serves the owners' interest in successfully perpetuating the business," said Smale. "It has to act as an independent monitor of management, asking the tough questions that management might not ask itself. I see that as an active, not a passive responsibility."

According to the guidelines, the board has a clear majority of outside directors. By 1995 there was only one insider, Smith, and the board had informally decided to leave the CEO as its only management member. Those independent directors select a lead director—in GM's case, Smale—who is responsible for coordinating the directors' activities. If the CEO were elected chairman, the lead director would be another member of the board. In addition to regular board meetings, the guidelines call for independent directors to meet alone in executive session or on a regularly scheduled basis. Without a regular schedule, Smale said management could see the directors' meetings as a threat, which was not what the directors intended. At GM, the outside directors meet three times a year, and Smith takes part in portions of the meetings. Under the guidelines, the outside directors have the responsibility to pick new candidates for the board with input from the CEO. But gone are the days when the CEO could load up the board with cronies or nonthreatening candidates friendly to his causes. Smale emphasized that guidelines weren't meant to be a threat to GM's management. He wanted the GM board to be a competitive advantage to the corporation. "In the final analysis," said Smale, "the board is responsible for the successful perpetuation of the corporation. That responsibility cannot be relegated to management."

Except for Smith, Harry Pearce, the top-flight attorney who shot through GM's ranks to become executive vice president in charge of much of its non-automotive business, best understands the role of the board. Since 1992 he has run EDS, Hughes, GM's locomotive group, Allison Transmission, and all of GM's corporate functions. Pearce has become, by responsibility and by design, the insider who is the link to GM's outside directors. He attended nearly every meeting of both the board and the NAO strategy board during the crucial early days of Fundamental Change. He was an early supporter of Ignacio Lopez's quest for change. "The lawyer—he understands what I tried to do," Lopez says.[2] Pearce was on the scene during the frenzied negotiations to keep Lopez from leaving, and he has played a key role in GM's legal fight against him. By corporate structure Pearce reports to Smith, but in reality he functions as Smale's man in GM's upper ranks.

It is to Pearce that Smale has turned to create the vision of what the corporation should be when the twenty-first century begins. "What's the persona?" Smale asked Pearce. What is it that is unique about GM that the nation, indeed the world, would miss if GM were to vanish overnight?[3] Thinking out loud on a gloomy February day in 1995, Pearce reasoned that GM's greatest role could be as technological leader of the world auto industry. "We ought to be the most creative and technically sound and technically advanced motor vehicle manufacturer in the world. And shame on us if we don't achieve that with the assets that we have," such as Hughes Electronics, GM's research labs, and its product development operations, says Pearce. "We ought to be such a leader and so creative that if we didn't exist, consumers in America wouldn't have the products that they ought to have."

Achieving that goal means transforming the workforce as rapidly as technology is changing, Pearce says. "The best companies know that they're never okay unless they are always searching for better and better solutions and are always challenging their people to find those better and better solutions," Pearce says. That is what Pearce is trying to do with a plan to transform GM's corporate staffs, which he calls Team One. As much philosophy as function, Team One attempts to make the branches of the company that support its business units into a vibrant source of ideas and innovation. Under Team One, members of management no longer stay boxed into their specialties. They take on broad bases of responsibilities— just as Pearce has—so that different perspectives are heard and taken into account. While his goal is not merely to reduce jobs, it is likely that GM's corporate staff, the "checkers checking the checkers," will be much smaller than its current size within a few years.

GM's public relations arm got a taste of what Pearce was up to in early 1995, when GM abolished Bruce MacDonald's job as vice president for corporate communications. MacDonald, who had run PR at Pontiac and Saturn during his thirty years in the business, got the post when Smith became CEO. Yet as NAO developed, many of the public relations staffers who had reported to MacDonald transferred to NAO. He was left with a small staff of corporate and international public relations specialists that was too small to justify a vice president's attention. Meanwhile, GM's ill-defined public profile was eclipsed by Chrysler's standout product lineup and Ford's financial success. The changes that Smith and his team were making remained a mystery, in part because GM's PR department had no idea how to articulate them or how to convince the managers that it was important to tell the story. In a move that GM did not announce (although it leaked to several journalists including the author), MacDonald's duties were handed by Pearce to Dennis Minano, formerly a member of the legal staff and vice president for environmental and energy activities, who had no formal PR experience. MacDonald subsequently took early retirement, leaving the PR staff abuzz with wonder and worry about what Pearce was planning for their department.

Pearce's idea for Team One echoes a concept called "bands of responsibility," which is being implemented at Allied Signal and at other companies where employees are being urged to acquire new skills and talents. They should not enter one function and expect to stay there for their entire careers, but instead have multidisciplinary resumes. Their job titles may not change when they get more responsibility, but, says Pearce, "The most important person at a corporation isn't always the chairman." At times it could be the chief engineer of a critical new car project or the head of a marketing division.

Team One falls right in line with what Smith has tried to achieve by sending key staffers overseas to gain international experience. In October 1993 Smith was faced with filling the presidency of GM Europe. Hughes, named president of GM's international operations, was vacating the job. It might have been logical for Smith to give the job to David Herman, president of Germany's Opel, or to Charlie Golden, then running Vauxhall. But Smith plucked Richard Donnelly, vice president in charge of GM's powertrain operations, for the European job. Donnelly was probably as surprised as anybody, but Smith's choice had a purpose. One of his goals for GM was to create a worldwide family of engines and transmissions, which are among the most expensive parts of a car to build. The powertrain strategy meant that Europe would develop small engines and diesel versions and NAO the rest. It needed careful coordination between IAO and NAO, and Smith felt Donnelly was the right person to oversee the job. Plus, Smith thought the wider responsibilities of GM Europe, for manufacturing and marketing, would be good experience for Donnelly to add to his technical expertise.

It has certainly been good for Hogan, coauthor of Fundamental Change, to take charge of GM Brazil. The Brazilian operation has been a key contributor to GM's booming Latin American operations, which are scheduled to double in size over the next few years, thanks to a major investment approved by the GM board in early 1995. Along with the Corsa, Brazil has added the Chevrolet S-10 small pickup truck to its lineup. On sales of $5.8 billion in 1994, GM's Latin American operations under group vice president Richard Nerod earned $828 million—a net margin of 14.2 percent, nearly triple Smith's goal for NAO. By the late 1990s Brazil will become GM's third-largest manufacturing site behind Germany and the United States. Hogan, badly needed back in NAO, has turned down offers to come home. "It is a million-dollar experience," says Hogan. "This is one the few places left where you have total responsibility, from the foundry to the GMAC. I'm just grateful to be here. There is nothing like having the responsibility for 25,000 people and their families."

Success stories like GM's Latin America operations and its disciplined international product development organization are becoming more frequent. But Smale, says Pearce, does not let management forget how much work lies ahead, particularly in NAO. "John's never totally satisfied, and that's healthy. He keeps us aware of what has to be done and he keeps us aware that half the journey remains to be done."

Clearly, there is no indication that the GM board is lessening its keen interest in what is happening. Yet when Smale ultimately steps down, many people would like to see the chairman's job return to a member of company management, namely Smith. There is a feeling that he is owed the job as a reward for the efforts of Fundamental Change and his leadership of the company in the years since. Smith laughs when asked if he wants it. "I don't get a vote," he says. More intriguing is who GM's board might select as its next CEO should Smith rise to the chairman's job during the next few years. The frontrunners include Hughes, who has transformed GM's international operations into a strong, competitive business unit that could prosper on its own, and Wagoner, if he is able to pull together NAO into a unit that functions as well as IAO. But both will have several chances to shoot for the CEO's job.

Quietly circulating are rumors that the job might go to Pearce. The idea is shocking to some young managers, who can't imagine that the next CEO will not be Hughes or Wagoner. Many find it hard to believe that the leadership of the company will not go to someone groomed in its automotive operations. But Pearce certainly has the best understanding of GM's non-automotive businesses. No one in the president's council has a better grasp for safety and engineering issues, which Pearce honed in his years of product liability legal work. With his twin responsibilities to GM's management and to the board, he has a foot in both arenas. Much as Smith did when he worked in New York and overseas, Pearce is quietly building a team of managers among those who report to him who could fill management posts at GM five and ten years from now. Says Stempel, who works closely with GM on electric car development, "I always keep Jack informed, but when I need a go-ahead [for a consulting matter], I talk to Harry." His name appears on many of the memos that deal with changes among GM's corporate staffs—like the decision to replace MacDonald.

Naming Pearce CEO would break with the old hierarchy that could be climbed only by an executive who had paid his dues. And it might assure an even faster pace of change than has occurred in the first hectic years of Smith's administration.

As Pearce's performance at the *Dateline NBC* press conference proved, he could easily be the best communicator ever to lead GM. No one would have to brief him on the wisdom of answering a particular question, for Pearce is a master of crafting thoughtful answers that seem to reveal more than they actually do. Picking Pearce would be a triumph for GM's outsiders as they try to open the company to the rest of the business world. Pearce could be a new kind of leader—the spokesman for the corporation on crucial policy matters confronting the company and the advocate within GM for progress and change. Opponents, however, protest his lack of automotive operations experience.

Pearce laughs at the speculation about his future. "I've got my hands full right now." Turning serious, he contends that GM managers have spent far too much time in the past dreaming and scheming about who will occupy the CEO's corner office on the fourteenth floor. "I think we got into trouble in the past because we had too many senior executives who had been taught that was the only road to success, so everybody had his or her eye on the corner office. That was almost built into the GM culture," says Pearce. "I think that's very unhealthy. There are senior positions at GM that are enormously rewarding. You don't have to be the chairman around here to be successful."

But it is an undeniable fact at GM that the CEO sets the tone for the rest of the corporation. Smith has easily been the most invisible man to ever lead the company. In the past GM suffered because of its culture of "doing what the boss wants." The system of unquestioned power led to CEOs who were tyrants. Stempel broke with the pattern to some extent and Jack Smith has smashed the practice into bits. During the first few years of his tenure, when the company needed to draw on suggestions from all corners to set itself back on a path to prosperity, Smith's style was just what GM needed. His consensus-based mode of operation, following decades of dictators, sent a message that voices would be heard and suggestions welcome. He may be the best-liked person who has ever sat in the corner office. But now, to move forward,

Smith may have to borrow from some of the old style of GM leadership. The GM community is crying out for direction—product development, marketing, finance, and labor relations. Only Smith has the position and the credibility to tell his employees and customers what GM plans to do and how it will get there.

Not until he got deeper into GM's problems did Smith realize how far-reaching they were. It was one thing to preach a gospel of common processes and common practices, and talk of the great savings GM could realize by using the same formulas to accomplish its tasks. It was quite another to see just how far GM was from being able to do so—and how stubborn some people inside the company were about dropping a way of life they'd known for decades. Even those who were most enthusiastic about Fundamental Change, such as its coauthor, Mark Hogan, are concerned GM did not change quickly enough when the pressure was strongest in the first years of Smith's administration. "I hope it gets done faster in the future," he says.[4]

Smith must now try to motivate an organization that lacks the sense of fear so pervasive in the terror-filled days of 1992. Hendry does not think a calmer atmosphere is such a bad thing. "A significant emotional event is one way of motivating people," he says, "and we were on the brink of a very significant emotional event in 1992. That got people's attention and created the motivation. Hopefully, those things only last a certain period of time." Lacking a crisis, the challenge for management is to find a way to motivate people who do not have ruin swinging ever closer like the sword of Damocles. That, Hendry maintains, is the responsibility of the NAO strategy board. "The job of change is far from over. And while I would like to think we are moving as fast as we were before, the issues that we are working on are a lot more difficult, and more complex."

Meanwhile, neither of GM's U.S. competitors are standing around waiting for GM to catch up. Despite Chrysler's record net income and sterling net margins, CEO Robert Eaton is not letting his company relax. A spate of quality problems on Chrysler vehicles in 1994 and 1995 made it ever clearer that

Chrysler could not stay financially healthy without top-notch products. Kerkorian's takeover attempt woke up Chrysler to the fact that management's leadership is not universally admired. Eaton has vowed to be the first Chrysler CEO in recent history who does not have to direct a turnaround. That vow seems to echo in every step he takes to keep Chrysler on track. In 1994 Chrysler paid off its unfunded pension liability, which had been $4 billion just five years before. With new minivans, restyled versions of its LH family sedans, and next-generation Jeeps in its product pipeline, and shaken by the Kerkorian threat, Eaton has plenty of reasons to stay focused.

Meanwhile, Ford CEO Alexander Trotman has as big a task as Smith in reorganizing Ford along global lines. The program, begun in 1995, is called Ford 2000. Ford dismantled its North American and international organizations, which GM mirrored, and created one large organization in which platforms and product development are centered in different parts of the world. Unlike Smith, who had to begin his task in a wretched car market, Trotman is attempting his reorganization in an atmosphere of fairly healthy sales. He prefers to make the tough moves at a time of record net income. "You do what we're doing from a position of strength. The timing is very, very good because the company is strong, with very good leadership and a good sense of teamwork," Trotman says.[5] Though Ford posted record profits in 1995, "We're not fine, and we don't find people saying that. There is close to unanimous view that now is absolutely the right time to be doing it." His ultimate goal is to get through the next downturn without losing money. Analysts say Ford has a better chance of doing so than either GM or Chrysler.

Along with the challenges posed by its restructuring, Ford is overhauling many of its cars and trucks, including the top-selling Ford Taurus and Mercury Sable, set to be introduced in the fall of 1995, and it plans to introduce a Lincoln sport utility around 1997. The vehicles pose a tremendous threat to GM, especially because Trotman's goal is to have the manufacturing capability to grab 30 percent of the U.S. car and truck market. When 1980 began, GM and Ford were nearly 30 percent market share points apart—GM had 46 percent of the U.S. market, Ford 17 percent. In 1994, the gap had closed to seven points, GM with 33 percent, Ford with 26 percent. Trotman, known throughout the company as an avid car enthusiast, is keeping close watch on his company's new model introductions. Vows Trotman: "Every one of them is going to be a home run. Quality has to be great. We have to launch them beautifully through the sales divisions. All of those millions we are spending have to be put on the street in the form of hardware in a super-professional way." Trotman is pushing his employees not to relax. "I'm proud of our company and what we've done. But I don't feel any sense of complacency at all. [I want Ford] never to sit back and think it's got the job done, because you never do."

Certainly, Smith would agree with Trotman. And it is up to him to make sure that others in GM feel the same way. Smith gets universally high marks for the financial near-miracle he and his team were able to bring off. But as the 1990s conclude, he must do more than coast through the steps of a turnaround program written years ago. He must show decisive leadership, and he must keep finding and promoting a diverse group of managers who understand his mission and are determined to carry it out. The men he nurtured in jobs in Europe, in Canada, and in the treasury department in New York have supported his insistence that GM embrace change. Yet a loyal band at the top is not enough to transform GM into a motivated, world-class company. The message must be sent deep into a middle management still entrenched in old ways of thinking. It is not a question of intent. The values Smith displays in his daily life, his insistence on "deeds, not words," his candor, kindness, and consideration of his associates are traits that will serve GM well. No one need worry about Smith's basic makeup. This is a man motivated by ideals not by greed. No scandal will wittingly touch this CEO.

But it is Smith's ultimate responsibility to make sure that the men and women who work for him understand and accept the same approach to business. He cannot be the invisible leader that he has been for much of his first few years as GM's

CEO. He needs to remember that GM employs more people than the city of Boston has residents. No Boston mayor could survive a year without making frequent sweeps through the city to talk to constituents and explain the changes he wants to make. When there's a crisis, the people want to see their mayor there. When the Celtics win the NBA championship, or the Red Sox the American League pennant, the people want their mayor leading the cheers. The same is true for the people of GM: They want to know that Smith is on the job in tough times, and they want to see him celebrate the victories.

UAW president Yokich is one who wants Smith to break out of his shell. "As much as I like Jack Smith, and I think he is the best CEO I've seen at GM, I think they've got him tied up to keep him away from me. I think they do that on purpose." Yokich blames GM's unfocused public relations department and the carmaker's cultural reclusiveness, not Smith's invisibility. Late in June 1995, the Motor City was euphoric when U.S. and Japanese negotiators reached a trade agreement that seemed to give Detroit automakers better access to Japan's car markets. Almost instantly, Chrysler made Eaton available for a conference call with reporters; Ford CEO Trotman came down to the lobby of Ford World Headquarters for a brief news conference. Smith, who'd given a speech the night before in New York, was nowhere to be seen, and GM did not even make a high-ranking executive available, such as Wagoner or Pearce. Reporters who phoned for comment had to settle for five minutes with GM's chief economist.

"I don't think Jack Smith has blinders on," Yokich said. "But he does not really have the support of those who should be more supportive of him. They should put him out front rather than trying to put him in his office and closing the door. They still try to hide things from him. That's wrong."

Smith, so admired by those who know him well, can easily be the kind of man whose ideas spark thoughts in others, whom Wall Street listens to for trends and the man his employees can talk about proudly. At Ford, people take a real interest in their spunky CEO, Trotman, a former Royal Air Force pilot who speaks his mind, loves the car business, has a sense of humor, and doesn't miss an opportunity to be Ford's public face. At Chrysler, Eaton is a determined, no-nonsense leader who can seem a bit imperial but who repeats and repeats and repeats his goals to make Chrysler fiscally sound. After the flash of an Iacocca, Eaton is just what Chrysler needed to keep its team aware of the fact that as the number-three auto company Chrysler cannot afford to fall asleep. He got high marks for his handling of the Kerkorian crisis, firing back at his biggest shareholder with decisive letters and statements. Both Trotman and Eaton give the impression that they love what they're doing. They seem to be looking to the future with great hope, full of ideas and goals and ready to take everyone else in the company along with them.

By contrast, Smith sometimes seems to still be battling the ghosts of GM's past. There is no way he can avoid it: They show up in person, when Robert Stempel and Lloyd Reuss and other ousted executives stroll the Detroit Auto Show. Sometimes, these are the only GM faces in sight because GM's current leadership is nowhere to be seen by the 5,000 journalists and 800,000 people who attend the show each year. Traces of the "old GM" have not yet been banished from the increasingly empty corridors of the GM building and the vastness of the GM Technical Center, no matter how much Smith and his team insist those days are gone. Too often, people in public relations and in the executive ranks slip and compare the GM of today with the company of a few years ago. "We're a lot better than we used to be" is one phrase that ought to be banished from the GM vocabulary.

One of Smith's challenges as the 1990s come to a close is to firmly toss aside what threatens to stall the progress that his team has begun to make, and keep his troops focused on the challenges that lie ahead. Says Roy Roberts, "What you have to do is say, 'A lot of this history is good, but this is where we want to go.' We have to have a burial for the things that are not good—an official burial—and say, 'These are the things we have to do as we go forward.'"

In the end, this philosophical purge will be one of Smith's greatest achievements. If he can transform GM's moldy ways of thinking and motivate its people to understand what GM's goals should be now and in the future, he will truly be a chief executive who can take his place alongside the greatest leaders of American business. Whether that happens depends on the personal investment he wants to make in assuring the future of GM and its people. It may simply be enough that Smith saved GM from certain disaster—not for his own gain, but for the greater good.

APPENDIX

GM's divisions and their share of total GM car and total GM vehicle sales

Division	% GM car sales	% GM vehicle sales
Chevrolet	32.8	48.9
Pontiac	19.2	12.3
Buick	17.9	10.8
Oldsmobile	13.9	8.9
Saturn	9.4	5.7
Cadillac	6.9	4.2
GMC	0.0	9.2

(Source: Autodata)

NAO net income, 1993 to 1999

1993: −$872 million
1994: $690 million
1995: $1.4 billion*
1996: $2.9 billion*
1997: $1.6 billion*
1998: −$1.0 billion*
1999: −$4.0 billion*

*estimate

(Source: PaineWebber/GM annual report)

GM new product introductions

1995: Saturn sedan
1996: Cadillac Catera
      Pontiac Grand Prix
      Minivans
1997: Oldsmobile Achieva
      Oldsmobile Cutlass Ciera
      Oldsmobile Cutlass Supreme
      Pontiac Grand Am
      Chevrolet Malibu
1998: Chevrolet CK pickup

Estimates as of spring 1995

(Source: AutoPacific Group)

293

GM U.S. car and truck sales to dealers (in millions), 1990 to 1994

Year	Cars	Trucks	Total
1990	2,762	1,469	4,231
1991	2,470	1,225	3,695
1992	2,503	1,369	3,862
1993	2,953	1,776	4,729
1994	3,049	1,967	5,061

(Source: GM annual report)

(Note: Figures include cars in dealers' inventory as of December 31.)

GM employment levels, 1990 versus 1995

Worldwide employment, 1990: 767,200

North American employment
Salaried: 96,400
Hourly: 355,800
Total: 452,200

Worldwide employment, 1995: 692,800

North American employment
Salaried: 72,800
Hourly: 274,400
Total 347,200

(Source: GM annual reports)

GM officers, 1990

Chairman and CEO: Robert Stempel
President: Lloyd Reuss
Vice Chairman: Robert Schultz
Vice Chairman: Jack Smith

Executive vice presidents:
  William Hoglund
  Robert T. O'Connell
  F. Alan Smith

Vice presidents and group executives:
  J. T. Battenberg III
  Gary Dickinson
  Robert Eaton
  Leon Krain
  E. Michael Mutchler
  Clifford Vaughn
  Marina Whitman

(and 37 vice presidents/staff officers)

GM officers, 1995

CEO and President: Jack Smith

Executive vice presidents:
  Louis Hughes
  J. Michael Losh
  Harry Pearce
  G. Richard Wagoner
  J. T. Battenburg III
  Michael Armstrong

Senior vice presidents:
  Richard Donnelly
  Donald Hackworth
  Robert Hendry
  Leon Krain
  Richard LeFauve
  Arvin Mueller
  E. Michael Mutchler
  Richard Nerod
  Clifford Vaughn
  Ronald Zarrella

(and 47 vice presidents)

(Source: GM annual reports)

NOTES

Chapter 1.

1. Interview with Jack Smith, March 1995.
2. Interview with Robert Stempel, February 1995.
3. Jack Smith interview, February 1994.
4. Interview with Walter Hayes, December 1993.
5. Stempel interview, March 1994.
6. Ibid.
7. Interview with G. Richard Wagoner, December 1994.
8. Stempel interview, March 1994.
9. Jack Smith interview, February 1994.

Chapter 2.

1. *On a Clear Day You Can See General Motors*, J. Patrick Wright, p. 23.
2. Ibid., p. 35.
3. Ibid., p. 167.
4. Interview with Robert Purcell, February 1994.
5. Interview with Roger Smith, March 1995.
6. Ibid.
7. *Comeback*, Paul Ingrassia and Joseph White, p. 120.
8. Interview with Donald Ephlin, November 1993.
9. Interview with Richard LeFauve, March 1994.
10. Interview with Donald Hudler, March 1994.
11. *Comeback*, pp. 171–172.

Chapter 3.

1. Interview with Sally Mahoney, October 1994.
2. Interviews with Donald Moran, George Sullivan, and Joseph Lane, October 1993.
3. Interview with Richard Quinlivan, October 1993.
4. Kathleen Kerwin, "Can Jack Smith Save General Motors?" *Business Week*, November 1, 1993.
5. Ibid.
6. Interview with Charles Golden, December 1993.
7. Interview with Louis Hughes, October 1994.
8. Interview with Kenneth Levy, December 1993.
9. Hughes interview, October 1994.
10. Interview with Jack Smith, May 1994.
11. Jack Smith interview, March 1995.
12. Ibid.
13. Hughes interview, *Car* magazine, January 1993.
14. Interviews with Jack Smith and Ignacio Lopez, March 1995.
15. Jack Smith interview, March 1995.

16. Ibid.
17. Interview with Lydia Smith, November 1993.
18. Lydia Smith interview, September 1993.
19. Ibid.
20. Lydia Smith interview, September 1993; Jack Smith interview, March 1995.
21. Interview with Arthur Krupnick, October 1993.
22. Interview with Mary Carroll Smith, April 1992.
23. Mahoney interview, October 1994.
24. Levy interview, December 1993.
25. Lydia Smith interview, November 1993.
26. Interview with Jim Farmer, April 1993.
27. Lydia Smith interview, September, 1993.

Chapter 4

1. Stempel interview, March 1994.
2. Interview with Lloyd Reuss, August 1991.
3. Interview with Mark Hogan, August 1994.
4. Hogan interview, August 1994.
5. Stempel interview, August 1993.
6. Stempel interview, March 1994.
7. Ibid.
8. Stempel interview, February, 1995.
9. Roger Smith interview, March 1995.
10. *Comeback*, Ingrassia and White, p. 277.
11. Hogan interview, August 1994.
12. *Comeback*, pp. 277–300, and interviews with Robert O'Connell, March 1993, and Stempel, February 1995.
13. Lydia Smith interview, October 1993.

Chapter 5

1. Hogan interview, August 1994.
2. Purcell interview, February 1994.
3. Jack Smith interview, March 1995.
4. Jack Smith speech at University of Michigan, February 1995.
5. Jack Smith interview, March 1995.
6. Ibid.
7. Stempel interview, August 1993.
8. *Comeback*, page 308.
9. Interviews by author for *USA Today*, October 26, 1992.
10. Stempel interview, February 1995.

Chapter 6

1. Wagoner interview, March 1995.
2. Hogan interview, August 1994.
3. Jack Smith interview, February 1993.
4. *Los Angeles Times*, February 17, 1993.
5. Jack Smith interview, February 1993.
6. Interview with Harry Pearce, February 1995.

Chapter 7

1. Jack Smith speech to the Chicago Economic Club, February 1994.
2. Lopez interview with John McElroy, *Automotive Industries*, September 1993.
3. Lopez press conference, Saginaw, Michigan, August 1992.
4. Author dinner with Lopez, November 1992.
5. Lydia Smith interview, November 1993.
6. Lopez dinner, November 1992.
7. Interview with Bill Hoglund, January 1994.
8. Jack Smith interview, March 1994.
9. Lopez dinner, November 1992.
10. Keith Naughton, the *Detroit News*, August 1992.
11. Stempel interview, March 1994.
12. Author lunch with Jack Smith, February 1993.
13. Lydia Smith interview, November 1993.
14. Interview with Ronald Haas, November 1993.
15. Lydia Smith interview, November 1993.
16. Lopez interview, March 1995.
17. Jack Smith interview, March 1995.

Chapter 8

1. Hughes interview, October 1992.
2. Lopez interview, March 1995.
3. Wagoner interview, March 1995.
4. Interview with Gerald Collins, March 1994.
5. Interview with David Herman, March 1995.

Chapter 9

1. *New York Times*, October 19, 1994.
2. Stempel interview, March 1994.

Chapter 10

1. Interview with John Rock, February 1995.
2. Lopez interview, March 1995.
3. Pearce interview, February 1995.
4. Hogan interview, March 1995.
5. Interview with Alexander Trotman, January 1995.

SELECTED BIBLIOGRAPHY

Gustin, Lawrence R. *Billy Durant*. Flushing, Mich.: Craneshaw Publishers, 1984.

Halberstam, David. *The Fifties*. New York: Villard Books, 1993.

Ingrassia, Paul, and White, Joseph. *Comeback*. New York: Simon & Schuster, 1994.

Jacobs, Timothy. *A History of General Motors*. New York: Brompton Books, 1992.

Keller, Maryann. *Rude Awakening*. New York: William Morrow & Co., 1989.

———. *Collision*. New York: Doubleday, 1993.

Nader, Ralph. *Unsafe at Any Speed*. New York: Grossman Publishers, 1965.

Sloan, Alfred. *My Years With General Motors*. New York: Doubleday, 1964.

Womack, James, et al. *The Machine That Changed the World*. New York: Rawson Associates, 1990.

Wright, J. Patrick. *On a Clear Day You Can See General Motors*. Grosse Pointe, Mich.: Wright Enterprises, 1979.

INDEX

301